Sacrament of Sexuality

SACRAMENT
OF SEXUALITY

MORTON T. KELSEY
and BARBARA KELSEY

AMITY HOUSE
WARWICK, NEW YORK

2H.6
R

8
Published by Amity House Inc.
106 Newport Bridge Rd.
Warwick, N.Y. 10990

ISBN 0-916349-06-3

ACKNOWLEDGEMENTS

From *The Sex Atlas* by Erwin J. Haeberle. Copyright 1978 by the Author. Reprinted by permission of The Continuum Publishing Corporation. —— From *Sexual Behavior in the Human Male* by A.C. Kinsey. Copyright 1948. Reprinted by permission of the Kinsey Institute for Research in Sex, Gender and Reproduction, Inc. —— From a Candace Pert Interview, *Omni*, 1982. Copyright 1982 by Omni International and reprinted with the permission of Omni Publications International Ltd. —— From *To Work and To Love*, by Dorothee Soelle. Copyright 1984 by Fortress Press. Used by permission. —— From *Sexual Morality* by by Philip Keane, S.S. Copyright 1980. With permission from Paulist Press. —— From *The Invisible Partners* by John Sanford. Copyright 1980. With permission from Paulist Press. —— From *The Sexual Celibate*, 1974 by Donald Goergen. Published by Seabury Press. All rights reserved. Used with permission. —— From *The Illness That We Are: A Jungian Critique of Christianity* by John P. Dourley. 1984 by the Author. Used with permission. —— From an article in *Your Church*, Jan/Feb 1975, "0-1-2-3-4-5-6-Changing Attitudes Towards Sexuality." Used with permission. —— Extract from *Someday I'll Find You*. Copyright H.A. Williams 1982, published in paper back by Collins Publishers, London. Used with permission. —— From *Sexuality and Spirituality* by John Moore. Copyright 1980. Reprinted by permission of Harper and Row Co. —— From *Marriage—Dead or Alive* by Adolf Guggenbuhl-Craig. Copyright 1977 Spring Publications, Zurich. —— From *The Pleasure Bond* by William H. Masters and Virginia E. Johnson. Copyright 1970 Bantam Books. —— From an article in *TV Guide* by Andrew M. Greeley, March 23, 1983. —— From "The Decree on Ministry & Life of Priests," *Documents of Vatican II*, Walter M. Abbott, S.J., general editor. Reprinted with permission of America Press, Inc., 106 West 56th St., New York, N.Y. 10019. 1966 All rights reserved. ——From *The Collected Works of C.G. Jung*, trans. R.F.C. Hull, Bollingen Series XX. Vol. 10, *Civilization in Transition* Copyright 1964, 1970 by Princeton University Press. —— From *The Collected Works of C.G. Jung*, trans. R.F.C. Hull, Bollingen Series XX. Vol. 9, I: *The Archetypes and the Collective Unconscious*, Copyright 1959, 1969 by Princeton University Press.

Contents

Introduction

There is very little on the market today that brings the perspective of Christian theology and spirituality to the whole matter of sexuality. Yet people are desperately in need of a practical theology of sexuality and love. Our good friend John Sanford was talking with us about sexuality and love one day and said: "I know a lot about sex. I know a lot about love. I know a lot about transference and when I add them together, I know nothing at all."

When we explore the subjects of sexuality, love, transference (the projection of romantic feelings onto another), and intimacy, we are getting into the very heart and mystery of being human—of that which distinguishes us from lower animals. Although we cannot penetrate and dissipate this mystery (nor would we want to), we do need to be as knowledgeable and understanding as possible on a subject that is the source of much pain, frustration, and misunderstanding—as well as the source of deep satisfaction and even ecstasy.

Only with hesitation and some trepidation do we take up the subject of human sexuality and its relation to spirituality and religious thought. We have a modern marriage; we share responsibilities and decisions and each of us has equal access to financial resources. We have a mutual understanding about sexuality and its meaning that has grown and deepened considerably over forty-odd years. We have a common spiritual life; we try to spend quality time with each other. However, our marriage and our rela-

1

tionship have not always been based on this kind of mutuality and equality. Both of us were raised in an era permeated with patriarchal Victorian ideas about relationships and sexuality. It has been a long and, at times, difficult struggle to come to genuine communication and equality.

We have confronted two issues again and again as we worked toward mutuality. First, we had to get over the notion that sex and sexuality were not quite nice and really could not be discussed. The study of depth psychology showed us that sexuality was a natural (and therefore potentially good) and pervasive aspect of human life and that it caused all sorts of psychological, social and physical problems when it was swept under the carpet and ignored. The word sex changed in meaning from "mere" sexual intercourse to a mysterious reality that extends to every part of life and can come to physical expression in intercourse and orgasm. We came to see that the negative attitudes toward sex of Puritans and Jansenists often resulted in a great amount of human misery. Second, we began to realize that there could really be no true mutuality in sexual relationships until it was understood that women, while different in some aspects than men, were of *absolutely equal value*. One of us was raised in a home where true equality existed sixty years ago; the other, in a bastion of patriarchal condescension. Philip Keane shows clearly in the opening chapters of his book *Sexual Morality* that any discussion of sexuality that fails to deal with these issues will not engage the deeper questions concerning this tantalizing human mystery.

Our book originated as two series of lectures we were invited to give at the Benedictine Abbey in Pecos, New Mexico—one for Catholic priests and one for clergy and laypersons studying to become better spiritual directors. We have found this abbey to be one of the finest Christian communities, and one of the most effective at mediating Christian spirituality to men and women of the twentieth century. We met to explore the meaning of sexuality, including celibacy, primarily as a way of deepening one's ministry. If priests, laypeople and members of religious orders are not knowledgeable about (and comfortable with) sexuality, they cannot be wise spiritual directors and guides to others. For sexuality is part of the human condition.

This book took on its present form during a two-month stay in Malaysia. Someone has called this country "instant Asia". During its British colonial past the Malay peninsula became home for a large number of Buddhist Chinese and Hindu Indians as well as the original Moslem Malay people. We came in daily contact with taxi drivers, waiters, guides, and beach boys who wanted to talk about their country and their religious values. We also have highly educated Chinese friends who live between Singapore and Kuala Lumpur, the capital of Malaysia. The population of Malaysia is about 50% Islamic, 30% Chinese (practicing Buddhism, and a mixture of Taoism and ancestor worship), 14% Hindu and about 6% Christian. The country has only recently achieved stability after having fought a ten-year battle against Communist guerillas. The attitudes toward sex and women were far different than those we were accustomed to. The place of women in Asia makes the worst conditions in the Western world look almost ideal. We shall say much more about this later.

One of the main points of this book is that sexuality can be a sacramental action. Calling sexuality a sacrament may seem strange or even blasphemous to those brought up with the idea that sex is an unmentionable, ugly or even evil necessity. We should remember that a sacrament is an outward and visible sign of an inner and spiritual grace. We suggest that sexuality is at its best an outer, visible, physiological sign of the inner and spiritual grace of love. Not all sexual behavior meets this definition, but when it does then our sexuality becomes a living symbol or sacrament of love. Sexuality in itself is neither evil nor good; rather, sexual expression can be seen as a many-pointed scale from evil and destructive sexual activity to a sexual relationship that can be a window into the nature of the self-giving love of God, a spiritual experience, a communion with Love or God. Sexuality is not the highest good, but it is a secondary good. It is very important to remember that any secondary good that is elevated to the level of highest good turns evil and destructive; it is also important to remember that when understood and practiced accordingly, a secondary good can lead us to the greatest good.

But this book is not directed primarily to priests and laypeople inside the Church. It speaks frankly on a host of subjects pertinent to all general readers—all who are not totally comfortable with their sexuality, but particularly men and women who are trying to make their lives whole and meaningful, whether they be single, married, celibate, or committed partners, whether they be adolescent or aged.

In the first chapter we will discuss the meaning and history of the word sexuality. This word means so many different things to different people that it is impossible to take up our subject with serious intent until we have defined what we are writing about. We will go on to examine sexuality from a physiological point of view—starting with the chromosomes and concluding with descriptions of the genital organs. We will go on to explore in the next chapter the development of our sexual identities. In the third chapter we will survey changing attitudes and theories that have been proposed by the scientific, philosophical and religious communities. Chapter four presents a religious and philosophical (for in the deepest sense these two cannot be separated) discussion of the place and value of women in our societies and religious institutions. A discussion of the sexual attitudes of Christianity, the Bible, and some other religions follows.

We then present a picture of what we believe mature, sacramental sexual relationships look like. Following this comes a discussion of sexuality in all committed relationships: in marriage, in the single life and in celibacy. Chapter nine discusses homosexuality, bisexuality, psychology and religion. The subjects warrant an entire chapter, for they are highly misunderstood topics although homosexuality is a significant lifestyle in the Western world. Chapter ten explores problems in sexuality and variations in sexual functions; the "problem" of masturbation, fear of homosexuality (quite different from homosexuality), premarital and extramarital genital sex, as well as a host of less common sexual expressions. Unless we understand the uncommon and sometimes destructive behavior evidenced in fetishism, transvestism, bestiality, voyeurism, genital exposure and other sexual anomalies we shall not be able to be open to people who suffer with these compulsions and are seeking help in dealing with them and relating them to their religious lives.

Chapters eight and eleven are attempts to describe the indescribable, the nature of love and the nature of spirituality. If sexuality is indeed a sacrament of love and love is one of the most central dimensions of the divine, we must certainly deal with these aspects of human life which are so little understood. We shall conclude in chapter twelve with a series of actual questions and answers which were asked and given at the Pecos retreats. They show concretely the concerns and questions of actual people and the kind of answers that can be given from the perspective we are presenting.

You may well wonder what our qualifications are for undertaking such an audacious task as writing a book on sexuality, particularly from a sacramental perspective. Qualification number one is life experience. We are in our forty-third year of marriage—years of difficulty, conflict, satisfaction and deepening, growing and maturing love. There are no storybook marriages; marriage is damned hard work and is an education in the school of life.

We have three children (also damned hard work and incredible satisfaction) and four grandchildren (not such hard work and still satisfaction).

Second, Morton has had fifteen years of formal Jungian analysis and Barbara has had five. Morton keeps up a running conversation at least every other week with some of his close psychologist friends; they listen to him and then he listens to them. Barbara has a psychologist friend she feels free to talk with occasionally. When we get into the depth of ourselves, we usually find unresolved problems in the areas of authority and sexuality. The latter is particularly likely if our heritage has been formed in large measure by Jansenism or Puritanism. Our Puritan heritage provides ample ground for years of reflecting and discussing the whole subject of sexuality.

Third, Morton is a marriage, family and child counselor licensed in the state of California, a member of the American Association of Marriage and Family Therapists and of the American Association of Pastoral Counselors. We attended together a workshop on sexual dysfunction required by California for Marriage Counselors. We have each listened literally to thousands of people in our parish ministry, in Morton's counseling practice, on retreats and at the University of Notre Dame. We have found very few people who, when they were honest, did not share real concerns about sexuality.

Committed Christians need to help the Church be a place where sexual healing and transformation can take place rather than a place of judgment, condemnation and fear. People outside the Church and sometimes with no answers to meaning and value need to be provided with tools to see life in more holistic ways. We all need to learn to see sexuality as a divine gift. We have been wonderfully and beautifully made and we need to have a total vision of life in which love and salvation permeate every area of our lives—including our sexuality.

We are grateful to the thousands who have talked with us and shared their concerns about sexuality. We regret that we did not know what we have learned through the years in the very beginning, and have thus sometimes done ill as well as good. We are grateful to those with whom we worked in analysis for the understanding, guidance and wisdom that they shared, particularly Max Zeller, Margaret McClean, Hilde and James Kirsch, Barbara Hannah and Franz Riklin. We are also grateful to our friends and colleagues. John Sanford has been a wise friend for thirty years and Andy Canale and Hal Perry for nearly fifteen. Doug Daher, Roy Fairchild, Sally Johnson, and Kay Kramer have read the manuscript and offered invaluable suggestions. We are grateful to our children for their questions and reactions to what we told them and for the honesty they demanded of us. Most of all we are grateful to each other for understanding, patience, commitment and caring, whether we were in conflict or at peace.

Both of us have been reading for years on this subject. We have appended a lengthy and incomplete bibliography (for this subject is enormous). We have found the various publications of Masters and Johnson of special help and particularly the popular summary of their work done by Nat Lehrman, *Masters and Johnson Explained*. Philip Keane's *Sexual Morality: A Catholic Perspective* has been stimulating; it is well footnoted and an excellent presentation of the pluses and minuses of the Catholic position. Donald Goergen's *The Sexual Celibate* brought the consideration of celibacy and sexuality together. Katchadourian and Lunde's *Fundamentals of Human Sexuality*[1] provides an excellent and well-supported technical study of sexuality; Haeberle, *The Sexual Atlas*, provides a more popular one. Carole Wade Offir's *Human Sexuality* is a readable and up-to-date study. We shall be referring throughout the text to numerous other books that deal with particular areas of concern.

Caroline Whiting had the tapes of the two Pecos conferences transcribed and edited them to give us an outline to work from. She also gave us valuable suggestions. Cindy Wesley put our handwriting and abominable typescript into readable form. She has also obtained permissions and prepared an index. The interest and encouragement of Richard Payne has been of great value in this work as well as in many others. John Whalen and John Neary have done another excellent job of editing our final manuscript and offering many helpful suggestions.

CHAPTER ONE

What Is Sexuality?

THE BIOLOGY AND PSYCHOLOGY OF SEX

What do we mean when we use the word *sexuality*? It has been used in so many ways that it is practically meaningless. The Latin derivation is *sexus*, which simply means to divide rather than to unite. It points to the fact that there is a difference between the male and the female. The word's first occurrence in English was in the year 1382 in Wycliffe's translation of the Bible. Then the word lay dormant until the year 1735. It didn't really become common usage until 1799 when the term *sexual intercourse* first appeared in the Oxford English Dictionary.

The next term to come into use, four years later, was *sexual function*, then *sexual organ* in 1828 and *sexual desire* in 1836. *Sexual instinct* appeared in 1861, *sexual act* in 1888 and *sexual immorality* not until 1911. We can easily see through the language how thought about sexuality was developing.[1]

How did people speak about sexuality before the word came into existence? There were more than 200 words for the various parts of the male and female sexual anatomy. Individual words, rather than a general term, were used. People spoke about lechery, about reproducing one's own flesh and blood, about kissing, embracing and fondling, about wantonness, lust, temptation by the devil, pollution and wasting one's seed. Each sexual act was treated separately. In fact, the word sexuality may be confusing rather than clarifying in that it lumps all our sexual activity—eros, passion, tenderness, affection, desire, marriage, intercourse, masturbation, homosexuality, fetishism, love, amour—into one category. Before we can say much that is meaningful about *sexuality* it will be necessary to look at the many different elements that have been lumped together without much thinking or discrimination.

Although people before the 19th century used a large assortment of terms for different sexual acts, they did not name a specific sexual drive. Before the development of formal psychology, human instincts and behaviors were not tidily separated from each other. Various functions of the body were not confined to compartments and physical needs were not categorized according to their differences. The erotic urge was not viewed as a separate and independent function but as part of the overall human state. All forms of life were related and shared commonalities. Differences and distinctions were minimized. Conscious and unconscious aspects of our psyches were not distinguished.

According to Erwin J. Haeberle, author of *The Sex Atlas*:

> This may explain why the expression 'sexual behavior' does not appear in any European language until modern times. It is not used anywhere in the Bible and was unknown to the classical Western writers from Homer to Dante, Shakespeare, Racine, and Goethe. As a matter of fact, even the word 'sexual' alone, which by now dates back several hundred years, only gradually acquired its great variety of present meanings. At first, it was nothing but a narrow, purely technical term and simply referred to the attribute of being either male or female.[2]

During the last hundred years the meaning of the words sex and sexuality has changed drastically. They no longer refer just to the differences between the sexes or to the act of reproduction. These words began to take on the meaning of an innate drive that pervades all parts of life and can lead to sexual intercourse and reproduction, but can also be repressed, sublimated or channeled into a sense of closeness between two people, into genital expression between members of the same sex, or into numerous other expressions that we will discuss later in greater detail. Much of this change in meaning was the result of the studies and writing of Sigmund Freud, one of the world's great creative thinkers. In 1905 Freud published

Three Essays on the Theory of Sexuality in which he outlined his theories about childhood sexuality, about sexuality as a psychophysical process like hunger with both physical and mental manifestations, and about psychosexual development. Freud continued to make additions and changes in all the successive editions of this work.

So *sexuality* gradually came, as Haeberle points out:

> ...to denote a preoccupation with sexual matters, and finally it came to mean the possession of sexual powers or the capability of erotic feelings. In short, it gradually turned from a relative into an absolute term. Thus by the 1880's one could discuss a person's sexuality as a special phenomenon all by itself. This phenomenon represented more than mere maleness or femaleness, and it was not necessarily always related to male/female encounters. Neither gender attraction nor any reproductive process had to be implied. Even solitary masturbation could now be perceived as sexual behavior, i.e., as an expression of someone's 'sexuality'[3]

In order to understand Freud's theory of sexuality it is necessary to see it in the context of the basic theory of personality that he described in his groundbreaking book, *The Interpretation of Dreams*, published in 1900. As Freud listened to people crippled with psychological problems he began to perceive the human psyche or personality as much more complex than most people at that time realized. It consisted of more than our conscious thoughts; the psyche was a battleground of three conflicting forces. There was first of all the basic unconscious, primal libido (Latin for lust) or id of which most of us are unaware; also repressed into the unconscious (and so forgotten) are unpleasant memories, particularly those dealing with forbidden sexual experiences. And then there was the human ego, or conscious self, often totally oblivious of its basic sexual roots or their expressions in childhood. Between the ego and the unconscious stood a *censor* or *superego* that kept us from remembering our sexual experiences, Oedipal wishes and other sexual fantasies and from knowing our essentially sexual nature. The censor even scrambled dreams that express our sexual nature so that we were kept in the dark about our essentially amoral, lustful nature. The superego was like a self-righteous conscience or puritanical parent horrified that anything so base as sexuality could provide the ground and base of our personality.

A diagram helps to put these three parts of the psyche in perspective. Eric Berne and his followers among other psychological contributions simplify Freud's system and label the three aspects of personality the child, the adult and the parent.

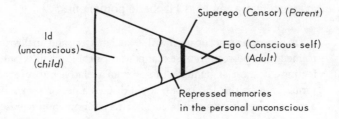

The word id is simply the German word for "it", the it that formed the basic stuff of personality. We like to think of it, however, as a shortened form of "idiot". Just like an idiot without control it would seek pleasure in any way that came to it, either masturbating in public (often seen in mental hospitals) or copulating at noon at the corner of First and Main. The id with its libido is utterly amoral and has no conscience or shame. If human beings were to rise above the animals the id had to be channeled, controlled and kept in bounds.

This control could be exercised through the unconscious superego that represses the id and even keeps us ignorant of our sexual nature. This repression could result in sexual disturbances or ordinary neurosis and psychosis, or it could be channeled into art and literature and create the "neurosis" of civilization. As long as humans were ignorant of their sexual roots they were run by the id one way or another. The goal of psychoanalysis was to bring all parts of the individual into awareness so that we could consciously bear the tension and have some control over our lives.

What Freud wrote about ego development forms the basis upon which much of modern dynamic psychology is based. The ego gradually emerges out of the unconscious and enables us to function as free autonomous individuals. It is what gets us around in the outer world, our capacity to function. A typical dream symbol for the ego is the automobile which gets us around from one place to another. Until we develop a well-integrated ego the impulses of the id are either lived out in inappropriate action or else automatically squashed by the superego and so we may find ourselves either acting out our sexuality or in psychological disturbance caused by repression. If we are to avoid these two undesirable alternatives we need to develop a strong ego that can honestly face our sexual nature and choose what our sexual path should be and at the same time resist the repressive voice of the superego.

According to Freud the ultimate force in the universe is the blind, pleasure-seeking libido of the id. Thus all life is but an expression of sexuality. All pleasure is sexual or a symbol of sex. Every action and symbol has sexual connotations. This attitude about sexuality has penetrated deeply into the thinking of the Western world. Many people accept this Freudian view without realizing its implications. The 1960 record "Songs of Couch and Consultation" was written by a song writer after he heard a newsboy hawking his papers using Freudian terms.

Jung never totally accepted Freud's view of sexuality as the single motivating force in human life and it was disagreement on this point that led to the final break between them. Jung acknowledged the importance of sexuality and of the pleasure that can lead to orgasm, but he believed there were other basic drives as well. Along with Adler he saw the manifold effects of the drive for power in human life. (Jung also perceived a drive for meaning, a need for meaning; this need could only be met by experiences of the transcendent, the holy, the numinous.)

One of the reasons we find Jung so helpful is that he built upon the foundations laid down by psychologists before him. He didn't go into reaction formation against them and deny what others had discovered. Jung only made two basic changes in Freud's picture of personality. First, he did not believe that the psyche was a system of self-deception; symbols meant what they signified and were not disguised sexual signs. Second, Jung agreed that we are motivated by sexuality and aggression, by selfishness and greed, by laziness and pride. But he thought that we also have a drive to wholeness. In fact, Jung actually spoke of sexuality as a symbol of wholeness and integration in the union of the opposites, and as an image of the Divine-human encounter, the experience of the numinous, which is the ultimate goal of human existence. In 1945 Jung wrote to P. W. Martin: "I'm not really interested in treating neuroses; I'm interested in the experience of the numinous."[4] He continued that the real therapy is bringing a person into touch with the divine and that when this experience has been profound, real and deep, one is relieved of the burden of pathology or mental sickness. Jung believed the depth of the psyche was directed toward meaning greater than itself. Other depth psychologists, Fritz Kunkel, Alfred Adler, and Otto Rank, came to this same point of view in their later writings. However, all three of these theorists died relatively young and never developed the religious implications as fully as Jung.[5]

THE PERVASIVENESS OF SEXUALITY

In order to understand how sexuality can affect every aspect of our being, we need to look more closely at Freud's theories about our sexual nature. Then we can decide how much of that theory we can accept, what rings true and what does not. We have great admiration for Freud; he was one of the world's great original thinkers. He developed a theory of the unconscious and showed that our behavior often results from impulses, desires and attitudes of which we are not aware or conscious. He braved the Victorian world of Vienna, probably more prudish than any city in Europe at that time, and gave data to support his thesis that sexual drives were responsible for shaping and misshaping our lives. His theories met with a storm of protest, but in a very few years were seen by people in many diverse professions to contain insights that human beings had long avoided.

Freud was primarily a physician dedicated to helping his patients overcome their emotional sicknesses, their hysterias, compulsions and other neurotic symptoms. In his early work he attributed most of this behavior to repressed memories of sexual trauma and abuse by parents or parental substitutes. Once he gained his patients' confidence by maintaining an accepting and entirely nonjudgmental attitude, they were able to remember these experiences and speak of them. Then they dealt with these experiences consciously.[6] In her book *The Drama of the Gifted Child*, Alice Miller gives a moving modern presentation of the effects of childhood trauma on fragile human beings, particularly gifted children. Sexual traumas are particularly destructive.

Freud abandoned this theory, however, and came to believe that a deeper conflict was the true root cause not only of all the misery of mental illness, but also the source and cause of art, literature, morality—indeed of civilization itself. The Oedipus Complex derives its name from the great Greek drama, *Oedipus Rex*, the story of the king who killed his father and married his mother. Freud claimed that he found in all patients, once their resistence was removed, the same kind of incestuous conflict; their loyalty and love for their parents was in conflict with a desire for the destruction of the parents of the same sex and an incestuous desire for the one of the opposite sex. This was the net-net of human existence. Blind, meaningless conflict-filled sexuality was at the root of our humanity and our lives, and had no ultimate meaning or purpose.[7]

It is one thing to maintain that sexual attitudes have a pervasive effect upon all human beings, and a negative effect upon many raised in a society or religion that has tabooed discussion of sexual matters. It is quite another to maintain that *all* human behavior (including art and religion) can be reduced to blind, irrational, meaningless sexual conflict. Many of the people who have accepted the pervasiveness of sexuality do not realize the full implications of Freud's thought and the necessity of modifying his views if life is to have any ultimate meaning. Many people with whom we have worked have shown us that sexual conflicts can cause all sorts of emotional problems. Anyone in our society with personality disturbances, particularly people under thirty-five, would do well to look into their personal history for evidences of sexual conflict. It is foolish to ignore, as some psychologists do, the effect of traumatic childhood experiences of any kind.

We believe that sexuality touches every aspect of human life. Sexual conflict and fears can upset our entire emotional and physical systems. They can raise havoc with our religious lives. But these are not the only factors that can have an effect on all parts of us. The drive for power and authority can do the same, as can dishonesty, the avoidance of the truth. Lack of meaning can bring on depression and affect everything from sex to sleep; usually concern with meaning occurs in the middle thirties but can sometimes appear earlier. To ignore or deny the naturalness and pervasiveness of human sexuality can lead to blindness about human beings and can result in disaster. It is an essential and pervasive element of our humanity. We get into trouble and absurdity, however, whenever we try to reduce all aspects of life to one element.

LEVELS OF SEXUALITY

In our explorations and studies over the years we have come up with thirteen different meanings for or levels of the word *sexuality*. The first level is that of chromosomal sex. Included here is a diagram that will help in understanding this aspect of sexuality. It is taken from *The Sex Atlas*.[8]

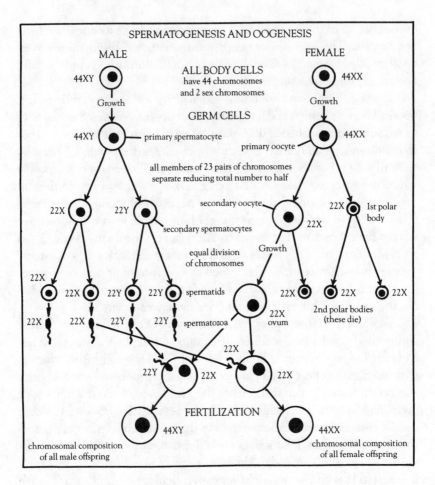

THE DETERMINATION OF SEX

The chart first compares the production of male and female sex cells and then shows the possible result of fertilizations.

1. Spermatogenesis and Oogenesis
While one primary spermatocyte eventually gives rise to four mature spermatozoa, a primary oocyte gives rise to only one ovum. The minute polar bodies which are formed in the process of oogenesis simply die and disintegrate.

2. Fertilization
All mature ova carry an x-chromosome, but the spermatozoa carry either an x- or a y-chromosome. Thus, the union of a spermatozoon and an ovum (fertilization) can result in either one of two possible new cells: one growing into a boy (the xy-combination) or one growing into a girl (the xx-combination).

Every cell in every human being contains 44 chromosomes, plus two sex chromosomes, 46 in all. In the female there are two x chromosomes. In the male there is an x and a y chromosome. Anyone who says there is no difference between male and female is simply not aware of the facts. The difference is inherent in the very chromosomal structure of the body.

Each cell microcosmically contains the plan for the entire human body. Cloning is possible for some living things because of this fact. We can actually see this in experimentation with frogs. It is possible to cut off a frog's leg but keep the point of amputation irritated and stimulated. The frog may under these conditions grow back an entire leg, perfect in every detail. The cells know when to make muscle, when to make bone, when to make nerve, as they reproduce the entire frog's leg.[9]

Several years ago Barbara had a severe accident and the only way the doctors could save her foot was to keep it raw. Then, up out of the depths of the foot, new flesh, bone and nerves developed. And then, finally, about six weeks after the first new growth, they were able to do a skin graft and she had a foot! Each cell is capable of the wisdom of the entire body/psyche, and this means that the basic difference between male and female goes right down to the chromosome.

Let us look at the reproduction process, the development of the embryo and the role of sex hormones. In each ejaculation the male produces somewhere between 250 and 500 million sperm cells. (Morton was talking to a Dutch priest one day who told him that, according to the catechism he learned as a young man, masturbation was a breaking of the fifth and not the sixth commandment. It was the killing of sperm cells. It had nothing to do with adultery.) The male's spermatocyte consists of 44 chromosomes and an x and a y sex chromosome. The female's oocyte consists of 44 chromosomes and two x sex chromosomes. How are they going to get together? They can't get together in this form. There is a long process in the female in which the oocyte with 44 chromosomes divides into cells with 22 chromosomes, and then one half dies off. There is another division, and the ovum ends up with only 22 chromosomes and an x sex chromosome. Likewise, the spermatocyte develops and splits into cells containing 22 chromosomes and an x and 22 and a y. As an ovum passes into the fallopian tubes, it is about the size of a dot at the end of a sentence on the written page and is visible to the naked eye. Interestingly enough, each sperm cell is 85,000 times smaller than each ovum (egg). Males continually produce enormous numbers of sperm cells. Women come into the world with only a limited number of ova, all of which are present at birth. Part of the reproductive process is maturing and releasing these eggs. At the time of maturity a woman's ovaries contain about 30,000 potential eggs.

The sex of the newborn child is determined by whether an x or a y sperm unites with the egg. If it is an x, then a female will be conceived. This gives a picture of the incredible complexity of the human body and of the reproductive process, all on the chromosomal level.

The possible implications of chromosomal sexuality for the nature of the psyche are interesting ones. What is noteworthy is that the female is fully female chromosomally, and the male has both male and female chromosomes in his cellular structure. What this difference in structure means for adult sexual functioning has not been determined. On the level of chromosomes men are bisexual beings—whatever that means. Rarely do other combinations of sex chromosomes occur. Sometimes there is the xxx pattern and also the single x. There is also the xxy combination and the xyy. The first two produce women often with other genetic effects. The person carrying xxy presents a particular body type and is not sexually very active. The xyy syndrome has received considerable attention as men with this syndrome appear very masculine and have been associated with crimes involving sexual violence. However, the xyy pattern has only recently been discovered and the evidence is not conclusive.[10]

The second level of sexuality is the hormonal, for our sexual development and behavior is influenced by hormones secreted by many of the different ductless glands. The male produces large amounts of the sex hormone androgen in addition to all sorts of other complicated hormones. When the sperm cell swims up into the fallopian tube, it meets the egg, the ovum, and fertilizes it. The fertilized egg grows for a while there, then moves down and attaches itself to the uterus. When the growing egg does not move down, a tubal pregnancy develops—which usually requires surgery. There are really three processes—fertilization, segmentation, and implantation— before the embryo can begin to grow.

There are few anatomical distinctions between the male and the female during the first two to three months after conception. Even the sex organs are the same. By about the third or fourth month some differentiation takes place: there is development of labia in the female and of the scrotum and testicles in the male. Then at four to five months there is further sexual differentiation—a penis in the male and a clitoris in the female. But up until this time we are bisexual creatures in the womb.

What causes sexual differentiation? And why are some people born with underdeveloped sex organs? Where the embryo has xx (female) calls, a group of hormones connected with estrogen is released in greater predominance than the androgens. If this is not the case, the person does not grow into a fully developed female. When the chromosomal combination is xy, more androgen and less estrogen are released and the person develops into a mature male embryo. Again, if there isn't enough of this hormone, the development does not take place. Of course all male bodies produce some estrogen and all females produce some androgens—not only during development, but throughout their entire lives. The quantitative balance of these two seems to make the difference. Hormones are continuously significant.

When a woman's estrogen stops flowing, she often will develop facial or body hair or other characteristics of maleness. The sexual development process is not really complete until puberty, which can occur from the age of ten up to the early twenties. Failure of an adequate supply of appropriate hormones can bring sexual development to a halt. This aspect of human development is very different from that of animals. Some men do not attain their full masculine body—full chest and hair—until the age of twenty-three or older. Women, however, usually develop earlier. The sexual hormones have a pervasive effect on human behavior, sexual and otherwise. A rise in androgen level in the blood has been correlated with increased aggressive action.[11]

The third level is that of gonadal sex, simply the differences in the actual sex organs. In the woman the ovaries, fallopian tubes, uterus, vagina and clitoris are the basic female organs. In the male the penis, scrotum, testicles, seminal vesicles, and prostate are the basic organs. One interesting fact about the testicles is that male sperm cells cannot live at body temperature and so the testicles have to descend in order for reproduction to occur. And this is one reason why some women cannot conceive—until their husbands start wearing boxer shorts instead of jockey shorts. The testicles have to be a degree or two below body temperature or sperm cells die off. After sperm cells are created they are stored in the seminal vesicles. The prostate goes through contraction at orgasm and ejects the seminal fluid, consisting of a mucousy type of fluid plus the sperm cells.

Occasionally in some people we find the sex organs to be incomplete and undeveloped. And sometimes we even find people with the gonadal characteristics of both sexes (the gonadal organs of both male and female).

Such individuals, called hermaphrodites, are considered unfortunate anomalies in our day and age, but in the time of the Greeks and the Romans and in many other cultures, they were often considered as more highly developed and complete human beings and were sometimes venerated as objects of worship.

Many years ago when we were in the Louvre we noticed that the floor was worn white on the back side of a particular recumbent nude statue. Being curious souls we walked back of it and investigated. There we saw turned toward the wall a first century Roman statue of a hermaphodite with fully developed breasts and a fully developed erect penis. This was considered a symbol of wholeness and probably was worshipped as a god in first-century Rome. In *Hosteen Klah* Franc Newcomb describes a Navajo medicine man whom she came to know very well. When he was an adolescent it was discovered that he had hermaphroditic characteristics. The Indians rejoiced as this condition gave promise of a great medicine man for he was endowed with the qualities of both the male and the female. This example shows how vastly different sexual views can be in different historical ages and in different cultures.[12]

In our own age sexual differentiation is seen as very significant and important. This leads us to the fourth level—the internal and external accessory organs and their behavior. For instance, the penis can only be adequately stimulated where there is little fear in the sexual situation. Whenever there is fear, the body is preparing for either flight or fight, and this puts a halt to assimilation of food by limiting the blood supply to that part of the body and increasing the blood available in the arms, legs and head. Survival takes precedence over digesting one's most recent meal. When the blood vessels leading to the abdomen are constricted the blood supply is not sufficient for the male erection. The penis is a spongy mass that can absorb a tremendous amount of blood so that it can become erect and hard. As we shall see in a further discussion, fear is probably the main cause of impotence and the inability to have adequate sexual intercourse. Fear closes off the blood vessels into the internal organs and into the whole abdominal area from which the penis and testicles derive their blood supply.

A woman has a similar response to that of the male, but it isn't as obvious. The inside of a woman's sexual organs changes when she is sexually aroused. She secretes a mucous that allows sexual intercourse to take place comfortably. There is also an increased tenderness. Oftentimes women have to be manually stimulated before they can have an orgasm by intercourse. And getting people to simply enjoy each other and stimulate each other may be necessary before an adequate sexual experience is a possibility. The woman who is afraid, or whose mind is busy with other thoughts, or who thinks that sex is ugly, awful or repulsive, or worries that her partner is not clean, will not be easily stimulated and may receive little or no pleasure in sexual intercourse. She may even dislike it.

The fifth level of sexuality is that of the secondary sex characteristics. Aside from the genitals, naked little boys and little girls up until the age of ten look much the same—it is very difficult to determine their sex. But then comes the second biologically timed release of sex hormones and the changes of puberty. Those males who lack the necessary hormones at this time can remain as undeveloped as children. One of Morton's friends in college—about fifty years ago—simply never entered puberty. You can imagine the cross this was for him to bear. His voice remained high, he had no facial hair, no development of the external sexual characteristics, and he never lost his baby fat. This situation was a real crisis for this young man. Marriage became impossible and he felt very incomplete. The same hormonal failure occurs in some females. Some women fail to develop significant breasts. In a society that views them as a sex symbol, this deficiency can cause deep psychological wounds.

In normal development in the male, the chest swells, hair develops on various parts of the body (first around the sex organs), the voice goes down, and the body is programmed for sustained and aggressive bursts of activity. The female body, on the other hand, develops to enable her to bear children and care for them. The hips grow larger, all the sex organs develop and then the breasts develop—usually by the time the woman is about fifteen. Studies show that females usually have more nurturing capacities and are less aggressively hostile. One author suggests that because of these characteristics it would be helpful for peace if there were more women in high levels of government.[13] It is fortunate, however, that the reproductive system lags behind the rest of development so that most girls are unable to conceive much before the age of fifteen.

In addition to these physiological factors in sexual differentiation and probably related to them there may be neurological differences. The brain researcher, Dr. Candace Pert, suggests that the brains of males and females may well be programmed in different ways. She believes that it takes greater skill to bear and raise children than just to fertilize a female, hunt and fight. We shall look at her suggestion in a later chapter.

Levels one through six, which we have just explored briefly, all deal with physiological aspects of sexuality. When problems or deficiencies occur in these areas they can be treated, if at all, only through medical intervention using surgery, drugs or other physiological procedures. Our only suggestion is that people faced with such problems seek the very best medical help possible. University medical training centers and large medical clinics are the best places to seek help. Levels seven through thirteen, however, are not primarily physiological in nature. We shall describe these remaining levels briefly at this point and then explore them in greater depth in the chapters that follow.

A seventh aspect of sexuality is gender identity, determined largely by sex assignment and rearing. This brings up the whole issue of how society views the roles of the different sexes. As Sandra Ben has pointed out, "The distinction between male and female serves as a basic organizing principle for every human culture. . .all societies allocate adult roles on the basis of sex and anticipate this allocation in socialization of their children."[14] Cases are reported where a perfectly normal female or male has been raised according to the gender expectations of the opposite sex. Such rearing will have an effect upon how we view ourselves as men or women, our social roles and our sexuality. Instances of radical role switching are rare, but subtle suggestions as to what our role should be can have an effect upon our gender identity.

The relationship of gender identity and sexual identity, our eighth level, is not well understood. Sexual identity is how we view ourselves in our sexual functions. Some women with a somewhat masculine gender identity still have a female sexual identity and some do not. The same is true of men also. We will discuss the many different possible kinds of sexual identity in the next chapter. The women's liberation movement has been attacking the gender role expectations of Western society. Many women and some men have come to believe that these gender expectations are the result of prejudices on the part of a maledominated society. This important subject will be explored after we have examined the matter of sexual identity.

Levels nine and ten deal with the social and religious aspects of sexuality —society's mores, religious commandments, taboos and customs. In a society where religion is central it is difficult to distinguish between customs and religious sanctions. Among the people of Bali, for instance, religion and mores are inseparable and nearly indistinguishable. Lyall Watson has described the same quality in rural black African society. We refer here to religion as socialized religion; later we shall speak of religion as the personal and experiential relationship with the divine: what we call the spiritual dimension. Cultural and individual religious expression can be closely related. However, in cultures where little value is given to the individual, or in societies where individual consciousness and experience are deemed very important, they can be quite separate. Religious rules on sexuality vary greatly from culture to culture as C.F. Ford and Frank Beach show in the important study, *Patterns of Sexual Behavior*.[15] We shall be referring to this work often as it is the only comprehensive work on this subject to date.

Perhaps the most benighted dimension of all is the legal dimension, level eleven. This is true at least in the United States, the Soviet Union and China. Many Western European countries have recently modified their laws regarding sexuality. On the other hand, Japan does not view sexual behavior as a matter of the state's concern as long as no violence is involved. Many states in the U.S. still have incredibly antediluvian laws on the statute books providing life imprisonment for husband and wife engaging in widely practiced sexual activity such as oral sex.

In most "civilized" societies a double moral standard exists in which women are more severely judged than men. However, in legal matters men (except in cases of prostitution) receive far more convictions than women. The facts about sex and the law must be read in order to be believed. Katchadourian and Lunde provide an excellent summary of the data in *Human Sexuality*.

Level twelve deals with the psychology of sexuality. Mature sexual relations are as much a matter of psychology as of physiology. How do we integrate the sexual aspect of our lives with intimacy, caring, love? What is love psychologically? Can sexuality be a sacrament of love?

If there is a spiritual dimension of life, there is a point where psychology leads to spirituality. We move on to the spiritual dimension of sexuality in level thirteen. What is the ultimate purpose and thrust of sexuality? We believe that the pervasive and nearly unquenchable fire of sexuality not only drives us to reproduction and companionship, but helps us to discover the very depth of ourselves, the various aspects of ourselves that we project out onto our beloved. Thus sexuality can push us toward consciousness and wholeness, toward salvation and even toward the inscrutable God of love. Augustine said that God made us restless so we might find in God the only adequate source of rest and wholeness. Those who have experienced the divine love that brings wholeness, peace, fulfillment and meaning testify that not only have they discovered the purpose of life, but they are then enabled to love other human beings with something of the same self-giving love that has been showered upon them by the Divine Lover. Many people find that mutual sexual ecstacy provides a symbol for divine union.

CHAPTER TWO

Formation of Sexual Identity and Attitude

The effect of parental modeling, behavior, and attitude upon children in the area of sexuality cannot be overestimated. Morton remembers his first sex lesson very clearly: "I was about five years old and was taking a walk with my mother down by our church. I recall seeing a little brook on one side of me and the church with a lovely stained glass window on the other side. For no reason I remember I suddenly asked my mother, 'Why doesn't Aunt Gertrude (my maiden aunt) have any children?' I knew immediately that I had trespassed into forbidden territory. Talk about consternation— my mother turned green, white and blue all at the same time. I don't recall her stammered reply, but I realized I should never ask anything like that again. Here was a *bad*, a forbidden subject."

A child picks up parental attitudes toward sexuality long before verbal communication. All you have to do is watch the average parents with a sexually "Conservative" background as they wash their child. They dig into the ears to get the dirt out and clean out the nostrils. The back and arms and legs and even the anal area are carefully cleaned. But what happens in the genital area? One quick wipe and on down to the feet? Children get the message: this is a bad area—don't touch.

According to a recent newspaper article in a Washington paper, Dr. Mary S. Calderone, author and adjunct professor in the New York University human sexuality program, says that parents who try to inhibit children from exploring their genitals may cause "sexual stuttering" (inhibitions in sexual functioning) later in life. Dr. Calderone advocates an acceptance of childhood sexuality and parental teaching of responsible attitudes toward sexual expression.

The article also pointed out that new research shows that a fetus in the womb has a sex life. Sonograms reveal that male fetuses have erections (one every five hours). Innate sexuality in the womb may also apply to females although ultrasound cannot demonstrate it. This research confirms Dr. William H. Masters' contention that "all the physical systems of the body are functioning fully at birth—with the exception of the reproductive system, which begins functioning at puberty."

OUR PERSONAL SEXUAL EDUCATION

Many parents do not express affection—to each other or to their children. And in more homes, whether poor, middle-class or rich, two subjects are very seldom discussed—sex and money. These topics raise parental blood pressure and touch anxiety hot buttons. Consequently, children learn not to see their parents as sexual beings, and this certainly inhibits and can even malform children's sexual identity. Morton's first formal familial sexual information came when he was seventeen and about to go off to college. His father took him aside and started to talk about the birds and the bees. His father was so embarrassed that Morton felt sorry for him. So he took him off the hook by telling him that he already knew about all that. Yet at that point Morton didn't even realize nocturnal emissions were normal occurrences. He had to wait until he was a junior in college rummaging around the college library before he learned that fact. This sort of thing contributes to sexual confusion and guilt and even contributes to a host of emotional problems that the psychiatric profession no longer likes to call neuroses.

Barbara's sexual education was as sketchy as Morton's and she describes it. "When I was four-and-a-half years old my only other sibling, a brother, was born. I had been praying for a brother or sister. Whether my mother had suggested this I do not remember, but I was not told that a baby was expected and I noticed no change in my mother's figure. Her friends didn't either as she hardly showed her pregnancy. She only became slightly plump.

"I went to stay for a few days with friends of the family at their home.

My father came over and took me home one day and he was cutting a door from my parents' bedroom into another bedroom (up to this time I had slept in a crib in my parents' room). He then told me that my mother was in the hospital. The doctor had brought her a baby boy—a little brother for me—and now I was going to have a bedroom of my own and the baby would be using my crib.

"I was sure that God had answered my prayers and was delighted to have a baby brother, but I was *not* delighted to lose my place in the parental bedroom. However, I worked out a system to get back into my parents' room and bed.

"When I was about 10 years old I began at that early age to mature. My mother one day explained that some day soon I was going to discover I was bleeding. She told me that I should be glad about it because it meant that I was becoming a woman. Then she told me that her mother had not told her and she was sure when it happened she was being punished for her sins and she was so scared she tried to keep it from her mother. Her mother finally saw the evidence and gave her the cloths (before the time of sanitary napkins or tampons), showed her how to fold them and said to expect this to happen every four weeks or so. This is all that my mother told me—I saw no connection between menstruation and having a baby and I believe I thought the blood came from the same opening as urine.

"During high school I became aware somehow that babies grew inside the mother. My mother then gave me a book to read which I am sure she thought would teach me all I needed to know. All I got out of it was that a boy and a girl loved each other enough to get married. The ceremony was beautiful and for days afterwards they sat at a lakefront and watched the beauties of nature (birds, bees and butterflies). Also they watched the sunsets and held hands. Occasionally he would hug her to himself. Finally the girl was 'in the family way' and had a baby. That is all I absorbed from the book. I read it years later with more knowledge than before and that is all it actually said!

"At seventeen years of age I still couldn't figure out what started a baby growing in a mother. My girl friends were curious also but no one seemed to be able to get the answer. This was before World War II yet the situation was, at least where I lived, still part of the Victorian era. I finally decided to ask my mother although I was sure before I asked that it wasn't the thing to do. She was ironing when I finally asked, 'Mother, what relation is a father to a child which grows in the mother? How does he have anything to do about the child?' I really didn't even know how to ask the question properly. My mother replied: 'Dear, you know I told you about menstruation when it was time for you to know about it; when you are old enough I shall tell you about the relation of a father to a child.' I went away to college that year and two months later my mother died so I never learned how old I needed to be to be informed. When I was about to be married she would undoubtedly have told me.

"In college most girls arrived as ignorant as I but there were a few more experienced ones and during the first week we were all enlightened. I must admit that those who knew the facts of life were pretty accurate in their knowledge as far as it went. We later took biology that taught us about reproduction and we had 'health' class which covered more personal information about sexual organs.

"One positive aspect of my sexual education was my parents' relationship; they were very much in love with each other and were affectionate not only toward us children but with each other. They hugged and kissed modestly in front of us. The message about intimacy and sex was not negative. There was something holy and good between married people but it was nothing that children, at least female children, should be bothered with. Childhood went into the twenties in our culture. 'Be children while you can, you will be adults soon enough.' Even in college I never found out about masturbation. I didn't even know one could do it until a doctor gave me Butterfield's book just before I was married!"

We lived in an age that had little radio, no television, vast parental control and few of the outside sexual stimulations that our children and grandchildren have been raised with. In many ways we had less to cope with in the sexual realm than our grandchildren and all the present younger generation will have. However, in our counseling experience few young people have received much more adequate information than we did from our parents. One reader of this material reported that in 1974 as a student at the very middle-class Colorado College for Women, many entering students were as ignorant as those Barbara described.

WHAT IS THE PROBLEM?

Most of the leading surveys on sexual education of children and adolescents reveal the same absence of parental instruction. John Gagnon and

William Simon have produced two excellent studies replete with data and sex researcher Aaron Haas has done the same. In one survey most sexual information was received from equally poorly informed peers (59% for the males and 46% for females). Printed material came in second percentage wise. Only 3% of the males and 13% of the females received their primary information from their mothers. Fathers were the main source of information for 6% of the males and 1% of the females.[1] Haas also points out that when teenage respondents were asked to rate six activities in order of importance—sex, athletics, doing well in school, friendship with the opposite sex, friendship with their own sex, and romantic attachments with someone, sex ranked fourth with boys and last with girls.

What is the source of our fear of talking about sexuality and sexual conduct? Why is the subject so delicate and forbidding for adults that they are uncomfortable discussing it with children? We believe the heresy of gnosticism that has permeated many of the sexual attitudes of the Christian Church is responsible for a great deal of the sexual negativity and unwholesomeness of our culture.

Gnosticism had an ancient history and has continued in many forms up to the present time. In many ways it was a creative force keeping alive ideas that the church refused to acknowledge. However, its influence in sexual theory has been one of the most negative influences within the church. All gnosticism does not continue the myth we shall describe, but the gnosticism that influenced the church contained it. There are many forms of gnostic belief. In the Protestant Church it helped form much of the point of view of Puritanism, and in the Roman Catholic Church it dominated the attitude of Jansenism that influenced the training of many men and women's Catholic religious orders. When we went to Notre Dame in 1969 we were surprised to find even more sexual repression among students raised in parochial schools than we had experienced in our Puritan background. In the Old Testament we find almost none of this negativity toward sexuality. In fact, sexuality, sexual relationships, copulation, childbearing and rearing were all considered perfectly natural, normal and acceptable.

In the New Testament, with the exception of a few passages in St. Paul, there are few negative statements about sexuality. It isn't until St. Augustine of Hippo in the late fourth century that we find the gnostic viewpoint about sexuality predominating. Early in the Church's life a conflict arose about the nature of evil that wasn't resolved until the end of the fourth century. The mainline Christians accepted the Old Testament as scripture and believed that the God revealed there was ultimate spiritual reality. Along with the Hebrews they believed that the physical world was an expression of the Divine, the direct creation of God, and therefore good. The gnostic attitude toward creation on the other hand sprang out of Persian thinking that saw two equal and opposite divine creative forces—the light and the dark. In the Persian view both the light and the dark were present in the spiritual world and in nature. The main purpose of human morality and religion was to support the forces of light and so enable them to conquer darkness and bring salvation to the universe.

Ultimately, however, a perversion of this Persian viewpoint developed and became a seductive Christian heresy. The dark force became equated with matter, with physicality and with the God of the Old Testament, while the light force became equated with spirit, spirituality, asceticism and Jesus Christ. In gnosticism matter was seen as ugly, recalcitrant, irredeemable and evil. The creation of human beings in this point of view was an imprisoning of pure and holy spirit in vile matter. If we believe that spiritual reality is a realm of bliss, harmony and ecstasy (what the gnostics called the pleroma) then the mingling of spirit and matter becomes a cosmic catastrophe rather than purposeful, orderly and good.

In the myth of gnosticism, such a cosmic catastrophe did occur; the realm of blissful spirit exploded and little fragments of spirit became imbedded in the earth where they became human beings. In the midst of such a catastrophe, how is salvation achieved? Through asceticism—by eliminating any attachment to the world of physical reality and by getting rid of emotional involvement and physical pleasure. However, there is something far worse than failing to be detached: bringing more soul or spirit into the world of matter thus becomes the ultimate evil—conception becomes the worst possible human act. Carrying this idea to its logical conclusion, one extreme Gnostic sect, the Manichaeans, taught that intercourse with preadolescent girls was not ultimately evil because pregnancy was not possible. Even the Roman Emperors were shocked by this idea and outlawed the sect.

Gradually the idea developed within this sect that anything to do with conception or copulation or sexuality or genital organs was evil or ugly. St. Augustine was a fringe member of the Manichaean sect for nine years and although he eventually disengaged himself intellectually, he never entirely disengaged himself emotionally. His little book *The Good of Marriage* has some passages on marriage that are well nigh unbelievable. Even normal sexual intercourse within marriage can be venial sin; the quicker married people abstain from all sexual relations the better for their souls. For Augustine all sexual acts or pleasure outside of marriage were mortal sins—acts sufficient to separate people forever from God and so consign them to hell.

The Church as a whole rejected this gnostic dualism: the Apostle's Creed was written to establish the goodness of the earth and the human and to declare that even the body is worth resurrecting.

Most of the Church Fathers—men like Justin Martyr, Irenaeus, Clement, Cyprian, Ambrose, Basil and Chrysostom—disagreed violently with gnosticism. The Fathers and doctors of the Church maintained that this viewpoint was utterly fallacious; it denied the possibility of the incarnation, God's coming in the flesh in Jesus. And St. Thomas Aquinas, whatever other theological failings he might have had, did affirm the goodness of the natural world and rejected gnosticism and Manichaean ideas. But the damage had been done; gnosticism had worked its way into Christian thought in the Western Church and expressed itself in Canon Law and moral teaching and still affects our sexual attitudes as we will show later on. In a culture where the body and its sexual feelings are often perceived as evil the sexual development of the children of that culture is bound to be warped.

One of the many areas affected by this viewpoint is the attitude toward masturbation, and we will deal at length with this topic later. Children are sexual beings and exploration of the body is natural; so nearly all children play with their genitals and many children masturbate at two or three. When parents slap their hands as a form of control, impressionable, sensitive children can be traumatized and sexuality itself is seen as bad, wrong or evil: children learn much more from parental acts and attitudes than most parents realize. Children are more influenced by what we do than by what we say.[2]

PARENTAL INFLUENCE

Let's look at some concrete examples of how parental attitudes tend to shape children's sexual identities. Certainly the lack of emotional affection and touch in many homes causes some youngsters to fail to relate sexuality and affection and such parental modeling can cause later sexual confusion. How parents treat the sexual interests and play of children can also have a profound effect upon the adult lives of those children.

In one family we knew well the parents expressed horror when their five-year-old son and a neighborhood girl were sharing their genitals, but no explanation was given. Then they showed equal horror when their son five or six years later was discovered in some homosexual play. Again tears and horror but no explanations. Then to put the frosting on the cake they expressed their thorough disapproval of the girl that this boy began to date as a teenager. Again they did not explain (indeed, there was never ever any discussion of sexuality). This disapproval blocked the young man's natural heterosexual drive. He had several homosexual episodes in his life before he realized that he really preferred a heterosexual adaptation. If the family had taken the son aside and said, "We are afraid this girl's family wants to corral you for the sake of prestige and money, and you know, sex is a pretty powerful force. Let's talk about setting some limits. . ." But no, the parents simply chopped off the heterosexual inclinations the teenager had.

One reason for dating in our society is to provide opportunities to develop heterosexual relationships in the context of caring and love. The idea that sex and affection are closely related is a relatively new social goal as Herbert Richardson shows in *Nun, Witch and Playmate, the Americanization of Sex*.

Another example of sexual confusion in a family we knew occurred when the parents took in a teenage girl the same age as their son. The girl was the most attractive young woman in his high school, so naturally he was sexually drawn to her. However, she was out of bounds for him; she was not to be touched. She was his sister and she wasn't his sister. The boy's natural heterosexual development was set back by this confusion in relationship. The situation could have been discussed and been a helpful experience; instead it became a roadblock in the teenager's masculine development.

One man, remarkably successful financially, once told us with pride that he had used a book on dog training as his guide in raising his five children. He also provided them handsomely with money even after they were married. It never occurred to him that children needed to develop independence. It was difficult for two of them to establish a comfortable sexual identity and two others remained dependent upon him until he died. Even in his declining years he had to ask others to speak to his children for him; he simply did not know what it was to listen or relate to them.

In another situation the father was the dominating patriarchal figure in a family with two sons and a daughter. His wife was cast in an inferior role of competent servant. Any opinions that she voiced were treated as ridiculous by her husband and ignored. The daughter worked for several years in counseling before she could shake off her own desire always to be right like her father and to be able to relate to another man as a human being who could care for her. The father complex can be as destructive for a woman as the mother complex for a man.

Many parents and guardians set limits for children in the matter of social contacts and dating without any explanation or discussion. The law is delivered from on high and cannot be questioned. Such an attitude reveals mainly the insecurity and fear of adults and often drives young people into reactions that can be disastrous. Few matters are more important or rarer in social and sexual development than communications between children and teenagers and the adults responsible for them. Most parents will need to do some digging for facts as well as do some honest soul searching and growing regarding their own sexual attitudes if honest communication is to be possible.

Despite the fact that it was not all smooth sailing in our relationship with our two sons and one daughter in their teenage years, we did try to answer all their questions honestly and completely and to talk very frankly with them on the subject of sex. One day we found one son reading a *Playboy* in the living room. Morton intervened in the conflict between him and his mother. Understandably she didn't want it on the rectory living room coffee table when the parishioners dropped by and she had informed him the next time it would be destroyed. We decided to give him one more chance and as long as he kept *Playboy* within the confines of his own room, it was within limits. *Playboy* may not be the best introduction to interest in the opposite sex but it was an interest in the right direction, to be encouraged, not squashed. One day two former counselees were visiting our son at home with us and we all got on the subject of sexuality. "Well," said my son, "if I ever had any questions, I just asked my father or my mother." This kind of familial interaction was inconceivable to our counselees.

The importance of communication between parents and their children of whatever age can hardly be overemphasized. Without listening to children from their point of view there can be no genuine caring and little communication on any subject, particularly on subjects charged with emotion. This is not the place to describe the process of communicating and caring for our families. Morton has dealt with this subject at length in *Caring: How Can We Love One Another?*. This book expresses our mutual experience in learning to communicate with each other and with our children. Growth in sexual understanding depends upon this kind of communication. When we have not experienced this kind of relatedness in the home, we seldom learn it except through some kind of therapeutic help. There can be no sacrament of sexuality unless there is love and there can be no genuine love where we have not learned to listen and communicate with each other.

It is most helpful for children and teenagers to see the naturalness of sex. Jung noted that young people growing up in farm country where the fertility of animals is necessary for survival don't get the same kind of negative conditioning that many city youngsters do. But a knowledge of the facts—and a willingness to talk without fear—on the part of the parents can go a long way in making a child comfortable with his or her sexuality. Certain books on the subject of where babies come from and on sexual maturity are helpful to have around and available for children.[3]

THE RANGE OF SEXUAL ATTRACTIONS

The sexual identity of a child is first fostered in the family and developed among peers and conditioned by the society in which the child lives. Five overlapping but different common sexual adaptations are found among human beings—heterosexual, homosexual, bisexual, celibate and asexual. (There are also the less common modes of sexual stimulation that have been called paraphilia or less frequent unconventional sexual behavior. We shall discuss some of those in a later chapter.) And there are many variations in each of these adaptations. As Kinsey pointed out we should speak of heterosexualities, homosexualities, bisexualities, celibacies, asexualities. Using the singular is very misleading. We shall treat this later on at greater length. Of course these are not entirely distinct and separable categories; they are more like concentrations of points on a many-pointed scale. Certainly we need to recognize that there may be parts of our lives in each category; we are very complicated creatures. However, children as they mature usually adopt one of these basic orientations. Part of our sexual identity is a willed decision or choice about what our behavior will be. Sometimes physiological and psychological factors override these decisions. Let us look at each of these five sexual adaptations.

People with a heterosexual identity will find themselves primarily attracted to people of the opposite sex for their sexual gratification. They see themselves as males or females and find themselves sexually drawn to their opposites. The continuance of the species depends upon this attraction and it is deeply rooted in our biological makeup. As we shall show a little later this does not mean that people with this identity may not occasionally feel some attraction to those of the same sex. Heterosexuality expresses itself in many different ways. The most common form in most civilizations is some form of marriage where the arrangement is according to the mores of that society and is considered more or less permanent. Then there are long term committed relations outside the rules of the society in which the people live. Many people consider themselves single and yet entirely heterosexual. They prefer occasional sexual unions or they are widowed or have been unable to find a permanent mate. Prostitution is still another sexual outlet for heterosexual males and Kinsey found that 69% of his white male sample had had at least one contact with a prostitute. By far the greatest number of rapes are heterosexual.

Human sexual feelings are not entirely biologically determined, for men and women can be exclusively attracted to the same sex for their sexual satisfaction and for experience of erotic intimacy. The words homosexual and homoerotic are derived from Greek words meaning attraction to the same sex. As we shall show later there are as many different kinds of homoerotic relationships as there are heterosexual. They range from permanent deeply caring unions to short-term relationships, to one-night stands, to rape. The percentage of people with a homosexual identity who consider themselves single is far greater than the number of those who are heterosexually inclined; a far larger portion of women make these long-term relationships than men. American society puts many roadblocks in the way of the more permanent kind of homosexual relationships.

Those with a bisexual orientation (and surveys show far more in this range than is ordinarily believed) have strong or moderate attractions sexually and emotionally toward both sexes. People in this position may be married heterosexually or in a long-term homosexual relationship. They may live a single lifestyle with sexual experiences with both sexes or they may opt for the celibate way of life. Some human beings are able to have warm, caring sexual relations with both sexes. The person with this orientation is often forced to face two different and seemingly opposed aspects of his/her inner life and can be driven to despair. But if the person can stand this tension he or she may find an inner wholeness. Society offers little direction or help for such people and there are very few support groups available for them such as have recently developed for those with a primary homosexual orientation.

Both the homosexual and the bisexual are quite different from the transsexual person. The latter feels like a woman imprisoned in a fully developed male body or a man imprisoned in a fully developed woman's body. These situations are relatively rare, but have caused considerable public interest because of the development of sexual surgery to change sexual identity. Except for operations on hermaphrodites, Johns Hopkins Hospital, one of the leading hospitals in the United States, began to phase out sex-change operations in 1978. They had discovered that those who underwent surgery were no better adjusted than those who did not. Again we stress that such radical medical action should only be taken in a center such as Johns Hopkins Hospital.[4]

Most of us usually think in terms of either/or distinctions rather than a many-pointed scale in which there are many different combinations between two quite different attitudes. One of the most important findings of Kinsey and his associates related to sexual behavior in regard to the three categories just mentioned. They presented a scale showing how exclusive heterosexuality shaded into bisexuality and finally to exclusive homosexual behavior.[5]

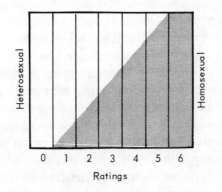

Less than 50% of the male population surveyed could claim that their sexual experience was totally heterosexual (and less than that if childhood sexual play was considered). Among women less than 60% could make that claim. On the other hand, exclusive homosexual activity varied from 1% to 3% among women and 3% to 16% among men. The best comment on these data is from Kinsey:

> Males do not represent two discrete populations, heterosexual and homosexual. The world is not to be divided into sheep and goats. Not all things are black nor all things white. It is a fundamental of taxonomy that nature rarely deals with discrete categories. Only the human mind invents categories and tries to force facts into separated pigeon-holes. The living world is a continuum in each and every one of its aspects. The sooner we learn this concerning sexual behavior the sooner we shall reach a sound understanding of the realities of sex.[6]

The research methods of Kinsey and his group have been questioned by some scientists. Kinsey's data upset a lot of our ideas about what actually occurred in human sexual behavior and shocked many people. However, most of the students of human sexuality agree that there is no other hard data available. Most of the surveys on partial aspects of human sexuality bear out the general direction of Kinsey's findings. What we have learned in counseling situations when people feel free to express whatever is bothering them, bears out to some extent the data this survey provided. We shall deal with many different aspects of this report as we go on.

CELIBACY AND SEXUALITY

This brings us to the subject of celibacy. The word itself comes from a Latin word meaning single or unmarried, but celibacy has come to mean either the permanent or temporary conscious abstaining from sexual activity. Abstaining may mean refraining from sexual relations with others that lead to orgasm or it can include cutting off sexual fantasies and masturbation or even ceasing any contact with another that produces erotic pleasure. Many different religious groups either require or advise celibacy as a permanent or temporary state.

As we shall show later the magisterium of the Roman Catholic Church states that celibacy in the strictest sense is required of unmarried people if they do not wish to fall into mortal sin. Members of religious orders, male and female, are required to take the vow of perpetual chastity, or celibacy. Most priests in the Roman Church are required to be celibate if they wish to be ordained, although there are some Church groups in communion with the see of Rome that do not require celibacy, most of them with Greek or Russian Orthodox backgrounds. The papacy is trying to eliminate these exceptions at the present writing, although inconsistently some married Episcopal priests have been accepted by Rome. In the Roman Church celibacy is not a matter of doctrine, but of discipline.

Among Hindus celibacy is encouraged among young people to encourage their growth in consciousness and among older people as a recognition of the illusion of the physical world. Ghandi believed that celibacy increased one's spiritual power. Total celibacy is required of some Buddhist monks and many serious followers of Buddha. In many warrior groups temporary celibacy was thought to increase the male's power, since relations with women were believed to be draining upon them. Uriah the Hittite, the husband of Bathsheba, had made such a vow and this caused King David great embarrassment as described in II Samuel, Chapter 11.

At the present time when sexual relations are perceived by many to be truly meaningful only within a loving context, many people opt for temporary celibacy until they find such a relationship and some never find it. Some even find that abstinence from sexual relations is an interesting experiment in our period of sexual freedom. *The New Celibacy* by Gabrielle Brown was published in 1980. She stated that people are more creative physically, artistically and intellectually if the water flowing into the "sewer is diverted to the garden". This sounds to us a little like gnosticism revisited.

Celibacy can be consciously chosen, temporarily or permanently: it may be required as a precondition for vocation; or it may be part of a socially enforced code for unmarried people. Although celibates may be asexual, most are not. Many celibates can, if they are conscious enough and wish to go this route, try to bring about the sexual union within themselves rather than through outer relationship. We have been invited as a team to several monasteries to explore with religious celibates and potential celibates the importance of recognizing both masculine and feminine aspects of their inner being and encouraging them to try to bring these quite different parts of themselves to an inner union. This wholeness can lead people to be open to God's love and their detachment from primary outer relationships can help them share with a wider group the love of God that they have experienced personally. One wise abbot told me that he doubts if men and women brought up without contact with each other can be fully human and reach their potential in ministry; the sexes usually need each other in order to discover themselves.

In some cases human beings are conditioned to be asexual, to have little consciousness of themselves as sexual beings or of sexual attraction to other human beings. In many patriarchal societies women are conditioned to think of themselves as asexual or merely responsive to male desire: in Victorian culture "nice" women were essentially asexual. Many people have pointed out the utter unfairness of a society that allows sexual feelings in only one sex.

Important experiments done with monkeys have demonstrated that baby monkeys who have contact only with a surrogate terry cloth mother and a bottle, rather than the warmth and affection of a real mother, tend to grow up to be asexual and cannot copulate.[7] Someone has remarked in referring to these studies: Are we to think that human beings are less sensitive to social environment than monkeys? Similarly it has been noted that children reared without fondling and touching also have many problems, some of them sexual. The studies of Dr. René Spitz show that up to one-third of the infants raised in aseptic nursing homes with very little human contact died of a disease known as mirasimus. When attendants were brought in to provide holding, fondling, and caring physical attention the death rate from the disease dropped to ten percent. If this deprivation can cause death it certainly can have an effect upon psychosexual growth, development and identity.

One of the reasons that sexual problems are so prevalent in much of Western society is the lack of warmth, affection and touch that we have received and that our parents and grandparents have received before us. A society or religion that perceives sexual contact as evil, dangerous, ugly or defiling often views touching as equally so because affectionate human touch can lead to sexual stimulations. Of course this is true—touch *can* be sexual. A member of a woman's religious order who had been raised in a very repressed sexual atmosphere told me that the way a certain male religious held her hand signified far more than fraternal friendship. But the dangers of a warm, touching atmosphere are far outweighed by the dangers of a lack of human warmth. Just as in monkeys, in humans who have been raised without human touch the sexual urge can be greatly diminished; sexuality can become merely a brutal aggressive act with little relationship to caring.

Asexuality is not the same as celibacy. People with an asexual adaptation do not express their sexuality either because they never fully matured, because their sexuality is repressed within them, or because they have consciously tried to suppress it. These people often put up a wall around their feelings and cut themselves off from emotional and sexual relationships with other people. Instead of moving toward wholeness and life they often retreat from it. Because of the repression of a vital aspect of their being they often have a host of physical and emotional problems. These people are not to be judged but offered the best of medical and psychological wisdom available.

As we will discuss in some detail, each of the first four of these sexual ways of life can lead to wholeness. In each situation the goal is to cease seeking for wholeness in and through another person, to cease using another person just for personal fulfillment. To come to potential wholeness we must find ourselves through these relationships and bring the various different and sometimes warring parts of ourselves before God so the Divine Lover may fashion a unity within us and enable us to go back into relationships with human beings more interested in giving than in receiving, in loving than in being loved. Such wholeness doesn't come easily; it is the result of a lifetime of work and struggle.

Whatever our sexual identity, we need to recognize that there *are* other identities and not be judgmental about others' sexual preferences. Many people who consider themselves heterosexual are vehemently judgmental toward individuals who express themselves in homosexual acts or speak of their homosexual feelings; such violent reactions usually betray an unconscious fear of their own homosexual component. And we *must* rid ourselves of the old wives' tale that one homosexual contact makes a person a homosexual. Nearly half the population has had at least one homosexual contact. Many of these occurred during the teens or early twenties. A sensitive person who has been convinced that one homosexual experience indicates an irreversible homosexual personality can be pushed into an essentially alien lifestyle and can even be driven to the verge of suicide by self-condemnation and confusion. We really need to clean the cobwebs out of the closet on this issue.

Carl Jung has made the profound and important suggestion that parents' unconscious attitudes will affect their children as much as their conscious attitudes and training will. These unconscious attitudes can be assimilated by the child's unconscious and may be lived out by the child without realizing from whence they came. The classical example is the child of a straitlaced minister who lives out many of the repressed desires of the parent. And if parents are scared to death of extramarital or bisexual or homosexual attractions and create an emotional scene every time their children display any of these characteristics, they can create a reaction formation, actually making the unwanted behavior more likely. This reinforces whatever influence the parent's unconscious has upon the child.

Sometimes the roots of male homosexual adaptation are seen in a family situation where there is a lack of relationship between father and son. If the father is not a person upon whom the son wants to model himself, and if the mother is warm, caring and affectionate, the son may identify unconsciously with the mother and may pick up many feminine attributes.

One young man of seventeen who came to Morton for counseling had shared his mother's bed from the time of his parents' divorce many years before until he was sixteen. This resulted in many, many problems; not the least of which was being cut off from his sexual feelings. His mother put him in a situation where any healthy heterosexual boy his age would feel sexual desires—sharing his bed with a woman—but in his case the object of the sexual attraction was forbidden. This young man developed serious problems because of this double-bind situation, which forced him to repress his normal sexuality. The sexual drives are strong; if they are cut off from the usual channels they can appear in many bizarre and antisocial acts.

Parental models can also have an effect on girls. For example, if a teenage girl is shown through parental modeling that the female has an inferior place in society, she may form a more masculine adaptation. This masculine identification can cause the woman all sorts of deep problems resulting from a wounded femininity and she may become what is known as a "daughter of the patriarchy",[8] suffering a father complex or an Electra complex. Until parents know themselves and are comfortable with their own sexual identities, they cannot help their children towards a healthy acceptance of their own sexual identities and towards their own wholeness. Sexual education, like most education that produces changes in attitudes, begins with parents.

It can help us understand how parents and society help form sexual identity if we look at the sexual attitudes in a culture quite different from our own. The following passage is taken from *Sexuality and Spirituality* by John Moore.

I was fortunate to be a member of an anthropological and botanical expedition to South America, an undertaking which at one stage took four of us into the Xingu area of the Mato Grosso of Brazil.

We stayed there for a period with a tribe of Indians who had had very little contact with the civilized world. It was said that their mode of living was about equivalent to that of the Stone Age. The implications of that I found totally impossible to comprehend at the time. To me they were fellow human beings—and very friendly and handsome ones at that—who happened to live in a very different way from the culture to which I was accustomed in Europe.

On the other hand, I could appreciate—since their ancient, natural and traditional way of life, and their relationship with the environment, were so different from mine—that their mental processes of assessment and reaction must be utterly at variance with those I was accustomed to expect. There was no possible way of bridging that difference to any significant effect; but that did not preclude our ability as human beings to live together in harmony, demonstrating through conduct our respect for each other. We could not converse but we could communicate simple messages through exchanging signs. There was very little we could offer them materially but they gave to us generously, especially food. They allowed us space in one of their large huts, where we slept in hammocks adjacent to one of their families. They welcomed us to accompany them about their daily occupations.

They had no clothing to cover their healthy, lithe, well-proportioned and, in the case of the men, muscular bodies. By the second day of our stay, our own clothing seemed an absurd encumbrance and we happily abandoned it. I felt self-conscious only for a short while—not at being naked in public, but due to my pale tenderness compared with their glowing bronze, a contrast I felt to be between my superficial sophistication and their naturalness. This abandonment of clothing not only provided a physical sense of freedom but a psychological one also. Of course, we all undress frequently, but either in private for specific purposes or, if in public, still retaining covering for the sexually-associated parts of the anatomy. Few people in the temperate, civilized areas of the world have the opportunity to remain naked and carry out all manner of daily occupations from dawn to dusk. In discarding our clothing in that situation, it was as if one had also discarded a habit (so that I am sure the double meaning of that word is not simply coincidence).

The action was not just the abandonment of a physical protection and defense but was effectively the abandonment of a psychological one also. This immediately removed a barrier of pretension (erected by us) from between ourselves and these so-called 'primitive' people. This in turn promoted a natural empathy; we had, as it were, nothing to hide from each other.

I had also not realized until that experience the extent to which clothing creates a false sense of modesty. As a man from a culture where women are seen continually clothed in public, it was at first novel to encounter them naked at all times. However, it was not in the slightest erotic; and that in itself furthered the sense of relief and freedom.

No doubt subtle factors unconsciously influenced the sense of its being inappropriate to become sexually aroused in their company but, at the time, it simply seemed that the nudity of those women did not invite it. It was as if mentally or physically they were not radiating or projecting sexual desire, thus being 'naturally modest' (or, rather, in that context it seemed that the concept 'modesty' was quite irrelevant).

To what extent the Indians modified their behaviour due to our presence I do not know. All I can affirm is that the whole time we were there, I did not observe a single overtly sexual gesture. Undoubtedly the tribe observed certain practices and disciplines with regard to sexual behaviour; and that implies a socially imposed code of conduct. However, to the extent that we were able to observe their daily lives, their obedience to that code did not seem to be artifically restrictive or to be followed for appearance's sake only. The impression gained was that of the *modus vivendi* being one that an unaffected, natural group would adopt in unthreatened conditions.

Certainly the experience proved to me that the covering with clothing of the genitals and breasts in the interests of modesty is an absurd pretence. One of its main effects is to generate a frustration and tension in members of the opposite sex which, in turn, can then cause detrimental repercussions in society. In modern societies, particularly in the case of women's clothing, the token covering of sexually-associated parts of the body in the name of modesty is actually exploited to arouse the opposite effect.

To what degree it could be said that the sexual behaviour of the Indians was influenced by a 'religious' factor is hard to determine. We witnessed an elaborate ritual for girls at the age of puberty, dances suggesting acknowledgement of metaphysical influence and communication, and evidence of respect for the dead. It is hard for us, accustomed to the consigning of features of our lives into separate categories, to comprehend an ethos where it seems no such categorization exists. I surmise that to analyze the behaviour of those people and to try to understand it in divisive, departmentalized terms—for example, its economic, political, social or religious aspects—would be to ignore, and probably destroy, the simple integrity of purely natural response to environment. It seems to me in retrospect that the conduct of their lives could most sensibly be comprehended as total attunement and obedience to the cycles and seasons they observed and experienced around them. For them it would be a time to be born and a time to die, a time to hunt and a time to fish, a time of fertility and a time for a woman to bear a child.

In such primitive societies, assuming they had no knowledge or means of contraception, could it be said that they only entered into the mystery of intercourse for the sacred purposes of procreating the species and of ensuring the tribe's survival? And that therefore the fulfillment of those purposes constituted in themselves the 'religion' of their lives?[9]

This passage gives a totally different view of the human body and sexuality than most of us are accustomed to. Sexuality is a part of the mystery of life, part of religion. Indeed the whole of living is seen as religious. Secular and religious are not separated. The sexual organs are in no way evil and sexuality is seen as a part of the holy mystery.

A tribe in New Guinea practices ritualized homosexuality between the young male adolescents and mature young men. Yet in this particular tribe there is almost no adult homosexuality. This homosexual practice is a ritualized part of life. We might expect such behavior to cause adult homosexuality. But for this tribe the lack of such ritual would destroy the very possibility of their becoming fully masculine.[10] We shall say more about this tribe later.

There are some tribes in the South Sea Islands where there is almost no sexual taboo surrounding genital touching and caressing. Little boys playing around with each other discover that they have erections and later on that in their roughhousing they have ejaculatios. They find it all a lot of fun and they have little negative feeling or guilt about it. Parents pay little attention to this sexual play. As they mature the boys and girls discover each other and make a natural transition to heterosexual involvement. If, however, adult men find themselves separate for an extended time from women they may revert to homosexual acts. Once returned to their families they return to an entirely heterosexual adaptation. Adolescent homosexuality has little or no effect upon the adult sexual orientation. These tribes have almost no exclusively homosexual adults. Some of these tribes do, however, have a strict taboo about shaking hands!

Let us look at a culture at the opposite extreme from these primitive groups with "permissive" sexual attitudes. We were surprised to find among the Moslems in Malaysia a very stringent sexual code. As much of a woman's body is covered as possible. Orthodox Islamic women appear for work in the big commercial centers dressed like pre-Vatican II nuns in full habits. The law of the land in Malaysia enforces for Moslems the Islamic law of *Khlawat*. Any non-Moslems caught making affectionate advances (and this may be as little as holding hands or a kiss) toward Moslem women are required to marry them, pay a fine, and convert to Islam. A Moslem man found in the same situation must also marry the woman and pay a fine. Hindu and Chinese people in Malaysia are governed by different laws and customs as long as they have no intimate relations with members of the Moslem majority.

Some highly sophisticated cultures such as the Japanese are nearly as permissive as the tribes that we described earlier. As a patient in a Japanese hospital, Barbara discovered a very different attitude toward the unclothed human body. It was as unnoticed by women as men in the Japanese bath. Virtually no laws exist in Japan prohibiting any kind of sexual behavior as long as it is not associated with violence; the expression of sexuality is considered a private matter with little legal, oral or religious implications.

In pointing out this cultural diversity, we are *not* suggesting a return to the happy and natural primitive state or Rousseau's romanticism. We are merely trying to show how different our cultures are when it comes to matters of sexual law, custom and taboo. We need to reflect carefully concerning our sexual attitudes, and check out the cross-cultural data, before concluding that our ways are the only possible behavior or that our customs represent the pattern of "natural law". We also need to be very careful about forcing our sexual mores on any other group. We shall even find marked differences within the different Christian communities.

CHAPTER THREE

Sexuality and Culture

In nearly every culture sexuality is seen in terms of the world view of that civilization. Where the culture has a dominant religious tradition, there is a close connection between religious belief and sexual taboos and practices. In some cultures having sexual relations with the temple priestesses was perceived as a means of communing with the goddess worshipped there. On the other hand, as we have already noted, many religious groups have seen abstinence from sexuality as necessary for a deeper level of religious experience and development.

In Asia Minor and Greece many cults of the great mother goddess flourished in the centuries prior to the emergence of Christianity. The male devotees of Cybele worked themselves into a frenzy, castrated themselves and laid their testicles on the altar. In Corinth at the temple of Aphrodite (another mother goddess) several hundred priestesses were available to provide sacred union with the goddess. Even daughters from noble homes sometimes served in these temples temporarily. This was not just prostitution as is so often found in the Western world; it was understood as communion with the goddess of the earth, a *hieros gamos* or heavenly marriage. Some anthropologists have viewed these practices as merely fertility rites to ensure a fecund earth, but they were more than just symbolic magic. St. Paul had great success presenting the Christian message to temple women disenchanted with this life. However, he had to remind them in one of his letters that they should no longer dress as sacred prostitutes for they had now changed their lifestyle. They should now act as demure, ordinary women.

In many temples in India there are explicit sexual carvings of many different kinds of sexual expression (no prudery here); these appear to represent wholeness or union with the divine. Gods and goddesses were often depicted in sexual embrace. In many cultures menstruating women are believed to be unclean or taboo. In front of a little Balinese temple close to the hotel where we were staying was a sign written in English and Balinese: "Menstruating women are asked not to enter for our holiness and your protection." In China one group of Taoists perceived the sexual union as the union of the yin and the yang. Thus the sexual union was perceived as expressing wholeness and harmony with *tao*, and union rather than orgasm was considered as the goal.[1] On the other hand in many religious groups total abstinence from sexual arousal was considered as necessary for detachment from this world and its illusions. What we believe about the ultimate nature of reality will influence how we think about sexuality and what kind of practices are encouraged or forbidden.

After years of thought and study we have come to see five quite different views about the meaning and value of sexuality: Western materialism, Eastern spiritualism, the sacramental view, sex as basically procreation for God, and the developmental view of depth psychology. In addition to these five paradigms, we must also examine the almost universal and perverse belief in woman's inferior position to man which can operate through any of these views. In this chapter we will examine the five sexual paradigms; we will reserve our discussion of the role of women for the following chapter.

MATERIALISM AND SEXUALITY

The idea that only the material world is real and significant is not unique to Western civilization. It was also the attitude and belief of several recurring schools of thought in China's long history and was one point of view in ancient Greece and in the Roman world. It is essentially the belief of Marxist communism and of most of the scientific community, and it has touched nearly every part of our modern world. If the only reality in the universe is material, matter, then mind, spirit and soul are *nothing but* temporary and insignificant by-products of matter; human values share the same fate.

This point of view is applied to human beings with brilliance and consistency by Melvin Konner in his book *The Tangled Wing*. We are *nothing but* what our genes have programmed us to be. Sexuality is simply the mechanical, evolutionary process by which genes reproduce themselves. The pleasure derived from sexuality, in this point of view, is merely a biological inducement to propel people into copulation so that the species may continue. It is interesting to note a recent discovery that shows that only apes—among all animals— experience anything like a human orgasm; the ecstatic orgasm is a basically unique human experience. Sexuality in this view is merely an invariable biological mechanism to bring us together and to force us to produce children and maintain the gene pool. As the biological organism increases in complexity it produces psychological inducements as well as blind compulsion to copulation.

It is no wonder that sociologists with this point of view believe in genetic engineering to improve the species; this technique removes those with inadequate genes from the gene pool and encourages those with superior genes to have more children. A May 5, 1984 article in the *New Straits Times*—an English Malaysian daily newspaper—describes the Social Development Unit (SDU), a governmental agency of the city-state of Singapore designed to create opportunities for college graduates of opposite sexes to mingle freely and to nudge them gently into wedlock. Prime Minister Lee Kuan Yew called upon the government to stop a decline in the island's national talent pool. The natural sex drive seems to be inhibited by college degrees and an increase in women's consciousness and needs to be stimulated. Observing the place of women in most oriental marriages it is no surprise to us that educated women in such a culture would hesitate to step into marriage.

Behaviorism is the most important psychological development within the materialistic world view. It teaches that our physical environment rather than our genetic structure shapes human beings. Mr. Konner is, quite understandably, violently opposed to this idea. People are changed, according to this school of thought, largely through reward and punishment (operant conditioning). This applies to sexuality as well as everything else. People can change if they desire to and will submit to proper conditioning. This point of view has legal overtones and ramifications in our society. If people break the sexual rules, they are punished. If they don't reform they are banished from the social group and put in prison. In B. F. Skinner's best selling novel, *Walden II*, the description of the behaviorist utopia, those who do not respond properly to conditioning are simply thrown out of utopia into the "uncivilized world". The rotten apples can not be allowed to contaminate the hedonistic happiness of the rest of the barrel.

Unfortunately, society usually deals with those who deviate from its standards on the basis of this theory. The prison system is also built upon this theory of punishment, and effectively turns most inmates into confirmed criminals. The only prisons that do not have an eighty to ninety percent rate of returning prisoners (recidivists) are those that break this behaviorist theory and provide an atmosphere of genuine concern for the individuals where people are really cared for rather than punished. And to make it worse, people with money or good attorneys seldom go to prison. Conditioning is a kind of manipulation and is the very antithesis of the view of Christ who suggests going out to the lost, to the inadequate, to those in prison and relating to them with concern and love. The film *Clockwork Orange* portrays the sinister character of conditioning and subtly contrasts this with the way of suffering love. The saddest irony is that prisons are the worst place to send sexual offenders if society wishes to "correct" them for it places them in a sexually abnormal situation.

Materialism tries to be value free; it holds that there are only material realities. According to this point of view values are unsubstantial and should be dispensed with. We know of no serious discussion of the depth and value of love from either of these two materialistic views. Both views contribute to our store of knowledge about human beings, but when either or both are taken as the total picture, they fail to take into account the full gamut of human life and experience, including sexuality, our capacity to love and religious experience. Sexuality is reduced to reproduction and pleasurable sensation.

Many Western humanists have tried to deal with sexuality and love while avoiding the whole matter of world view. Carl Rogers and Eric Fromm are two excellent examples of this. They both see the importance of sexuality and love; they emphasize the importance of love in sexual experience. They are not, however, able to deal with the religious dimension of sexuality and love. Sometimes people with this humanistic viewpoint become incurably romantic and fail to see love as related to procreation on one side and religious experience on the other. Like the troubadours of late medieval France they separate love, procreation, and committed relationship to the detriment of all three.[2] Still another example of romanticizing sexual experience for its own sake is found in the array of pulp and slick magazines and books available in every newsstand. The "feeling" of love and the experience of sexual pleasure have become an end in themselves and relate to nothing else.

SEXUALITY IN THE EASTERN WORLD

A least one-half of the world has been touched by the great religious traditions of India, Hinduism and Buddhism. Although the Chinese and other Far Eastern people have modified Buddhism, its fundamental framework has had profound effect on the thinking of that half of humanity. Few Westerners have spent much time in the East or know much about the history, life or culture of the Orient and the rest of Asia; they simply do not know how different that world is. And yet, according to one survey several years ago, some eight to ten percent of the people in America have been touched by Transcendental Meditation or some form of Yoga, or have been involved in some Eastern religious sect. How easily we bury our heads in the sand.

There are nearly as many variations of thought and practice in Hinduism and Buddhism as denominations in Protestant Christianity—maybe even more—and any generalization will be false to some degree. Yet there is a basic framework common to those religions emerging from India. This world view can almost be described as the mirror-opposite of Western materialism.[3] Its basic idea is that the spiritual world is real and the physical, material world is illusion. This view has very specific implications for sexuality. Sexual feelings and love are states in which the emotional, spiritual and physical touch. If indeed the universal and spiritual, that which is beyond space and time, is the only genuinely real aspect of reality, then sexuality and even human love can easily be viewed as experiences that drag human beings back into illusion, away from reality and salvation.

Buddhism as taught by Buddha is a remarkable and consistent way of life by which human beings are taught to escape from the inevitable suffering and meaninglessness of this transitory and illusory world. Buddha discovered and taught a method of detachment from all emotions and desires which tie us to this world and its chaos. Once free we can experience the bliss of enlightenment or *nirvana*. Obviously one of the most powerful desires is sexual; this must be conquered before we are free. In lower animals it even takes precedence over survival. Monasticism, asceticism and celibacy are therefore almost a necessity for attaining the higher levels of enlightenment. Buddha also taught compassion; indeed once he had been enlightened it was his compassion that induced him to give up *nirvana* to help his fellow human beings. But this compassion is not directed toward the outer situation of suffering persons, but rather toward providing a method of overcoming the universal agony of humankind; to help people to become enlightened and free. It is seldom concerned with relieving oppression and poverty or improving the economic system or helping people overcome sexual problems.

Much of the same fundamental view of the universe is also found in Hinduism, out of which Buddhism sprang. The inner eternal rather than the outer event becomes the important focus of life. Not only the physical world, but the ego itself is illusion in this world view, and what we do with our lives, how we grow and develop as discrete individuals in space and time are relatively insignificant. There is little biography in either of these traditions; individuals as such do not count. Our task is to detach ourselves from this illusory world and merge with Brahman and so avoid returning by reincarnation to this miserable existence. Several of the Hindu pantheon of gods are understood as expressing the very nature of love, but again it is not love that seeks to help make this world better, but rather love that provides deliverance from this world.

Robert Johnson, the author of *He*, was in India with a Hindu guru and gave alms to a beggar. The guru rebuked him, telling him that he was interfering with the man's karma. Robert replied that he was doing it for himself and not the beggar. The guru agreed that was permissible.

From this point of view the idea that human sexuality or love might lead to the divine or have eternal consequences is nonsense. The *Bhagavad-Gita* is very clear on this point. At the conclusion of the great Hindu classic, the *Ramayana*, the king and hero leaves his beloved wife so that he can come to true holiness. After the long struggle to be with each other and their blissful union and their ideal reign, they must separate to achieve spiritual maturity. Only alone can the king enter the spiritual world unhindered and unencumbered; intimate loving and sexual relationships can block ultimate spiritual growth if they are important to the individual. They are not a bridge to the divine. Gandhi tells in his autobiography of reaching the insight that he must abstain from sexual relations with his wife if he were to attain full spiritual power. He also advised those within his ashram to do the same.

The idea that the physical world is illusion can be very dangerous for Westerners, as Jung has pointed out again and again. Without the rich spiritual wisdom and mature spiritual guidance to be obtained from Hindu gurus as well as the discipline required, Westerners can trip themselves into playing with religious ideas or even into psychosis. Several counselees of ours used Eastern religious ideas to avoid real-life problems and created a worse situation for themselves. The practice of Zen Buddhism in Japan leaves some novices in a state known as Zen madness; they are caught in a world of inner images and cannot pass through to *satori* or back to ordinary existence.[4] Peter Coukoulis in his book *Guru, Psychotherapist, and Self: A Comparative Study of the Guru-Disciple Relationship and the Jungian Analytic Process* describes the lives of several Hindu saints. From the point of view of Western psychology some of them appear to have lost their ability to deal with physical reality and to have suffered psychotic episodes. Sexuality and love can give us extravagant notions about our beloved at times and keep us hopelessly entangled in this world, but they can also keep us rooted in the real physical world in a healthy way.

Romantic and sexual attachments can lead to the dead end described in Hinduism or Buddhism or can force us to look for a savior. What is the best path for one person may be the worst for another. Salvation for each individual will depend on his/her unique nature and history and this includes the kind of sexual practice proper for that person.

SEXUALITY AS SACRAMENT

We have already alluded to another world view that states both the physical *and* spiritual worlds are real. This basic belief was common to both the Hebrews and the Greeks and was the frame of reference of the Roman-Persian world into which Christianity was born. The eternal, the spiritual, is real and permeates the physical; the physical then becomes a carrier of, an expression of, a sacrament of the spiritual. Concrete physical reality is part of the ultimate nature of things and is also of eternal value. The creative divine reality can operate through us material human beings and when it does these acts can be truly valuable and holy.[5]

We have already seen how gnosticism came to influence Christianity with its devaluation of the physical world and sexuality, but this point of view has never been representative of the mainstream of Christian thought. As a matter of fact gnosticism is a variation of the Eastern view. Both of these views devalue the physical aspect of reality; one perceives matter as illusion and unreality in any ultimate sense; the other believes that matter is an actual, concrete evil. In both points of view salvation is achieved through knowledge (gnosis is the Greek word for knowledge) of the way that frees us from being trapped and through a strict control of those actions and emotions that keep us embroiled in either the unreality or in the active evil that wars against the spirit. In this view of sexuality, love, which is so closely related to it, becomes a hindrance to salvation.

In his book *Myths to Live By* Joseph Campbell looks to the Eastern religions for ultimate meaning. The weakest chapter in the book is on love, for he can find no Eastern myth that provides a central place for love in that tradition or that sees human love as a pathway to God. In 1984 at a talk given by him at his 80th birthday celebration Campbell said that he had returned to the Western view of reality because he saw it as a more complete view of existence.

Although a misunderstanding of Plato contributed to the gnostic tendency in the Christian Church, Plato actually taught that love was one of the four ways by which we are given access to the world of the Ideas, the spiritual domain.[6] In both the *Symposium* and the *Phaedrus* he describes the process by which love leads to the divine. Plato believed that a beautiful soul is out-pictured in a beautiful body. In the first stage of love two people fall in love with the beautiful body of the other through physical attraction. As they come to know each other more intimately they come to love the psyche of the person more than the body. They fall in love with the beautiful soul of the other person. Love (Eros) then drives the lovers to seek the God who, as source of beauty and goodness, has created the beautiful person, soul and body. According to Plato genuine love can be a ladder that leads to God. Some of the rungs on the ladder may be missing, however, and we need to be careful as we climb. We are not mature if we get stuck on the first rung, the physical.

Jesus of Nazareth shared the Hebrew belief that God made the physical world in all its complexity and the spiritual world as well and that both were good. He believed that we can share now in a spiritual dimension of reality and taught his followers that they could communicate with Abba, the heavenly father, as a present reality. He also believed in a host of heavenly beings that influence our lives. The incarnation and resurrection of Jesus are the supreme examples of the importance of both aspects of reality. Jesus characterized the essential nature of God as love and taught his followers that their best pathway to God was to love all people as unworthy of their love as his disciples had been of his love—love that was supremely expressed in his coming among men, emptying himself of his divine power, teaching, healing and then dying and rising again. This divine drama was presented to out-picture God's love and provide saving power over the evil that attacks us in so many ways.

When the Church has been most alive and vital it has lived love, not abstract love with no feeling or sexuality in it—what Berdaeyv has called "glassy Christian love". Love with its feet grounded in sexuality and its heart and head in the kingdom of Heaven became for Christians one essential part of the pathway that leads us to God. Dante described love as the reality that moves the human soul as well as the sun and other stars in his monumental *Divine Comedy*. Charles Williams has portrayed the power and religious value of love in his seven novels, but particularly in *The Greater Trumps, Descent into Hell*, and *All Hallow's Eve*. He has also provided one of the finest modern theological presentations of this idea in a little pamphlet entitled *The Theology of Romantic Love* and in his magnificent study of Dante, *The Figure of Beatrice in Dante*. He pointed out that there were two ways of coming to God, the way of negation (*via negativa*) that finds god through withdrawing from the world and the way of affirmation (*via affirmativa*) that seeks God through the world. He maintains that a committed relationship with another person can lead on to wholeness and God as well as withdrawing from them. One's beloved can become the symbol that opens the way to God. Dante's love for Beatrice was probably never consummated by sexual intercourse, but she became a living symbol of "love" that saved him, guided him and eventually brought him to the beatific vision. Since our book is about love and sexuality and their relation to the religious way we shall be examining the affirmative path in greater detail as we proceed. On this path sexuality becomes an essential part of coming to religious fulfillment.

PROCREATION FOR GOD

In the first pages of Genesis God is recorded as saying: "Let us make man in our own image, after our likeness. . . Male and female created he them. . . Be fruitful and multiply and replenish the earth and subdue it." (Genesis 1:26, 27, 28.) The implication is clear. The earth is God's creation and is good and it is the *religious* duty of human beings to fill the earth and to enjoy it. This is a holy task.

And then God called Abraham to sire a holy people who would be God's people in a particular way. This nation is begun by God's special action through the miraculous conception and birth in the aged Sarah. This people will be God's people and even though they have such a problematic beginning they shall be as numerous as the sand on the seashore or the stars of heaven. It is the holy responsibility of this people to increase and multiply.

No woman was to be left childless. It became the responsibility of a deceased husband's brother to have sexual relations with the widow and raise up a family for his brother. The story of Onan in Genesis 38:9-10 bears this out.

Judah then said to Onan, after his brother Ur had died:

> Take your brother's wife and do your duty as her brother-in-law. But Onan, knowing that the child would not be his, spilt his seed on the ground every time he slept with his brother's wife in order to avoid having a child for his brother. What he did displeased the Lord and therefore he killed him.

Onan was probably practicing contraception by withdrawal. The need to increase the population of the Hebrew people probably lies behind this prohibition of contraception. Later this spilling of seed was extended to cover masturbation as well. Indeed masturbation is often referred to as onanism.

The emphasis of the Jewish law on procreation had a very practical basis. The Jews were surrounded on one side by the Egyptians and on the other by the Babylonians. They needed every single warrior they could muster. Because children were so badly needed in this small nation and the biology of sexual reproduction so little understood, it was thought sinful to waste any semen. While we were in Malaysia the government was urging all Moslem families to have at least five children for much the same reason. The country is underpopulated and has Thailand on one side, Cambodia on another and Indonesia on a third side—all greatly overpopulated. It should also be noted that only the Moslems are urged to multiply—the Moslems do not wish to lose their political and religious power. They, like Israel, consider themselves a holy people, the only true worshippers of God. It is their religious duty to cover the earth.

In Bangladesh and India there are basically two reasons for having a large number of children: first, children are the only social security in these countries; second, children will guarantee that the parents are decently buried and given the proper entrance into the next life. In China, where ancestor worship is still strong in spite of forty years trying to suppress it, bearing children is important so that the souls of the ancestors will be given adequate respect and worship and so that one will become an ancestor to future generations and will have someone to worship and honor one's self.

When the procreation of children becomes a central purpose for human sexuality, it often follows that procreation is seen as the *only* moral reason for human sexuality. Fr. Keane writes: "To the extent that St. Augustine did break with the 'sexuality is evil' notion, he tended to place himself in the 'sexuality is for procreation' school."[7] He goes on to say that the average Catholic was given no other direction for thinking until the *Code of Canon Law* in 1917 and the *Casti Connubi* of Pius XI in 1930. In each the mutual help that spouses gave one another was described as a secondary but nonessential good of the marriage relationship.

During the Middle Ages it was believed that women were merely the garden in which the little new people were planted and grew. The sperm was seen as being a complete potential new life in itself. Thus any conscious "spilling" of the semen was tantamount to murder and a breaking of the commandment forbidding murder, rather than the one relating to adultery and impurity.

Even Vatican II, liberal in so many ways, stills sees procreation as the main purpose of marriage: "Marriage and conjugal love are by their nature ordained toward begetting and educating children. Children are really the supreme gift of marriage and contribute very substantially to the welfare of their parents. The God Himself who said 'It is not good for man to be alone' (Gen. 2:18) and 'who made man from the beginning male and female' (Mark 19:4) wished to share with man a certain participation in His own creative work. Thus he blessed male and female, saying: 'Increase and multiply' (Gen. 1:28)."[8]

Richardson suggests in *Nun, Witch, and Playmate* that the Protestant reformation introduced a new individualism into the Church and this brought about a revolution in our ideas of marriage. Individual human beings are no longer just a part of the family or the social group or of the past. When this change occurs and people marry because of their own personal desires and preferences, then society is changing. Within this framework the personal relationship, the personal affection and sexual communion, is the the essence of the marriage and children become a nonessential secondary good. He wonders: "Is it merely an accident that of all the people of Europe, the men who had the courage first to leave their homelands and settle in America were predominantly Puritans and spiritualists—those in whom the idea of personal marriage had come to fullest consciousness?"[9]

SEXUALITY AS DEVELOPMENTAL PROCESS

A fifth viewpoint toward sexuality emerges from the psychological study of human beings and of children in particular. Freud challenged the prevailing idea that children were asexual and theorized that the pleasure principle-libido-id sex drive was the basic life force and that it developed through certain well-defined stages and only emerged as loving genital sexuality at maturity. He also believed that any individual who remained stuck in one of the earlier stages of sexual development suffered not only sexual problems as an adult, but other personality disorders as well. Freud came to his conclusions largely through the study of emotionally disturbed people through pathology. We do not view Freud's stages nearly as definitively as he did, but they are the basis of so much theorizing about human development that they need to be sketched out.[10]

Freud states that we pass from stage to stage in our sexual (libidinous) development: from an oral stage to an anal stage, toa phallic stage, to a latency stage (throughout this period children were polymorphous-perverse), and finally to the stage of genital maturity. During the oral period of development the libido is largely expressed in sucking through the mouth and Freud maintained that people still primarily interested in oral-genital activity and those still intent on putting things like cigarettes or pipes in their mouths are still caught in the oral, dependent stage of psychosexual development. In the anal stage we begin to learn to control the bowels and find pleasure in both this control and its release. Erikson sees this stage as one of learning autonomy. People who are very miserly or constipated are said to be anal-retentive. They find it difficult to let go of anything or to hold on to things when appropriate.

The third stage of development is the phallic, when sexuality becomes associated with the genitals. (Note the sexism of calling it a "phallic" stage.) At this period, which occurs sometime between three and five in most children, the sexual organs become the object of interest and manipulation, often resulting in orgasmic masturbation. There is also a real interest in exploring the sexual apparatus of others of the opposite sex and the same sex. Freud also believed that at this stage the Oedipal drama was reenacted in all children. Oedipus was the Greek king who unwittingly killed his father and married his mother and is celebrated in a Greek drama entitled *Oedipus Rex*. Freud states that the young boy is attracted to the mother and the young girl to the father. If the child is able to resolve this conflict, then he or she passes on to the next stage. Freud saw this unresolved Oedipal conflict as the root source of most of our emotional problems. Psychoanalysis is the instrument he developed to help people resolve this conflict at a later period in life.

Childhood sex play according to this theory is a natural part of the growing up process. Why so early? This early age in children corresponds approximately to the time at which most other animals come to sexual maturity. Freud saw this early childhood sex play as the emergence of the developing sexual energy in the biological mechanism which is deferred in the human being some eight to fifteen years until puberty for fulfillment. Although we had learned about sex play from counselees as young children, we were surprised to find how much data was available on this subject. Orgasm for little girls and orgasm without ejaculation in boys is very common behavior from three on. It is amazing how prejudice can blind our eyes to such facts. Both Katchdourian and Lunde and Carole Offir present conclusive data on the sexual activity of prepubescent children.

If we truly believe this theory of sexual development we will no longer be horrified when we find children in sexual play. If they are very young we will merely say to ourselves, "Oh, so he or she is beginning to mature sexually." If the child is older we will explain to him or her that some things are done in public and some things are not and that there are times when actions are appropriate and times when they are not. Trying to stop sexual play in young children (particularly when the parent is upset and confused and ashamed) is more likely to reinforce that practice in the child's mind by attaching importance to it. On the whole, girls are less likely to masturbate and engage in sex play than boys, probably because the female genital equipment is much more hidden and less easy to stimulate. The best stance parents and responsible adults can have is to ignore it, explain it when necessary and treat the whole matter as casually as possible.

It is difficult for us brought up in a sexually repressive society to realize that masturbation and sex play are a normal part of growing up. For the Church to view such sexual play as mortal sin and teach this to children is a refusal to face reality and the facts of child growth and development. It is as serious as condemning Copernicus or burning Giordano Bruno at the stake; it is like still maintaining that the sun goes around the earth.

According to Freud, this stage was followed by a latency period, approximately ages 5 to 12, in which interest in sexual activity died down or was directed in other directions. However, the only hard data available indicates that sociosexual play increases in males during this period and decreases in girls only after the ninth year. There is good reason to see why girls in a society fearful of pregnancy out of wedlock would be discouraged from such play as they approach puberty.[11]

Freud also believed that all children were polymorphus-perverse. By this he meant that they would try any kind of sexual play including masturbation, playing doctor and undressing others or being undressed, inserting objects in the anus, prepubescent intercourse, heterosexual or homosexual genital-oral play, anal intercourse, exploration of animals' genitals and dressing in the clothes of the opposite sex. Again, the data which we have suggests that in the period described as latency this play increases rather than decreases for boys and only decreases in girls after nine years of age. It would seem at least for males that the flame of sexuality once ignited throughout childhood continues to burn with increasing vigor.

One of the most common of these polymorphous-perverse activities is homosexual contact. Kinsey's data bears out this contention. It is the most common form of childhood sex play for males up to puberty, accounting for the sexual activity of 21% to 30% of the boys from nine through thirteen. Among girls in the same age bracket it is still more common than heterosexual play, but only amounts to 8% to 9% of sexual activity. Even into puberty, homosexual play continues to be a significant percentage of sexual activity for both male and female.[12]

This data has led some students of sexuality to see the homosexual stage as a normal stage of development operating in late childhood and early puberty. It is easier for most of us to relate to the known than the unknown; in addition society separates girls and boys to a large extent. We can observe this homosexual interest in "crushes" that are not primarily physical but nonetheless emotionally meaningful and also in physical play among members of the same sex anywhere from nine to seventeen years old. Crushes with members of the same sex can prepare for and even lead to the ability to deal with the unknown, the opposite sex. Freud, however, did not explicitly call attention to this as a stage of development. Gagnon and Simon in their study of human sexuality state that adolescence rather than childhood is the critical period in sexual development. They point to the fact that most males learn about orgasmic sexuality in the social group with other males and even engage in competitive contests to determine who can shoot the fastest or farthest. Sexuality then becomes an activity detached from relationship and caring. These authors conclude that such a homosocial introduction to sexuality "can lead to a capacity for detached sexual activity—activity whose only sustaining motive is sexual. This may be the hallmark of male sexuality in our society."[13]

This detachment may be caused or at least encouraged because of the stigma associated with homosexuality—the boys may fear that emotional involvement in this type of situation may mean that they are homosexual. Emotional involvement with other males is seen as a greater indication of homosexuality than physical contact. It took one counselee several years of work before he could remember the extent and emotional involvement in his teenage homosexual play. It was a great relief to him when he was able to confront it and be released from the repression that made him forget it.

Freud viewed polymorphous-perverse activities as normal for children, but believed that these activities should be outgrown as people attained the genital stage, the last stage of human development, in which two people of the opposite sex meet in loving sexual union. The very name polymorphous-perverse carries a negative value judgment. Freud developed psychoanalytic treatment in order to free individuals from oral and anal fixations and from the problems surrounding the Oedipal conflict, to help people come to terms with "mature" sexuality and make adequate heterosexual adjustments. When sexual aspects of life fall into place, according to this theory, our lives run more freely, with less of our energy spent in repression and neurotic avoidance. In our counseling experience we have found that sexual fear and tension can certainly cause a host of emotional and physical problems. These, however, are not the only tensions and fears in childhood as Alice Miller shows so well in *The Drama of the Gifted Child*.

It is often helpful in talking with people who have sexual problems to be able to reassure them that coming to mature sexuality is a developmental process and that in most cases growth can occur if growth is really desired. This knowledge lifts a tremendous burden from many people who had considered themselves hopeless deviates. It is much easier to accept that one may be undeveloped than that one is all askew. This knowledge can also help us treat children's sexual play in a much less fearful and condemnatory way, realizing children pass through these behaviors and stages. They are most likely to pass on to maturity when their sexual play is ignored rather than blown out of proportion by ill-informed and moralistic adults. When these behaviors seem excessive then a psychologist should be consulted. Punishment usually reinforces undesirable actions, increases their incidence and causes guilt.

The real problem in lack of sexual development isn't one of failing to meet standards set by conventional morality; it is getting stuck in one particular stage because for one reason or another we have been kept from the responsibility of full life. Freud viewed adult homosexuality as failure to resolve the Oedipal conflict or getting stuck in the polymorphous-perverse behavior of childhood. For him homosexuality was more pathology than immaturity and as he states in a well-known letter to a mother distressed about her son's homosexuality, he saw it as nearly impossible to treat. In our discussion in a later chapter we show that many psychologists do not view homosexuality as either pathological or immature.

The attitude towards homosexuality is not the only limitation of Freud's view of sexual maturity. His emphasis on genital sex as the only truly mature sexual act can also inhibit playful sexual relations among heterosexual couples which may contain elements of the various earlier sexual stages. Freud's attitude can even cause a kind of prudery about sexuality.

As we have shown, Freud interpreted all of human existence in terms of sexuality. In this matter three of his former associates—Jung, Adler and Rank—differ from Freud; although they accepted many of his ideas about developmental patterns, they didn't see sexuality as the only significant factor in development. Jung believed that sexuality on all levels is an inevitably important drive and also a symbol for the experience of the union of the opposites, of wholeness, of the numinous, of the Divine. (At times he is infuriating as he assumes that his readers are acquainted with Freud's writings and that the reader will know when he does not agree with Freud, and when he is in agreement. Jung does not spend much time on ego development or the importance of sexuality in emotional disturbance. This has led many people, including some "Jungians", to believe that these were not important for him).

Someone has said that Freud saw life, love and human development in art and civilization as symbols of sex. Jung viewed sexual experience as an important reality in itself *and* as a symbol of wholeness and life. According to Jung, human life does not come to its ultimate fruition until human beings come to realize that there is a Reality superior to human consciousness that human beings can experience. The highest levels of human maturity, growth and creativity come from relationship with this Reality beyond the human psyche and available to it. Both Rank and Adler came to a similar position in their late writings. Rank died at fifty-five and Adler at sixty-two while Jung worked and wrote until three weeks before his death at eighty-five. Some of his most important writing took place during the last twenty years of his life and emphasized the religious needs of human beings. We met Jung when he was in his eighties and never have we met anyone with more vigor, incisiveness, personal dynamism or spiritual understanding. He was certainly not losing his acumen in old age.

From Jung's point of view each individual has a unique destiny which extends beyond the limits of the material world. The task of the analyst or psychologist is not to mold a person to some preconceived model of maturity or just to unscramble their confusions about sexuality and authority. Rather, it is to accompany other people in the voyage of discovery as they seek to understand their own individual way and then aid them in achieving their destiny. The task of the psychologist on this level is that of the midwife who allows birth to take place. Jung once said: "Thank God I am Jung and not a Jungian." Unfortunately some Jungians, unlike Jung, get so caught up in archetypal ideas that they fail to see the importance of childhood traumas, authority conflicts, and sexual tensions. Therefore they fail to enable people to deal with these aspects of life and so do not provide the necessary personal ego base from which growth through numinous experience is possible.

Some of Freud's insights are particularly useful in resolving problems that keep people from functioning as adults. Jung's unique contribution provides ways for people *who have achieved effective adult participation in life* to deal with the problems of meaning and transcendence. In some particularly gifted people both of these concerns must be dealt with in late adolescence and early adulthood. We have often remarked that with most people under twenty-five with problems of inadequately facing adulthood we use Freudian ideas while Jung's broader perspective is more helpful for people who have lost their sense of meaning and are floundering in despair. Sexuality and love are important in both of these struggles. It is difficult to use sexuality as a path toward God and meaning until we have come to terms with our personal sexual problems and neuroses.

Many people in our society—consciously or unconsciously— view sexuality as evil. Sexuality is not evil. It is no more intrinsically evil than my will to power, my desire for dependency, my drive to create, my thirst for knowledge, or my passion for chastity. All of these drives are good in the service of God, the Divine Lover. Evil arises when any of these drives becomes autonomous or the central purpose of life and is thereby given over to the destructive forces in reality. So the questions we must ask ourselves are: How am I using my sexuality? Am I using it as the central focus of my life for momentary pleasure, or for power, or as an end in itself? Or am I using it to facilitate love, relationship and spiritual experience in my growth and development and in the growth and development of my partner or spouse and those around me?

Once we arrive at this understanding of sexuality, then we find it easier not to judge ourselves or others. None of us totally achieves this goal. Nearly every one of us has some remnant of all the various developmental stages within us—remnants that we need to be kind to and not repress, but *not necessarily* live out. Indeed living out whatever pops up from the psyche can be destructive and even lethal. This is the task: to recognize honestly whatever remnants of immaturity there are within us, to deal consciously with them, to bring them to God, to ask for help so that they do not run us, and then to ask for the transformation that is possible through God's love and the courage and humility to bear what is not changed. And finally to ask that this creative tension of our imperfect lives may bring us more often and more intimately into God's presence and love.

Achieving sexual maturity is very seldom an easy task for any individual human being. Nearly all of us have some sexual hang-ups. The problem of developing sexual maturity is complicated because mature sexuality necessarily involves another person and this means dealing with another person's sexual fears, doubts and inhibitions as well as dealing with our own. For the last five or six thousand years nearly all "civilized" cultures have solved this problem by viewing women as inferior to men and subject to them. Only half the population was given the option of freedom in developing toward sexual maturity. And men were given a false view of sexuality by having submissive women available. It was a "no win" situation for both sides. Before we can even look intelligently at the Christian view of sexuality we need to examine the pervasive propaganda concerning women's inferiority. True sexual maturity involves mutuality and this is impossible except among equals.

We shall also find a much more liberal view of sexuality in matrilineal cultures or societies; in them the Mother Goddess usually enjoys the center of devotion. The value and importance of women usually goes along with a view of reality in which sexuality is valued, perceived as good and even sometimes understood as holy. The value of women and sexuality usually wax and wane together.

CHAPTER FOUR

The Patriarchal Putdown

Of course there are differences between women and men; anyone with eyes can tell that. But in addition to the physical differences, there are differences in customs and attitudes, in dress, in expectation and, in our patriarchal culture, huge differences in opportunity. It is a neat trick to disentangle which differences are biological and which are due to cultural conditioning. It is even more important to answer the questions: Why is it that in nearly all major cultures in our world today women are looked upon as physically, emotionally, and mentally inferior? Why are they viewed as defiling, polluting, dangerous, and seductive; as meant to serve men; as good only for cooking, children and church? Why is their reason for being, in many societies, to satisfy the sexual needs of men and to care for their homes and offspring? Like many things that are taken for granted, once the questions are asked and the matter is out in the open, the obvious becomes the absurd.

In order to answer the questions we have posed let us first of all look at the biological evidence for differences in ability, attitude and behavior. Then let us move on to history and try to reconstruct how the present attitude developed. Then let us examine the patriarchal view of the Old Testament which, although more benign in its attitude toward women than many of the world's cultures, is quite representative of the patriarchal view of women. After examining this view we will look at the teachings of Jesus on the subject and see how different they are from the view of the Old Testament. We shall then try to understand how the patriarchal view of the Christian Church developed out of the teachings and practice of Jesus of Nazareth. Next we will turn to depth psychology, which suggests that there is a feminine aspect of personality in males and a masculine aspect in females. We shall look at Jung's theory of the anima and the animus concerning these contrasexual aspects of each of us. Jung and his followers have developed a potentially useful tool in helping give women the equal place they deserve in human civilization.

The reader may wonder if we are not wandering from our subject of the sacrament of sexuality. However, there can be no genuine heterosexuality, no mutuality and honest sexual communication until men and women are perceived as equal in value as well as in what they value. Without this kind of equal exchange human beings do not, can not, reach the potential of love of which they are capable. Without this kind of love sexuality does not come to its full sacramental value as an outward and visible sign of the kind of love that can lead us on to Love, to God. One reason some women involved in Women's Liberation have turned to lesbian relationships is their failure to find this kind of mutuality from men.

BIOLOGY AND EQUALITY

Many feminists in recent years have declared that there are no significant biological differences between men and women other than those dealing with reproduction. It is certainly understandable that women who have been denied education and opportunity should wish to reject the idea that females were inferior or different from the males of the species. However, tough-minded women scientists have established a solid base of data that shows that the differences of the behavior between women and men are in part biological. The work of Margaret Mead in her *Male and Female* published in 1949 demonstrated that men and women can be trained to have very different social roles than are common in our society. In some of them women are more assertive and vigorous than men; they bear and raise the children as a matter of necessity, provide most of the food and leave the men the leisure to play, squabble and plot. However, even in these societies, indeed in nearly all societies where there was murderous violence, it was perpetrated by men. Even the dreams of men and women tended to be different in a cross-cultural study of seventy-five tribal groups.[1]

In the work of Maccoby and Jacklin, *The Psychology of Sex Differences*, the studies of supposed differences between men and women are evaluated and found wanting. They found studies demonstrating no significant gender differences in either direction in the following areas—tactile sensitivity, vision, discrimination learning, social memory, general intellectual abilities, achievement striving, self-esteem, crying, fear and timidity, helping behavior, competition, conformity, imitation. There is weak evidence of gender difference only in the areas of tactile sensitivity, fear and timidity, in compliance and less assertions of dominance—these are slightly more common in women. "In the realm of cognitive abilities, there is good evidence for superiority of girls and women in verbal ability, and of boys in spacial and quantitative ability."[2] Only in the area of aggressive behavior was there a marked gender difference with most studies showing boys and men exhibiting more physical violence of a serious sort. In addition studies of young children who have not been fully socialized confirm these conclusions and show a greater aggressiveness for men and a greater nurturance for women even though the culture may blunt these differences by training. Most societies try to add training *on top of* biological tendency and train young women to be more nurturing; one of the societies studied tried to do the opposite. The same is true of the training that boys receive in self-reliance and assertiveness.

What causes these differences? Certainly one reason is the greater presence of the male hormone testosterone and the whole physical backup system that encourages its greater production in males of the species. This steroid not only promotes muscle growth in teenage human males when it is poured out in great abundance, but also affects the brain and behavior. For centuries animals have been castrated to reduce their aggressive behavior and in some societies this practice has been carried out on some criminals. One Johns Hopkins Medical School professor recently lectured on the effect of administering hormones that counteract testosterone in male patients imprisoned because of aggressive sexual behavior towards boys and young men. Some patients found great relief. A correlation between the first arrest of juvenile males and an early adult high level testosterone was established in one study of prison inmates.

Some progress has been made in tracing the pathways through which this hormone actually affects brain development. It is now quite clear that the brains of female mammals is female unless it is modified through the genetic signals provided by the Y chromosome. A fascinating confirmation of this hypothesis has been provided by a study of an abnormal sexual differentiation found in a rural section of the Dominican Republic. Certain individuals at birth appeared to be females and were treated so until puberty when a delayed surge of male hormones made men of them. Instead of developing breasts and other female sexual characteristics, they were provided with male sexual organs including descended testicles. Incidentally, although reared as girls most of them passed into male identification without great problem.

The male appears to be a derivative expression of the "natural" female mammalian plan. Perhaps this might account for the fact that the basic physiological system of the female is generally better and more durably built than that of males. Women live longer by quite a few years, have better cardio-vascular systems as well as other bodily functions. One wise intern once said to me: "The women should be the ones standing up on buses and trains; they are so much more durably constructed." On the whole the female appears to be the fundamental plan. Males are probably created to foster reproduction and to provide variety impossible in nonsexual reproduction. An unconscious recognition of this truth might be responsible for some of the male fear and reaction formation that has developed in the patriarchal society.

Candace Pert shook the scientific world with her part in finding the opiate receptor that led to great advances in brain study and research. In 1982 she was interviewed by the science magazine *Omni* and her remarks summarize the best thinking about male and female differences in a framework that we find most congenial:

> Well, at a certain level of consciousness, it's very upsetting for a women to think she's any different from a man. I went through that phase in the late Sixties. I wore a lumberman's jacket and boots and really denied any difference between men and women except for the most obvious difference in sex organs. But of course you need a whole different brain circuitry to operate those different sex organs. So I think, in a few years, we'll be able to look into the brains of a man and a woman and see differences. At Stanford recently researchers found an area in the rat brain that was bigger—it contained more neurons—in males. And wherever you have different neurons, those

neurons are secreting different neurochemicals. So, yes, I think we'll be able to figure out the chemical coding for the differences between the sexes.

OMNI: But why should there be sex differences in the brain? Is it because evolution favored different characteristics in males and females?

PERT: Yes. Of course men and women have entirely different attitudes toward sex, and those attitudes are hard-wired in the brain, not learned. Men derive an evolutionary advantage from spreading their seed as much as possible. Women, on the other hand, need to choose a male who will stay around and take care of them and their offspring. So I'd expect to find a part of the female brain that is devoted to (making) that kind of choice.

Women are programmed to fall in love with whomever they make love with, no matter how ludicrous the person. As soon as they look into the eyes of their partner they've had it. Men can act as if they're really in love, but it's [a case of] out of sight, out of mind.

The brain doesn't know the Pill was invented. Women are programmed since time immemorial to get that guy back to take care of any offspring that might ensue. After all, our mothers had babies, our grandmothers had babies; women alive today are the result of a long line of women who reproduced. When a woman chooses not to have children, it's a momentous decision, at odds with her programming.

The female brain was designed to enable her to teach another organism to survive. I think the reason why the x chromosome is bigger than the y chromosome is that it takes so much more information to produce a brain that can raise a baby to the point where it can survive than a brain that merely impregnates and runs. Evolutionary theories have made too much of the bands of cavemen working together to hunt down a bull, and they've forgotten the women back at the cave, who have chosen which men to mate with, and I do think it's a choice. Maybe when we look for the origins of language, we should look to the cavewomen communicating with their offspring and with one another.

OMNI: What about violence? Are men innately more aggressive than women?

PERT: Each sex has to grapple with its own hard-wired programming and I think the female program is easier to deal with. Women don't realize how much men have to struggle to control themselves. In their early teens, when testosterone starts to surge, young men feel angry. There is now a proven connection between violent behavior and elevated testosterone levels. A Y chromosome is a real cross to bear. It's a predisposition toward angry, violent, competitive, macho behavior. The biggest problem *women* have is that of controlling their sexuality so it doesn't do them in.

OMNI: But is the male "program" evolving, in your opinion, now that communication and peaceful coexistence are more important survival skills than physical prowess?

PERT: Yes. There was an article in *Newsweek* about men like the late John Lennon staying home to take care of their children. We've come a long way. Men have gradually developed paternal feelings and bit by bit the concept of monogamy has grown. So men are becoming more civilized. Someday they may be as civilized as women.

The women's movement is also a sign that the female element is becoming respected by our society. It's a sign of the civilizing process, of the evolution toward peace. It's interesting that the main reason why many people oppose the Equal Rights Amendment is that they are threatened by the idea of women going into combat. Well, I think once you have women in the trenches, you'll have no more war. My feeling is that if there had been women in every trench during World War I, the women on both sides would have communicated with one another, and they all would have celebrated Christmas Eve together.[3]

As the data come flooding in there is little doubt that there are significant biological differences between men and women. However, the differences point to superiority in females in the very areas which may be necessary if civilization is to survive. There is no biological evidence of the inferior position of women. The most recent survey of the material is *Myths of Gender, Biological Theories About Women and Men* by Anne Fausto-Sterling.

CONJECTURAL THEORY

In *Surprised by Joy* C.S. Lewis expressed the masculine fear of women with his characteristic incisiveness: "You may add that in the hive and the ant-hill we see fully realized the two things that some of us most dread for our own species—the dominance of the female and the dominance of the collective."[4] Any study of either the hive or the ant-hill shows how superfluous males can be except in the act of insemination of the female. Some societies of ants number a million individuals sustained by one queen. After the nuptial time the males are destroyed and the life of the hill continues as a purely asexual female enterprise. Warriors, workers, nurturers—all are female.[5]

Writing the history of the period before recorded history is difficult to say the least, but some hints can be given of the structure of social development. From all the evidence available, it seems that for hundreds of thousands of years the basic ideology of humanity was to be found in the culture of women and women's mysteries. Society was not matriarchal (we have no evidence of a society in which women exercised domination and power) but it was matrilineal. It is not known when human beings first realized that men contributed something to the creation of new life; there was never any question, however, that a baby was the woman's baby, and so it was natural to trace family and traditions along the female line.

For thousands upon thousands of years human beings in these matrilineal societies lived largely by the hunt. Even the gradual shift from a hunting to an agricultural society was connected to feminine mysteries through the lunar cycle. William Irwin Thompson writes of the roles of masculine and feminine in this period of human development: "The rise of lunar notation (keeping track of time by the phases of the moon) and the beginnings of an observed periodicity upon which all human knowledge is based was a feminine creation. Agriculture and the rise of sedentary villages and towns were feminine creations. But civilization and warfare were not; they spelled the end for the Great Mother. The father had appeared on the historical scene and was going to do battle with the mother's brother, and in that revolutionary struggle the most long-lived tradition on the face of the earth was overthrown. So recent and so revolutionary is that struggle that to this day men have not forgotten, and the slightest stirring of the ancient mother can send them running for their swords and guns. . . Man has cut the umbilical cord to the Great Mother with a sword, and the sword has been hanging over his head ever since."[6] We agree with this statement if we can simply insert for the word civilization—a word so filled with positive connotations—the phrase "what we have been taught to believe is civilization". At present maledominated "civilization" appears to be on the verge of total self-destruction.

When women developed agriculture they spelled the end of their influence. There could be no real, permanent accumulation of wealth in the hunting culture. But grain could be stored and accumulated. In Anatolia in the cities of the sixth and seventh centuries B.C. wealth had begun to accumulate. Still these cities show evidence of dedication to the Mother Goddess and little evidence of war. Since there was no need for the hunt men became somewhat peripheral. And then they began to realize that wealth needed to be protected from other men. Men then turned what they learned from the hunt against other human beings and modern warfare was born. Modern "civilization" was developing. Women were necessary for the continuance of their families and their power and so women were placed in an inferior place, made slaves or at least servants of men and subject to their wills. Thompson shows how this took place in Mesopotamia and Egypt and how myths developed to justify their rule—their patriarchy.

We can also see the same development among the Sambia in the Eastern highlands of New Guinea. Stanford anthropologist Gilbert Herdt spent parts of two years among this stone age tribe. In *Guardians of the Flutes* Herdt describes this culture, which was probably just emerging from a matrilineal social structure. As he gained the confidence of these remote people he learned of secret initiation rites in which ritualized fellatio was practiced by the young boys upon physically mature male initiates. It was believed that only so could boys grow into men. Women were seen as dangerous and sexual intercourse with them drained life from men. These people even developed a mythology of the totally male origin of life (through male parthenogenesis). The author speculates that one of the purposes of their initiation rites was the rooting out of all feminine, relational, nurturing qualities; in a society in which war was the male's main occupation it was necessary to train young men away from nurturance and into aggressiveness if these young men were to survive.[7] One is reminded of Aristophanes' bawdy comedy, *Lysistrata*, in which the women, fed up with the continual warfare their husbands were engaged in, banded together and refused any sexual relations until the men ceased their warring. Comedy and humor often reveal truth that human beings can only bear as they are laughing.

THE RESULTS OF THE PATRIARCHAL PUTDOWN

Except for some agricultural tribes such as the Navajos relatively untouched by the influence of "civilized" cultures, there are few places in our modern world where women have continued to exercise the influence and status they had at the dawn of human development and in early agricultural societies. Some social groups combine remnants of matrilineal tracing of families with the development of patriarchy, but as men took more and more power to themselves even lineage began to be traced through the male side. In both Matthew and Luke, Jesus' ancestry was traced through Joseph even though both authors wrote of the virgin birth! Were it not a fact it would be difficult to believe that slightly under one-half of the population could or would subject the other portion to what amounts to perpetual servitude. Let us look at some random facts.

In the longest lasting, continuing human civilization—that of China— women were seldom educated and were viewed as an inferior species. For many years they were hideously crippled by foot binding to make their sub- jection and dependence complete. Female children have been regularly exposed and left to die throughout Chinese history. In an effort at absolutely necessary population control the Chinese government has decreed that each family may have only one child and the government is enforcing this law with heavy fines. Talking with the Chinese in China, Hong Kong and Malaysia we found a consistent attitude toward women: the birth of a girl is almost as much of a misfortune as the birth of a boy is reason for rejoicing. A trial in China in 1984 (and reported in the daily newspaper prepared for foreigners) convicted a man who drowned his four-year-old daughter when a fortune teller advised him that his wife was pregnant with a son. Although few of the upper eschelon in China's government are women, women probably fare better there now than ever before in Chinese history and are given economic equality with men in the same job—something American women are still fighting for.

In India women have been treated as less valuable than men for cen- turies. The very practice of child marriage well described by Gandhi in his autobiography made women subject to men from an early age. For over two thousand years many Hindu widows practiced the custom of sati (or suttee) by jumping into their husband's funeral pyre so that they might ac- company him into the other world and serve him there as well. It was never suggested that the husband do the same for his wife. Sati is a vivid symbol of woman's place in that culture. Hare Krishna groups share this Hindu background. The role of women as servants in these groups is quite clear.

Buddha must have had a strong heterosexual drive as he taught that women were a snare and should be avoided. Celibacy is common among those who take Buddhism seriously. Few women achieve sainthood or are counted among the redeemed in Buddhism. Unfortunately we find some- thing of this same attitude in such illustrious Christian leaders as Augustine and Ignatius of Loyola. Some women graduate students at Notre Dame could hardly read the *Spiritual Exercises* of Ignatius because of its disparaging comments on women. In Hinduism nearly anything is possible and women sometimes attain great admiration as spiritual leaders because of the veneration of Kali (or Parvati as most Hindus prefer to call her). And we must also note that until Indira Gandhi's brutal assassination, the political leader of India was a woman. On the whole, however, women's place in Hindu culture is still inferior.

A thorough treatment of the incredible way that patriarchal society has treated women in India is provided by Mary Daly in *Gyn/ecology*. She also describes in detail the cruelty of the century-long Chinese practice of footbinding. In addition she gives documented support of the practice of performing clitoridectomies on young girls and also the practice of infibulation and excision (sewing up the labia and then opening the vaginal canal at the time of marriage to a prescribed size). At the present writing, there is evidence that these practices occur over large parts of Africa among many of the tribes. She sees the witchburning of the Middle Ages as another example of patriarchal cruelty to and fear of women.[8]

Undoubtedly Mohammed improved the status of women in Ancient Arabia, but he still allowed men to have four legal wives, and concubines beyond these four were common among the wealthy and the political leaders. There is no suggestion that a woman might have four husbands. A visit to the sultan's former harem in Istanbul shows clearly the cloistered, slavish existence of the Sultan's wives. Here again women were viewed as inferior and as a threat and so must be veiled and covered like nuns. Islam may be the fastest growing religion in our world; it has cut a swath from Arabia east through India, Bangladesh, Malaysia, Indonesia and the Philippines. In India it became very popular as Islamic conquerors took over northern India and released the outcasts from the caste system. They also abolished the sati. The Taj Mahal, one of the most exquisite buildings in the world, is simply the tomb erected by a Moslem ruler for his favorite wife who died after bearing their thirteenth child. On the whole, the idea of equality between men and women in these three religious traditions is nearly unthinkable.

In the Graeco-Roman-Persian world the same attitude prevailed. Unwanted infant girls were exposed (left in the wilderness to die). An affectionate letter of a man to his wife has survived from Roman times in the sands of Egypt. The husband concludes by telling his wife to keep their child if it is a boy, but to expose it if a girl. In Mary Renault's historically accurate novels of ancient Greece, particularly *The Last of the Wine*, we see portrayed the place of women in classical Greece. Women were seldom taught to read or write and were unable to relate to their educated husbands. Women were little more than breeding machines. Men turned to other men for affectionate relationships and no wonder many educated women today fail to see ancient Greek society as anything but sick.

In early Rome the father, the *pater familias*, had the power of life and death over his wife and children. Later women were given more legal equality and in late Roman times there was a "unisex" period lamented by most moralists. In this period men and women dressed in a similar manner and one has to know the Roman customs of dressing to discern whether a tombstone is that of a woman or a man. Some historians have suggested this equalization of male and female contributed to the collapse of the Western Roman Empire. The barbarian conquests didn't improve matters. From the point of view of most of these tribes, daughters were viewed as the chattel property of their fathers. As the barbarians took over the Roman Empire, the Church adapted. In order to release the father's property rights in his daughter to her husband, a question was inserted in the customary wedding service: "Who gives this woman to be married to this man?" And the father replied, "I do."

One of the reasons that adultery was considered so heinous was that it was a property violation. In most patriarchal societies property became more valuable than people. The husband "owned" his wife and his property was trespassed in the adulterous act. In addition, adultery meant that a child born by his wife might not be his own, and someone not his "natural" heir might inherit his property. (As we have already noted, a woman never has any doubt that the child is hers!) In countries where property passes through the eldest son, as is traditional in Great Britain, this becomes even more important. Adultery by the Queen was an act of treason because it muddled the whole question of succession. Henry VIII beheaded Anne Boleyn because she was suspected of it. A man might have sexual affairs outside of marriage with impunity, but the property value of a woman was diminished when she was involved in such affairs. Thus the double standard concerning the moral evil of sexual relationships outside of marriage developed in the West.

Still another cruelty perpetrated upon women by patriarchal society has been the idea that women are asexual beings. According to Victorian standards a woman was not a "lady" if she enjoyed sexual experience. As we have already seen, sexual adequacy is greatly conditioned by our attitudes toward it; thus many women have been robbed of their sexual birthright by conditioning. In addition, some societies have gone so far as to perform clitoridectomies upon women to guarantee their sexlessness and to be more certain that they would be faithful. Even in our age, women taught to think their sexual feelings shameful have been known to have the clitoris removed by surgery.[9]

How did such an absurd idea arise—the idea that women were inferior to men and should serve men? We have seen that there is no biological or psychological evidence for this attitude. Part of the responsibility goes to the patriarchal tradition of the Old Testament absorbed by Christianity. However, an irrational attitude of this kind is usually the result of fear and a reaction to fear, an avoidance of fear by projection. We suggest that men have felt far more dependent upon women than they have been willing to admit. They recognize that women possess a physical creativity that men do not have. Remember the ants: one male is all that is needed to service a colony of a million ants. And then we believe that deep in the heart of many (most?) men can be found the primordial fear that if the mother had not nurtured them, given them the breast, they would have died. In addition there may be an awareness that women have provided the foundations of human culture and men have been peripheral in its development.

As patriarchal institutions took a firmer and firmer grip on society and displaced the matrilineal ones, males had to reinforce their rickety sense of superiority and did so by subjugating women as they would a country they had conquered. Even "history" came to be "his" story, an account of wars, politics, conquests, great adventures, male Olympic Games, kings, rulers, bishops and popes. This even infected Biblical history. Religious leaders within these male societies found themselves overwhelmingly attracted to women and blamed this on the seductiveness of women (about all that was left to them) rather than on their own weakness and uncontrollable sexual desire. This is a perfect example of projection. As we shall show shortly, of all the major religious leaders of humankind only Jesus seemed to value women equally with men.

It is truly amazing how unconscious men can be of the position of women in our society. Most women have even been blind to it because they have been conditioned by patriarchal society. The idea of woman's secondary value is so pervasive and deep that it takes a lot to jar us out of it. Morton thought he was quite liberated when he was rector of St. Luke's Parish. It took a truly liberated woman with a Ph.D. degree to show him how patriarchal his attitude still was. Dr. Ollie Backus joined the staff of the church and did what few wives who wish to maintain a marriage would dare to do: she confronted him every time his unconscious patriarchal attitude leaked out. He owes an enormous debt to this brilliant and courageous woman. Barbara later suggested rather doggedly that Morton read Marilyn French's *The Woman's Room* and this helped complete the transformation. This book should be required reading for all men; conscious women already know what it so clearly says. Morton's attitude towards women priests changed when he came to know many of the nuns at The University of Notre Dame. They were the finest ministers and pastors to be found anywhere. How ridiculous that a community of women must import a *man* so that the central service of the Church, the Eucharist, can be celebrated. Morton also began to see the necessity of removing sexist language in his writing if he was to treat women equally. He began to read feminist literature and realized that one of the most important tasks facing all human civilizations is granting to women and men an equal dignity and value. Total equality in sexual relationships and companionships is one of the heroic challenges before us.

PATRIARCHY IN THE OLD TESTAMENT

One of the reasons that most men in the Western world do not view women as equals is that they have been raised on the ideas and laws of the Old Testament; the ideas of Jesus on the subject have hardly been heard. The basic view of the Old Testament is similar to that of ancient Mesopotamia described at length by William Irwin Thompson in his book *The Time Falling Bodies Take to Light: Mythology, Sexuality, and the Origins of Culture*. The God of the Hebrews, like the heroes of the Gilgamish epic, was in reaction formation to the mother goddess and her cult.[10] Women were viewed much the same as they were in Ancient Sumer. Let us list the ways in which women were downgraded in the Old Testament:

1. According to the curse on Eve in Genesis 3:16 women were to be subject to their lord (Baal), either the father or the husband. The law was clear. The main value of the woman was to provide children for her hus-

band and the lot of a childless wife was almost intolerable. This was modified by the natural affection of some of these men for their wives, but legally the women had few rights.

2.   Women were viewed almost as property or chattel. This is the logical result of the idea of husband as lord. As a matter of fact, wives and concubines were often inherited by the eldest son (II Samuel 3:7, I Kings 2:22). The only basic difference between the wives and the concubines was that wives usually had better social connections and someone to stand up for them. Often wives were taken in war or were bought. Jacob had to pay for his wives with years of hard work. Deuteronomy 21:10 provides the rules for a wife taken in war as part of the spoils.

3.   The real reason that sodomy was seen as such an outrage was that it *womanized* a man. It put a man in the position of a woman. There was little horror at the one who was the active person in that act.

4.   Polygamy was one consequence of women being seen as property. The wealthy man might have as much property or as many wives as he could afford. When Sarah could not bear a child, she gave to Abraham her Egyptian serving girl (slave), Hagar. Hagar conceived and Ishmael was born. Then Sarah herself conceived (through Yahweh's special mercy) and bore a child. When Isaac was weaned, Sarah forced Abraham to send Hagar and Ishmael out into the desert. This certainly shows little value for Hagar or her child and doesn't sound like the solution that Jesus would have suggested.

The relationship of Jacob, Leah and Rachel and their children was scandalous by modern standards or by Jesus' values. Here a patriarchal, polygamous marriage is portrayed with all the tensions and problems inherent in such a relationship. If it was this bad between two sisters, imagine what it was when a new favorite wife was introduced into a family. We can hardly blame Leah's children for the hostile feelings they harbored against Rachel's offspring, Joseph in particular.

5.   The Mosaic law on divorce treated women like property which a man could dispose of as he desired. Divorce was simply taken for granted (Leviticus 21:7, 14; 22:13, Numbers 30:9). This was only a male prerogative. He might do it for any reason, although some schools of Jewish thought required more justification than a mere whim of the husband. Of course, adultery on the wife's part was always seen as just cause. The husband merely

prepared a bill of divorcement and formally handed it to his wife. This practice is described in Isaiah 50:1 and Jeremiah 3:8. The laws on divorce are the logical consequence of the inferior position of woman totally subject to her "lord".

6.   Few things are more demeaning to women than prostitution. Again the Old Testament takes it for granted. A man might have several wives and concubines and take care of his sexual needs with prostitutes, but the woman had to remain always faithful. The death penalty could be leveled against her if this law was violated (Deuteronomy 22:13-29).

Two kinds of prostitution are described in the Old Testament. First there were pagan temples sacred to the Mother Goddess and then there was ordinary commercial prostitution in which men satisfied their sexual needs.

The Hebrews did not exterminate all the pagans in Palestine after they migrated into it. For many years they lived among these people who worshipped the Mother Goddess and accepted many of their practices. In order to separate the Jews from these religious influences anything to do with these pagan temples was forbidden—dream interpretation, fortune-telling or having sexual relations with their priests or priestesses. Particularly abominable was taking part in the rituals of the high places and having relations with the priestesses; this was viewed as idolatry and apostasy by the law. The downfall of some of the great kings of Israel and Judah was attributed to their violating this law. Male as well as female prostitutes were available in these temples and transvestitism was not uncommon. The law prohibiting the "abominable" practice of wearing the clothes of the other sex (Deuteronomy 22:5) is not only interesting in itself, and because some fundamentalist Christian groups follow it today, but also because Joan of Arc was finally sentenced to death for breaking this law.

Undoubtedly these pagan practices were degrading to both the men and women involved in sacred prostitution, but it was probably better than prostitution purely for financial gain run by the Mafia. In the United States today most prostitution is a grim, horrible business that is destructive to all participating. It is one form of slavery still existing in the underworld where young women and men are sometimes held in virtual captivity.

Leviticus 19:29 enjoins fathers (mothers would have had little to say about it) not to force their daughters into prostitution for gain. Commercial prostitution was simply taken as a matter of fact and there is no law directly prohibiting it. The children of harlots were, however, outcasts as shown in Deuteronomy 23:2 and Judges 11:1ff. In the practical advice of Proverbs the father speaks to his son, warning him against adultery because he may fall in love and get snared by the woman, and also against the "strange women" (probably the temple prostitutes). Instead, Proverbs continues, one can buy an ordinary prostitute "for a hunk of bread" and avoid these risks. (Proverbs 6:23-7:27.) Little or no consideration was given to what prostitution does to women. One of the great Old Testament heroines was Rahab, the harlot, who protected Joshua's spies and led to the downfall of Jericho. She is spoken of with admiration in the Epistle to the Hebrews. This passage assumes prostitution just as St. Paul's writings never reject the idea of slavery. However, Jesus' emphasis on *mutual* love makes prostitution as utterly unthinkable as slavery. Prostitution is slavery for a limited period: one person buys another person's body for a period of time.

7.   Under the law, Jewish women were declared unclean during menstruation and after childbirth. Menstruation is viewed with horror in Leviticus 15:19. It is also interesting that a woman was unclean for one week after the birth of a boy but for two weeks after the birth of a girl (Leviticus 12:1ff.). If a man had relations with a menstruating woman the law declared that both of them were outlawed from the community, cut off from the fellowship. As is true today in Bali, the menstruating women were viewed as defiled, tainted, almost outcast.

8.   This brings us to the double standard for women. Men were free to have several wives and concubines and even visit prostitutes as long as they were not connected with pagan temples. A woman so involved could be slain according to the law. The ferocity of the law is seen in the conclusion of the story of Onan. After Onan died, his father, Judah, promised his daughter-in-law Tamar that when his next oldest son, Shelah, was old enough then he would provide her a child. Judah did not live up to his agreement and so Tamar played the harlot and enticed Judah to sleep with her. After three months it was reported to Judah that Tamar had played the harlot and was pregnant. Judah said, "*Take her out and burn her.*" It was only when Tamar produced a pledge that Judah had given her that Judah admitted the fault was his, not hers. Few stories better reveal the patriarchal attitude of the Old Testament. Behind all this patriarchal law and custom, however, lurks a hidden matrilineal note. In 1970 an Israeli court decided on the basis of an old law not to give Israeli citizenship to a child who had an Israeli father but a gentile mother.

Here and there in the Old Testament we detect a similar respect for the feminine. Evidently the Hebrew people had passed very recently from worship of the mother goddess. This may in fact account for a violent reaction formation found in the patriarchy there. Abraham may have been a member of the mother religion before his call by Yahweh. In the wisdom literature, wisdom (translated in the Greek as Sophia) is perceived both as a human skill and as a feminine creative aspect of the Godhead similar to the Logos of John I. Several attempts have been made to rescue the Old Testament from its patriarchal bias. A book edited by Clare Fischer, Betsy Brenneman and Ann Bennett, *Women in a Strange Land*, offers some of the most convincing studies of the feminism underlying some parts of this great book.

Hosea, the great prophet of the eighth century Northern Kingdom, comes closer to Jesus' message of unconditional love than any other figure in the Old Testament. Whether his story is reality or allegory we do not know; the message is the same in either case. Hosea was directed by God to marry Gomer, one who would pour out her love upon others in adultery. The prophet then goes out to seek her after she has strayed away and takes her back. His continued love and willingness to take back his wife are symbolic of God's love for adulterous Israel which has strayed after other Gods. The God portrayed by Hosea is a God of never ending, irresistible love. This prophet's message is a far cry from the words of Judah when he hears that Tamar is pregnant.

9.   In his book *The Resurrection of Jesus* Pinchas Lapide points out how ridiculous it would be in a fabricated story of the resurrection for Jesus to have appeared first to women. According to Yalkut Shimoni I, 82, women are not allowed to give testimony before a court because Sarah denied her disbelief that God could make her pregnant in Genesis 18:15.

JESUS AND WOMEN

Jesus proposed only three basic changes in the Old Testament tradition, his Judaic heritage. The first was that the kingdom of heaven was at hand and that we could participate in it now: human beings did not have to wait for the Day of Yahweh in the distant future. The second was that God was essentially characterized by love: God was Abba, an incredibly loving father with many of the best qualities of a mother. Because of this we were to give to our *neighbor* the same kind of love that God gives us. In the third change, Jesus expanded the meaning of the word *neighbor*: the neighbor is not just the member of the family or of the people of Israel, but all people. God loves all human beings, good and bad, just and unjust, and makes his sun to shine on them all. The Divine Lover cares equally for men and women, slaves and free, rich and poor, children and adults. All human beings may turn to God no matter what they have done and they will be received as a loving parent picks up a crying, hurt child. The third change means that we human beings are to see all other people as our neighbors—regardless of race, religion, sex, age, social status, or education.

We very much doubt that any such message has been given by any other major religious leader and embedded in the sacred scripture of that leader's followers. Nowhere else do we find the idea that every human being has infinite value and worth, that each human being is an irreplaceable child of God. No one person can be sacrificed for another or used as a thing by another. There are no distinctions as to our innate value. All this because God *is* love. The radical implication of his teachings is just beginning to unfold *two thousand* years later. Jesus set out immediately to rectify the state of women. They were not just to be used. They had infinite value in and of themselves. He attacked the accepted divorce procedure of the Judaic law largely because it put women in an inferior position. Jesus saw that all relationships must be I-Thou relationships. No one is to be treated as an it. All people are to be treated as God treats us. This is the touchstone. We become followers of Jesus as we love other people with the same kind of self-giving, unjudging love as he gives us.

If we are to treat the enemy, the stranger, the acquaintance with caring and love, how much more will we need to treat those we love and those who love us with this kind of love. In spite of the Jewish divorce law, family life among the Jews at the time of Jesus was probably more caring than anywhere else in the Roman world. If this basic principle is actually put into practice, then women will have a right of choice, consideration, love, companionship, mutuality and sexual equality. How we treat other human beings becomes the final test of how religious we are, how deep and real our fellowship really is with God, the risen Jesus, the Divine Lover. Our religious maturity is measured not by our ecstacies, trances, visions, vigils or feelings of peace, but by how consistently we treat others with fairness and equality—the foundation stones of any love worth the name. We become followers of Jesus as we love others as he has loved us.[11]

When Jesus' attitude toward other human beings is truly understood we realize first of all that none of us really follows the way that Jesus pointed out and lived. We fall and try again. Sexual relationships, above all others, need to be expressions of love, caring and mutuality. The patriarchal view of women and children becomes absurd. Slavery becomes absurd. Prostitution becomes absurd. But it has taken 1900 years for Western society to begin to take seriously the implications of Jesus' teaching with regard to women—longer than it took to legislate against slavery, child labor and child abuse in most "Christian countries".

In the story of the lost sheep, the shepherd searches for it until he finds it and then he picks up the strayed sheep and carries it home on his shoulders—a perfect picture of tenderness. When the disciples told the women not to bother the great man with their squalling brats, Jesus was angry, called the little children to him and picked them up in his arms—showing love, tenderness and sound psychological knowledge at the same time. When children are valued, women are automatically valued along with them. In his book *The Kingdom Within*, John Sanford points out the complete wholeness of Jesus; his personality reveals a full development of all the psychological functions and of masculinity and femininity as well. Mother Julian of Norwich, writing in the fifteenth century, referred to Jesus as she. And yet contrary to male chauvinistic fears this full development of both sides of his nature did not make Jesus less of a man, but more of one. How many men have faced opposition, condemnation, torture and excruciating pain and death with greater equanimity and courage?

WOMEN IN THE CHURCH

The point of view expressed by Jesus about the place of women and their values is not found consistently in many places in the Bible either before or after Jesus. This confronts us with a problem. What is authoritative in this holy book? The Jews have long realized that the Old Testament needs to be interpreted by the later understanding of devout Jews, the Mishna and the Talmud. Christians need to look at the Bible through the eyes of Jesus of Nazareth, who is the *final authority* on matters religious and moral. What others have said or written— even elsewhere in the Bible—needs to be checked against what Jesus was and taught. If it is not consistent with Jesus' revelation, the ideas of others need to be questioned. Some Biblical literalists see the Bible rather than the person of Jesus, living, dying, rising and still present as the final revelation of God. This fundamentalist attitude often allows people to avoid the radical message and practice of Jesus and turn back to the less stringent demands of the Old Testament and its demeaning patriarchy.

Although there have been some women leaders in the Christian Church and many women saints, few women have achieved institutional leadership. One reason for this may be Paul's introduction of the concept of male as lord and master in Colossians 3:18-21 and Ephesians 5:22-33. Although some scholars doubt that this latter passage is from Paul's hand it is viewed as equally authoritative by Biblical literalists. The Ephesians passage is more extreme than the other. Colossians merely states that women are to be obedient to their husbands; Ephesians states that women are to submit to their husbands for husbands have authority over their wives just as Christ has authority over the Church. Women are to submit to husbands just as the Church submits to Christ. Rather a strong statement if one believes that the Church owes its life and existence to the continuing presence of the risen Jesus. Of course it also says that men are to love their wives as Jesus loves the Church. The history of the Church's treatment of women, love and sexuality bears out that men just delivered from the idea of male supremacy by Jesus' own teaching took this passage as all they needed to ignore the strong demands of radical Christian love and equality, just as they used Paul's passages on slaves submitting to their masters to continue slavery. Some of our minister friends in the black Baptist Church have pointed out to us that they do not accept the idea of the literal inspiration of scriptures as many Baptist groups do; these blacks *knew that there was something wrong in Paul's pronouncement on slavery* and this has given them a wider view of Biblical inspiration.

In Paul's first letter to the Corinthians (11:1-16) he goes into a long diatribe about women covering their heads in Church, because the beauty of their hair seduced the angels and resulted in monstrosities. By covering their hair women show that they are safely under their husband's authority and are not out of bounds. And women are not to speak in Church, again to show that they are under a man's authority. (14:34-35.) Of course this passage is also used as a reason to deny the ordination of women. We feel that this particular proof text is one of the least authoritative in the New

Testament and even Paul comments that he did not receive these rules from Christ.

In recent years several excellent studies have shown that women played a much more important part in the life of the Early Church than scholars with a patriarchal bias had realized. That for which we have no place in our world view we simply do not observe. We have noted the same lapses in scholarship in regard to healing and the use of dreams as scholars had no place for these experiences in their world view. In her book *In Memory of Her: A Feminist Reconstruction of Christian Origins*, Elizabeth Schussler Fiorenza shows how patriarchal most Biblical study has been and then reconstructs the life of the Early Church from the point of the women who participated in it. In *Sexism and God Talk*, Rosemary Radford Ruether lays down the foundations of a theology in which women are viewed as equal to men and have equal input into the Church and its life.

However, in the sixteen hundred years from the acceptance of Christianity by the Roman Empire to the beginning of the twentieth century, women played little part in the organized life of the Church. They were peripheral, an epiphenomenon at the edge of the Church. There were startling exceptions where very holy women organized communities and had an incredible impact upon the Church. St. Catherine of Siena was largely responsible for resolving the scandal of triplicate popes. St. Teresa of Avila was admired for her extraordinary religious experiences and has been declared a doctor of the Church. The mystical side of Christianity is amply represented by women, but in the years when this aspect of Christianity has not been central, women's influence has waned. The emphasis on celibacy also put marriage and women in an inferior position. Only in the twentieth century have women and some men realized that a nondemocratic and an un-Christlike patriarchy had taken possession of the institutional Church. Since then some women have been ordained and taken a position in the leadership of the Church in many Protestant denominations. (The annual convention of one large Protestant denomination that will remain unnamed, however, recently decided not to extend ordination to women because Eve had been taken in by the Serpent!)

The great danger of the patriarchal Church is that it views God in patriarchal terms as does much of the Old Testament. In this situation we fail to see how different a picture of God is presented by Jesus of Nazareth. According to orthodox Christian theology, Jesus was the outpicturing of God for humankind; Jesus reveals the essential nature of God. Dorothy

Soelle, an incisive German theologian, is one of the best minds in theology today. She comments on this fact in these words:

> But I am speaking of a dream, or rather a task that is waiting to be done—the dream of a more human society. This dream-task begins with two objectives which are the basis of every emancipation: self-criticism and criticism of society. Unfortunately I find that even today, after the emancipation has supposedly been accomplished, most women in our society still stand dumbfounded before these two objectives.
>
> Instead of self-criticism we encounter either lamentation or self-glorification, a lot of loneliness on the one hand and a lot of "mother's day" on the other. . .
>
> And instead of criticism of society we find accommodation to the status quo. . .
>
> Thus the emancipation of woman by way of social criticism can take place only if man will become liberated at the same time, only if he frees his consciousness from the modes of thinking which presently dominate it.
>
> Theology has a part in shaping and determining these thought patterns, even for people who have a secular selfunderstanding. It is important to recognize under which god one has been socialized. The "male God" is a fundamental part of our culture. He is a being whose most important activity is rulership. Theologically, power becomes omnipotence, and rulership becomes world domination— total control and determination of all things, as at Auschwitz. The male God is the ruler of the universe, he has created the universe and has the power to intervene in it at any time. He is autonomous, totally independent of his creation. His rule is overall and he himself needs no one. This ruler derives neither stature nor happiness from having created any of us. He is, in theological terms, *aseity* (self-derived existence) raised to infinite power.
>
> One must ask why people speak and think of God in terms of such *aseity* and omnipotence. In order to answer this question we may use the method developed by Ludwig Feuerbach. He holds that this God corresponds to a deep-seated fantasy of mankind. Men, too, wish to be self-sufficient, autonomous, dependent on no one. They too would like to be omnipotent rulers. Probably all of us, even women, have dreams of omnipotence, but these dreams find their verbal expression in the religion fabricated by men in the interest

of men. The highest satisfaction men can imagine is to be autonomous and independent.

Actually, *Christian* faith can arise only if we dismiss this God
once and for all. For if anything can be said with assurance about
Christ—in contrast to this male God who is of course adored equally
by many women—it is that Christ had no special prerogatives or
privileges. Privileges are an integral part of the omnipotent male
God; they are his essence. Christ, however, did not want any privileges; he abandoned them. In mythological language he left heaven,
assumed servant's clothes, became vulnerable, hungry, thirsty, and
mortal. The astronauts, when asked what God looked like, are
reported—in a joke—to have answered, "She is black." When will
we, all of us, begin to love and honor this God who is without power
and rule? When will we rid ourselves of the male God and reach
that point in faith where we can radically turn to Christ, without fear and without desire for special privilege? When will we be
emancipated?" [12]

And only emancipated people can relate with freedom with each other,
with open communication without fear. Only for such emancipated people
can sexuality be a sacrament of their free caring for each other and commitment to each other.

ANIMUS AND ANIMA

For centuries psychology was a part of philosophy, a matter of introspec-
tion and speculation. Most of the philosopher-psychologists were men and
on the whole they presented a masculine set of values. Some of the most
influential of these men never married—Kant, Nietschze, Kierkegaard,
Schopenhauer. These men were a product of their society, and it never occurred to them that women could be equal with men.

But it was Freud, who thought that he was presenting a scientific theory
of psychology, who made one of the most lasting and most vicious anti-
feminist attacks. Freud saw women as deficient men (rather than men as
altered women as biology seemed to show). His idea of penis envy lies at
the base of everything that he had to say about women. Everything in his
background seemed to contribute to his blind prejudice. He was raised in
a Victorian patriarchal family. His wife never questioned his attitude and

most of his days were spent with neurotic women. His views on the subject are found in a late paper, "Femininity" in *New Introductory Lectures on Psychoanalysis*. Betty and Theodore Roszak quote a long portion of this diatribe in the book they edited, *Masculine/Feminine*. They summarize Freud's argument. Freud maintains that "penis envy" results in the following attributes: passivity, dependence, sexual frigidity, and general incompetence. "Women, doomed to an unrelieved 'genital deficiency' and lacking the strong male superego, fail to develop any capacity to create culture. They are natural-born homebodies, scatterbrains, and parasites."[13] How Freud could maintain this point of view in the face of Havelock Ellis' writing and data is hard to understand. The damage done by Freud's thought is almost immeasurable.

Not all psychologists have followed this point of view. Both of us have been nurtured on Jungian thought. Jung believed that in the unconscious depths of the man there is a feminine archetype or primal aspect. And biology certainly bears that out. Jung calls this the *anima*, the Latin word for soul. Jung believes that men never approach wholeness and individuation unless they deal with and integrate this aspect of themselves. Jung also believes that in every women there is a masculine aspect or archetype that he calls the *animus*. And Jung contends likewise that women who do not come to terms with this masculine aspect are often run by it and so fail to come to wholeness. The process of coming to maturity involves for both men and women coming to terms with their contrasexual natures.

This is rarely possible where men and women are not in honest, open, equal relationship. As we shall show in a later chapter, falling in love can be the prod which forces us to grow up. I have already quoted my wise abbot friend who said that men raised entirely apart from women are likely to be peculiar; women seem to be less vulnerable to separation, but are still in danger. Falling in love (at least in its initial stages) is the projection of the man's largely unconscious feminine aspect or anima out upon a women. In the same way the woman projects the masculine aspect of her unconscious upon the appropriate (or inappropriate) man. One of the leading psychiatrists involved in family therapy, Dr. Carl Whitaker, has said: "The greatest ordeal in life is marriage—it is the central focus for enlightenment and the natural therapeutic processes in the culture." Coming to wholeness is no easier within the analytic situation.

This idea of Jung is very much like the idea of the *yin* and the *yang* central to Chinese thought and to the profound book of Chinese wisdom,

The I-Ching. The masculine and feminine principles are intertwined and represented by the well-known symbol:

yang

yin

The goal is to keep these polar principles in balance. When one part suffers the other is damaged. Both are absolutely essential to wholeness and harmony. Jung views the balance of masculine and feminine in human beings in a similar way.

In 1927 in the aftermath of World War I Jung was asked to speak on the subject of women in Europe at that time. His article has a prophetic note about it. Jung wrote that at the beginning of our Christian era three-fifths of the population of the Roman Empire were slaves. "Every Roman was surrounded by slaves. The slave and his psychology flooded Italy, and every Roman became inwardly a slave. . .The explosive spread of Christianity which might be said to have risen from the sewers of Rome— Nietzsche called it a 'slave insurrection in morals'—was a sudden reaction that set the soul of the lowest slave on a par with that of the divine Caesar . . .Something similar is happening to women in present-day Europe. Too much that is inadmissible, that has not been lived, is accumulating in the unconscious, and this is bound to have an effect. Secretaries, typists, shop-girls, all are agents of this process, and through a million subterranean channels creeps the influence that is undermining marriage." Jung goes on to say that the terrible male casualties in World War I robbed women of any access to real relationship with men except through the breaking of tradition.[14]

Jung also believed that women carried an aspect of divinity and that men could not come to wholeness without relating to this principle. He states this clearly in his spiritual autobiography, *Answer to Job.* In it he identifies with Job and sees him standing against an unreasonable side of God but supported by the advocate, God's feminine side, Wisdom, Sophia, Mary. In the last pages of this book Jung shows how deeply he was impressed by the recent dogma of the Assumption of Mary: At last the feminine was put alongside the masculine trinity where it belonged.[15]

Many women were attracted to Jung's thinking as it offered them a depth psychology that gave women equal value to men. Many of the most important thinkers in Jungian psychology have been women—Frances Wickes, Esther Harding, Barbara Hannah and Marie Louise von Franz. These people have found that the idea of the masculine/feminine polarity of human nature gives them a base for discussing both the uniqueness of women and men and also the similarities between them

Men and women have equal potential value. They carry it not in their naked masculinity or femininity, but as they try to be whole human beings inwardly uniting both the masculine and feminine. We are not suggesting that men become women or that women become men. Then we usually have monstrosities. In order to be quite clear we repeat that we are not suggesting that women take over men's roles or that men take over women's roles, but rather that each person seeks a new role expressing the wholeness of his or her being. Each person is to be viewed as an individual and each is to find his or her unique destiny under God. Some hardline aggressive masculine attitudes will have to be changed and softened. The feminine values of relating and nurturing need to have more universal acceptance. God never intended for our world to be a storehouse of destructiveness that might explode at any moment. In a demolished world sexuality disappears as well as everything else.

CHAPTER FIVE

Sexuality, the Bible and Christianity

The attitude of Christians and the Christian Church has been mixed regarding the place and value of women in society and the Church. The Church's view of the place of sexuality in human development and experience has also varied, from seeing sexual expression as an evil to be renounced for the sake of one's salvation to perceiving sexual love as a symbol of the Divine-human encounter and as one major pathway to an experience of the God of Love. Let us sift through these different attitudes looking first at the various viewpoints to be found in the Old Testament, in the teaching and practice of Jesus and in the teaching and practice of his followers as recorded in the New Testament. Then let us look at the early history of the Church's thinking on this subject. The Roman Catholic Church developed a consistent point of view dating back to late Roman times right up to the present and expressed it clearly through the statements of the magisterium, the authoritative voice of the Church. We shall examine these statements in some detail, because the Roman Catholic Church is the largest single Christian body and because the same attitudes underlie many Protestant beliefs. We will look critically at this point of view in the light of the history of marriage and the developmental theory outlined in an earlier chapter. Then we shall draw some conclusions and see how this religious view has influenced the Western legal system.

SEXUALITY IN THE OLD TESTAMENT

The Bible as we now have it is a library of books written by different authors over a period of nearly twelve hundred years. The Old Testament contains many different strands written and edited by different authors over a period of a thousand years B.C.E. Some of its reliable traditions may date back much further. Some of the writers seem to have been able to hear and express their experience of divine inspiration more clearly than others.

The Bible does not provide one consistent view of sexuality and love; a careful reading reveals a number of very different attitudes, some of which have already been mentioned in previous chapters. We can identify four major Old Testament attitudes. The first is what we would characterize as the earthy, natural view found in many of the narrative sections of the Old Testament. The second is the patriarchal attitude that sees sexuality as the particular privilege of men that unfortunately colors a large portion of the Hebrew law. Sexuality for procreation is the third view and the one most common in the books of Deuteronomy and Leviticus; anything thwarting procreation therefore becomes evil. In addition these books contain a vast array of laws regulating sexual behavior. The fourth view is characterized by an emphasis on romantic love, on Eros, on the sexual longing and joy of two people in love: this is the attitude of The Song of Songs. Sometimes this romantic longing and love are seen as symbolic of God's love for his people.[1]

SEXUALITY AS A NATURAL PART OF LIFE

Throughout most of the Old Testament narrative, sexual intercourse of a man and woman is seen as a good and natural part of life. However, since procreation and maintaining the family line were so important, little emphasis was placed on the sexual experience of the two involved. Little prudery is found in these stories. Explicit references to sexual relations were not avoided. Some of these accounts make *Peyton Place* seem mild indeed. Rape and incest, for example, are frankly described. When Morton was in seminary the story of the rape of the Levite's wife in Judges 20-21 was passed over with a shudder. This brutal narrative is also avoided in most *Stories of the Bible* volumes even though it accounts for the near destruction of the tribe of Benjamin. There is no hint in the Old Testament of the later gnostic attitude that the physical world, and thus sexuality, is evil. The Old Testament writers in general see the physical world as good; in the Day of Yahweh it is this physical world which will be redeemed. Sexual relations were perceived as good because they produced children; however, sexual experience must be confined within the limits of the law and the law regarding sexuality is quite specific and detailed. We shall show later that some of these regulations make much more sense than others in the light of the psychology of human psychosexual development.

The Old Testament abounds in stories of the naturalness of human sexuality. One of the most touching and explicit tells how Ruth asked Boaz to marry her. The events related in this story are particularly important in Judaeo-Christian tradition, because Ruth and Boaz were the great-grandparents of King David, the ideal Hebrew man and king. Let us listen to the story.

> Then Naomi, her mother-in-law, said to her, 'My daughter, is it not my duty to see you happily settled? And is not Boaz, with whose servants you were, our kinsman? Now tonight he is winnowing the barley at the threshing-floor. Come, wash and anoint and dress yourself. Then go down to the threshing-floor. Do not make yourself known to him before he has finished eating and drinking. But when he settles down to sleep, take careful note of the place where he lies, then go and turn back the covering at his feet and lie there yourself. He will tell you what to do.' And Ruth said to her, 'I will do all you say.'
>
> So she went down to the threshing-floor and did all that her mother-in-law had told her. When Boaz had eaten and drunk, he was in a happy mood and went to lie down by the heap of barley. Then she came quietly and turned back the covering at his feet and lay there. In the middle of the night the man started up and looked about him; and there lying at his feet was a woman. 'Who are you?' he said; and she replied, 'I am Ruth, your maidservant. Spread the skirt of your cloak over your servant for you have right of redemption over me.' 'May Yahweh bless you, my daughter,' said Boaz 'for this last act of kindness of yours is greater than the first, since you have not gone after young men, poor or rich. Have no fear then, my daughter, I will do whatever you ask, for the people of Bethlehem all know your worth. But, though it is true I have right of redemption over you, you have a kinsman closer than myself. Stay here for

tonight, and in the morning if he wishes to exercise his right over you, very well, let him redeem you. But if he does not wish to do so, then as Yahweh lives, I will redeem you. Lie here till morning.' So she lay at his feet till morning. Boaz rose before the hour when one man can recognize another, 'For' said he 'it must not be known that this woman came to the threshing-floor.' Then he said to her, 'Bring the cloak you are wearing and hold it out.' She held it out while he put six measures of barley into it and then gave it to her to carry. And she went into the town...

Meanwhile Boaz had gone up to the gate of the town and sat down, and the relative of whom he had spoken chanced to come past. Boaz said to him, 'Come here, man, and sit down'; and he came and sat down. Then Boaz picked out ten of the town's elders and said to them, 'Sit down here,' and they sat down. Then Boaz said to the man who had the right of redemption, 'Naomi, who has come back from the country of Moab, is selling the piece of land that belonged to our brother, Elimelech. I thought I should tell you about this and say: Buy it in the presence of the men who are sitting here and in the presence of the elders of my people. If you want to use your right of redemption, redeem it; if you do not tell me so and I shall know, for there is no one but you to redeem it except me, though I come after you, myself.' And he said, 'I am willing to redeem it.' But Boaz continued, 'On the day you purchase the land from Naomi, you purchase Ruth the Moabitess also, the wife of the dead man, and so restore his name to his inheritance.' And the man with right of redemption said, 'Then I cannot use my right of redemption, without jeopardizing my own inheritance. As I cannot use my right of redemption, exercise the right yourself...

Then Boaz said to the elders and all the people, 'You are witnesses this day that I buy from Naomi all that belonged to Elimelech, to Chilion and to Mahlon. You are witnesses too that I buy Ruth the Moabitess, Mahlon's widow, to be my wife, to keep the name of the dead man in his inheritance, so that the dead man's name may not die out among his brothers and at the gate of his town.' All the people at the gate said, 'We are witnesses'; and the elders said, 'May Yahweh make the woman who is to enter your House like Rachel and Leah who together built up the House of Israel.'[2]

The book of Ruth is a sensitive portrayal of the faithfulness and dedication of two women to one another. It is also an explicit account of the naturalness of human sexual relations that would be difficult to explain to a Sunday School class that had not previously had some sex education. What actually occurred that night on the threshing floor between the two is not described. However, we are told that she was to make herself as attractive as possible—to anoint herself (put on her best perfume) and wear her best clothes. We shall see when we listen to the words of The Song of Songs that Hebrew writers were not unaware of the power of physical attractiveness in love and sexuality. It is clear that Boaz did not find Ruth unattractive. In the time of the story, when sexual relations were not viewed with the horror of the later gnostic Christian Church, it is possible that sexual intercourse took place. The official Roman Catholic Church, as well as the majority of Protestant denominations, would declare that Ruth's actions were wanton and that she committed venial if not mortal sin. If we were more concerned with global injustice and poverty, abandoned children and starving people we might view sexual expression in a more kindly light. Sometimes we lay emphasis on some sins in order not to see others.

SEXUALITY AS THE PRIVILEGE OF MEN

Evidently Ruth's forwardness was not totally out of place in her culture. Her actions give a different picture of the place and power of women than is given in the legal codes of Israel. And yet Ruth was bought along with her land. Her actions are a case of human love getting around the patriarchal laws. These laws are still there and have important sexual implications that support the abominable double standard under which women live in most cultures today; in the Western world women are just beginning to be freed from this standard. In the patriarchal view, sexuality was a good and beautiful thing for a woman within marriage as long as it did not interfere with the pleasure of males. If the male was not satisfied he was free in Hebrew culture to divorce his wife, take another wife or visit a prostitute. Women were not given the same options. Tamar was nearly burned because she appeared to be indulging in prostitution as Judah actually did. This double standard was easier to enforce because women often carry the evidence of their sexual relations in pregnancy.

This double standard still persists in most cultures. Even in our Western society the woman bearing a child out of wedlock has an infinitely more difficult time in most instances than the man responsible for impregnating her. "Boys will be boys" is a familiar justification, and men are not too severely criticized if they have an extramarital affair or visit a prostitute. We have already noted that Kinsey found that 69% of his population of white males had visited a prostitute. We have already noted the horrors of clitoridectomies and associated practices, for making sure that the woman's sexual pleasure does not get in the way of the man's.

Most prostitution is practiced by women. If there were no demand for these services they would most likely not be offered. In the sexual freedom of the matrilineal society or even the polygamous one, there is little need for harlots. The Mormons boasted that there was almost no prostitution when polygamy was practiced in Utah. Prostitution is often the result of the patriarchal devaluation of women and their sexuality. Sexual experience is bought and sold and women are viewed temporarily as slaves, as the man's property. Many studies detail what prostitution does to women physically, psychologically and spiritually. Indeed some of the most frequent users of drugs are prostitutes; only by numbing themselves with drugs can they continue their practice.

Polygamy was another patriarchal solution to meeting male sexual needs. Yet how is it possible for women to express themselves freely in a polygamous marriage? A study of the difference between romantic, passionate love, friendship and caring shows how unstable sexual passion can be.[3] Imagine the situation of the first wife in a polygamous marriage who was ignored because of the passionate relationship with a new wife. She was virtually a prisoner of a household where she might have physical security for herself and her children (who might be valued by the husband); however, her sexual needs might be totally ignored. Some women who have had an adequate and happy sexual life and then have been divorced and denied sexual experience, have described to us the almost physical pain that this unsatisfied need created. The stories of Sarah and Hagar and Rachel and Leah and their children show the dangers of polygamous marriages when one wife is truly loved and the other just used. Polygamy is probably less damaging when romantic love is kept out of the picture and it is simply a matter of social custom.

The viciousness of the customs persisting in the Turkish Sultan's harem for many centuries gives another example of what polygamy can do to women and their sexuality. Islamic law still allows a man to have four wives in most countries where it predominates while women can have but one husband.

In Hebrew society a woman could be divorced at will by her husband for nearly any whim. Of course, it was impossible for women in this situation to have security and the communication that is necessary (as we shall show later) for the development of truly mature sexual relations. Sexual mutuality was particularly absent when women were taught that their husband was *baal*, their lord. And, ironically, the lot of most divorced women in Hebrew society was prostitution for survival. When it is realized how fickle romantic passion can be, easy divorce laws *available only to males* can be seen as another devaluation of the feminine and female sexuality.

When people object that these Hebrew ideas have been largely abandoned they are not looking at the facts. In our society women who are as forward as Ruth would be avoided by most men except for an affair; they are considered by the male majority as not quite nice. We shall see in a later chapter that performance anxiety is one of the leading causes of male impotence. Often when men are expected to perform they are unable to get erections. Many males have found that they can avoid this problem if they relate only to submissive women where mutuality is not involved.

Morton was brought up in a Victorian patriarchal household. There was deep affection between his mother and father, but the idea of sexual or intellectual equality was not even considered. It is possible to have real affection even within that kind of marriage, but it is in spite of the patriarchal nature of the arrangement. We believe that one reason for Morton's mother's sickness and untimely death was not being permitted to live out her potential. Phyllis Rose has described what patriarchy can do to women in her book *Parallel Lives, Five Victorian Marriages*.

SEXUALITY FOR PROCREATION

In most of the Old Testament the only real purpose suggested for marriage and sexuality was to produce children. The Hebrew people were God's chosen people and were meant to populate the earth. Any practice that was not directed toward that goal was seen as a defiance of Yahweh's will and could result in the worst of tragedies. When this principle is carried to its logical conclusion then sexuality for communication is totally ignored. Later when gnostic ideas became influential, then even sexuality for procreation was viewed as an actual evil.

The drastic penalties prescribed for those who transgressed sexual laws could certainly have given rise to the idea that Yahweh was terribly upset by our failure to live up to the sexual code outlined in Deuteronomy and Leviticus. One reason for these rules was the presence of the mother goddess cults common among the Canaanites with whom the Israelites shared Palestine. As we have already noted, men who had relations with "temple women" were viewed as breaking their commitment to Yahweh; such practices were viewed by the prophets and the legal codes as idolatry and apostacy and were subject to the death penalty. The downfall of the great kingdom of Solomon (as well as of the kingdoms of other kings) was attributed to the fact that many of the people participated in these cults. Men as well as women were available in these temples and so homosexuality came under the same drastic ban. Sometimes the temple people wore the clothes of the opposite sex, and so transvestism came under the same death penalty. This may have resulted in the law prohibiting the "abominable practice of wearing the clothes of the other sex" that we mentioned earlier. This particular prohibition is found in Deuteronomy 22:5. Deuteronomy 22-24 contains many prohibitions including one that says that the man with crushed testicles or without a penis cannot be admitted to the assembly of Yahweh. Candidates for priesthood can not be deformed in any part of the body including the sexual organs. Leviticus 19 and 20 contain similar decrees. Breaking sexual taboos often called for the death penalty, seldom carried out in Israel but sometimes invoked in the Christian Church during the Dark and Middle Ages. Some of these laws and the punishments prescribed are brutal and savage. Anything to do with these pagan temples was forbidden, including dream interpretation and fortune-telling.

The Old Testament even viewed nudity within the family as offensive to Yahweh. We have already seen that many cultures not influenced by this tradition are not offended by the naked body. In the account of the fall in Genesis 3:7 Adam and Eve ate of the forbidden fruit, their eyes were opened, and they realized that they were naked (and that this was somehow wrong). They sewed fig leaves together to make loincloths. Later they made skin tunics. Nakedness here represents the state of innocence before the fall. One commentary states that what was good before has now become evil and the sin of indecency has been invented.

Noah was the first to plant the vine and the first to get drunk. He was lying naked in his tent when his youngest son Ham came in and saw him lying naked. He went out and told his brothers what he had seen. They, then, walked in backward so as not to see their father's nakedness and covered him with cloaks. Because of Ham's "sin" he and his descendents, the people of Canaan, were cursed by Noah and made subject to the descendents of Shem from whom the Israelites are descended. Leviticus 18 expressly prohibits family nakedness. The same horror of nakedness runs through Hebrew literature although David danced after a victory and offended his wife. Nudity within the family was viewed almost as incest; nakedness in this culture was acceptable only in legitimate sexual intercourse.

It is difficult to understand this attitude toward nudity. Perhaps nudity was common in the Pagan temples. Perhaps the offensiveness of the graven image may have carried over to the human body. We have already mentioned Barbara's experience in a hospital in Japan where we discovered that Japanese men or women did not even notice a person's nudity. The passage quoted in the first chapter tells of the same attitude among primitive people. Kenneth Clark's excellent study, *The Nude, A Study in Ideal Form*, suggests that in Christianity where the Word became *flesh*, a new view was presented that was quite different from the Hebrew view. The body was even capable of carrying the Divine image. Leo Steinberg's fascinating book, *The Sexuality of Christ in Renaissance Art and in Modern Oblivion* confirms this thesis with sound scholarship.

When nudity is seen as an offense to God, human sexuality becomes problematic to say the least. When one is ashamed of one's body it is difficult to give it freely to another person and communicate sexually with another. We have talked with many people whose fears in this area crippled them sexually. In light of the psychology of human psychosexual development we doubt that Old Testament prohibitions against nudity, masturbation and many other sexual acts have any more current application to our day than the food laws and regulations about slavery. However, in a culture like ours that has prohibited portraying the human body and is somewhat hung up on the subject, nudity can be provocative, seductive, titillating and lewd. The acceptance of the human body and lack of fear about it in the presence of those with whom it is appropriate, does not constitute flaunting nudity or exploiting the nudity of others in any way. There is a difficult line to hold between reacting toward an unwise set of attitudes and coming to a sensible new approach within the family.

It is difficult for most human beings to understand that an action may be equally valuable for several different reasons or purposes. The idea that sexuality is for procreation alone destroys the meaning of sexual love at least in theory. This Old Testament attitude has influenced the devaluation of sexuality in much of our Christian culture, as we shall see later on. It influences the Church's teachings on contraception and sexual freedom within marriage.

Paul believed the end of the world was at hand and suggested that it was wrong to bring children into those chaotic times. Since procreation was the only legitimate reason for sex, Paul's attitude was that sex should be avoided. He may not have known that there was such a thing as contraception, and he would have been influenced by the story of Onan if he had known of it. Thus he simply recommended that people avoid marriage and children. During the decaying and hopeless conditions of the Dark Ages, Paul's words made sense to many; the birth rate dropped drastically as people could not bear to bring children into that world.

One does not have to look far to see how inappropriate the Hebrew view of sex solely as a means of populating the earth is for our time. The problem in our world today is not *underpopulation*. We have spent a considerable amount of time in Southeast Asia, India, Bangladesh and China. The problem of overpopulation is everywhere evident. The rich do not suffer in overpopulation, but the poor do. The abandoned children in Brazil and much of South America as well as in Bangladesh and Southeast Asia are a scandal. Poor women who are abandoned by unreliable men cannot provide for both the child and themselves and so are forced to abandon their children. Bringing unwanted children into a broken world seems to us a worse moral breach than interfering with conception. Even in developed and economically healthy countries, most families can only raise so many children without falling into poverty. Some of the most tragic counselees with whom we have talked were children who were basically unwanted and whose birth created problems for their parents.

Religious leaders need to rethink and reformulate the idea that sexuality is just for procreation. They will be aided in this if they study some of the findings of depth psychology, sociology and population studies.

SEXUALITY AS ROMANTIC PASSION

We are grateful that the Bible was never really censored and that it contains Job's angry cry against God, David's failings, the skepticism of Ecclesiastes and the magnificent description of romantic love in the Song of Songs. This brings us to the fourth quite different view about sexuality in the Old Testament. The Song of Songs was attributed to Solomon for we are told in I Kings 11:1ff that Solomon had seven hundred wives of royal rank and three hundred concubines. However, we doubt that Solomon knew much about the kind of mutual sexual longing and love that is expressed there. How degrading such a harem would have been to the women involved, but Solomon was not criticized for the number of his wives, but rather that some of them were foreigners and that he followed their *religious* practices.

Let us listen to the lovers in The Song of Songs speak to each other. First of all the maiden speaks. (In the Moffat Bible it is a maiden who speaks. In the Jerusalem Bible the woman is called a bride for obvious reasons when we consider the inflammatory nature of the poetry. The following translation is from the Jerusalem Bible.)

> Let him kiss me with the kisses of his mouth.
> Your love is more delightful than wine;
> delicate is the fragrance of your perfume,
> your name is an oil poured out,
> and that is why the maidens love you.
> Draw me in your footsteps, let us run.
> The King has brought me into his rooms;
> you will be our joy and our gladness.
> We shall praise your love above wine;
> how right it is to love you. 1:2-4

The woman then speaks to her beloved and a dialogue follows:

> —While the King rests in his own room
> my nard yields its perfume.
> My beloved is a sachet of myrrh
> lying between my breasts.
> My beloved is a cluster of henna flowers
> among the vines of Engedi.
>
> —How beautiful you are, my beloved,
> how beautiful you are!
> Your eyes are doves.

—How beautiful you are, my Beloved,
and how delightful!
All green is our bed.

—The beams of our house are of cedar,
the paneling of cypress.

I am the rose of Sharon,
the lily of the valleys.
—As a lily among the thistles,
so is my love among the maidens.
—As an apple tree among the trees of the orchard,
so is by Beloved among the young men.
In his longed-for shade I am seated.
and his fruit is sweet to my taste.
He has taken me to his banquet hall,
and the banner he raises over me is love.

Feed me with raisen cakes,
restore me with apples,
for I am sick with love.

His left arm is under my head,
his right arm embraces me. 1:12-2:6

The chorus asks the woman what makes her beloved so desirable and attractive and she replies in a fourth poem:

My beloved is fresh and ruddy,
to be known among ten thousand.
His head is golden, purest gold,
his locks are palm fronds
and black as the raven.
His eyes are doves
at a pool of water,
bathed in milk,
at rest on a pool.
His cheeks are beds of spices,
banks sweetly scented.

His lips are lilies,
distilling pure myrrh.
His hands are golden, rounded,
set with jewels of Tarshish.
His belly a block of ivory
covered with sapphires.
His legs are alabaster columns
set in sockets of pure gold.
His appearance is that of Lebanon,
unrivaled as the cedars.
His conversation is sweetness itself,
he is altogether lovable.
Such is my Beloved, such is my friend,
O daughters of Jerusalem. 5:10-16

In the fifth and last poem of these songs of love the youth tells the
chorus of the beauty of his beloved:

How beautiful are your feet in their sandals,
O prince's daughter!
The curve of your thighs is like the curve of a necklace,
work of a master hand.
Your navel is a bowl well rounded
with no lack of wine,
your belly a heap of wheat
surrounded with lilies.
your two breasts are two fawns,
twins of a gazelle.
Your neck is an ivory tower.
Your eyes, the pools of Heshbon,
by the gate of Bath-rabbim.
Your nose, the Tower of Lebanon,
sentinel facing Damascus.
Your head is held high like Carmel,
and its plaits are as dark as purple;
a king is held captive in your tresses.
How beautiful you are, how charming,
my love, my delight!

In stature like the palm tree,
its fruit-clusters your breasts.
'I Will climb the palm tree,' I resolved,
'I will seize its clusters of dates.'
May your breasts be clusters of grapes,
your breath sweet scented as applies,
your speaking, superlative wine. 7:2-10

This poem is pure, exotic, graphic love poetry that glorifies and celebrates physical beauty, attractiveness and passionate physical love. Romantic love and physical sexuality are joined together in this song of love and placed in the canon of sacred scripture. How did this writing come to be included in the Old Testament? One Jewish tradition dating to the first century B.C.E. ruled that anyone singing The Song of Songs in a tavern would be expelled from the synagogue. The rabbis were well aware of the poem's inflammatory nature. This little book is a glorification of romantic love almost without parallel in literature. Were it not found in the Bible and allegorized it would certainly have been banned in Boston for centuries.

In both the Jewish rabbinical tradition and in the Christian Church this book has been viewed as symbolic of God's love for Israel and the Christian community and also of the divine-human love relationship. In the book of the prophet Hosea, Yahweh's love is compared to that of Hosea who lovingly takes back his unfaithful wife, Gomer. The prophet may have actually lived out this symbolism as a way of impressing the message of God's love for the people of Israel. Seldom in religious writing has the unfailing, continuous love of God been better expressed. In all this symbolism our deepest and most intimate sexual relationships with our beloved are perceived as symbols of an even greater love that God bears for us. We find this theme developed in many Christian mystics but particularly in St. Bernard of Clairvaux and St. John of the Cross.

SEXUALITY AND LOVE

Before leaving the Old Testament, let us look at the value placed on love and forgiveness in several Old Testament stories. Few narratives reveal more tender compassion than Joseph's love for Benjamin and his other brothers and his forgiveness of them. In his elegy at the death of Jonathan, his closest friend, David sings that his love for Jonathan was greater than for any woman.[4] The greatness of David is attributed in large part to his incredible love for his soldier followers, and to his compassion and love for his traitor son Absalom. Even his murderous love for Bathsheba is portrayed as a sign of his capacity to love. One reason the Psalms were attributed to David was that they so often speak of God's love. The law of Leviticus also states that we are to love our neighbor as ourselves.[5] Jewish tradition maintained that this was one of the two basic commandments of the law. The Hebrews were such earthy, embodied people that this love was not a glassy intellectual concern, but an emotional, total love carrying some of the quality depth psychologists attribute to sexuality. Jesus picked up on this tradition and made it central to his teaching, changing it only by extending the meaning of the word neighbor from those of one's own nation to all humankind, from those of masculine social status to women and children and slaves.

JESUS AND SEXUALITY

Although Jesus made very few changes in the tradition of his people, he did present the idea that God was an incredibly loving parent with many of the best qualities of mother and father. Abba cared for us all, good and bad, and made the sun to rise on the good and the evil, on the just and the unjust, on those who follow the sexual laws and those who deviate from them. Like the father of the prodigal this Divine Lover is not interested in punishing those who mess up their lives but in offering new possibilities and opportunities. Jesus accepted crucifixion and death and rose again to bring new life to all who needed it. The only group he consistently criticized were those who felt that they were living righteous lives, those who were like the unconsciously self-righteous Mrs. Turpin in Flannery O'Connor's short story "Revelation."

Jesus spoke directly to the subject of adultery. In Jewish law this term referred to having sexual relations with another's wife. In the Sermon on the Mount Jesus said that not only those who actually commit adultery are guilty, but any who have looked upon a woman with desire or who have longed for another's wife are equally guilty. Then Jesus was reported by Matthew to use characteristic exaggeration and say that one should root out such behavior. If the eye offends, tear it out and if the foot offends, cut it off. Jesus was trying in this passage to show that none of us can live up to law. None of us are in the position to judge another. All of us are imperfect and impure; therefore we should not judge.

In the story of the prodigal, the father (who was a symbol for the compassionate Abba-God) does not reject or punish the returning son who has not only probably visited prostitutes as his brother sneered, but has also broken the ritual law and tended *pigs*. Having had these questionable sexual relationships did not keep the father from expressing his love as has been the case in many "Christian" families. The prodigal was lucky that he met his father before he met his elder brother.

The account of the women who broke in and anointed Jesus at the home of Simon the pharisee is found in two quite different settings. Walter Wink, the Biblical scholar, has suggested that the account in Luke 7 is the earlier and that it expresses the essence of Jesus' attitude toward sin and forgiveness. A woman breaks into a party of men in Simon's house—a scandalous action for a woman. She is called a sinner, a Greek word used for idolators and notorious sinners; she may even have been a temple prostitute. She stood behind Jesus where he reclined Roman style at the table. She wept and her tears flowed so freely that they moistened his feet. She then wiped them with her hair, kissed them repeatedly and then anointed them with an ointment, *myros* in Greek. What was Jesus' reaction to the wild behavior of this totally unconventional woman? First of all he rebuked Simon for his lack of hospitality and then he told a parable about how the debtor who received the greater remission of debt will be more grateful than the one who received less.

Turning toward the woman, Jesus said to Simon: "Do you see this woman? I entered your house and you gave me no water to wash my feet, but she has washed my feet with her tears and has wiped them with the hair of her head. You did not give me a kiss of greeting, but from the time she entered she has not ceased to kiss my feet affectionately. You did not anoint my head with oil, but she has anointed my feet with precious ointment. And so I say to you: 'Her many sins have been forgiven, because she has loved deeply; but the one who is forgiven little, loves in the same measure.'" Then he turned to the woman and said: "Your faith (in love) has saved you, go in peace." Jesus spoke no higher praise of any person in the entire Gospel narrative.

Not only did Jesus not single our sexual offenses for special castigation, he actually selected these sins as examples of sins that can be forgiven and ought to be forgiven. He saw that all of us fail in our principal voca-tion: none of us loves God or our neighbor as God does and none of us is in a position to judge. Even though Jesus was often portrayed as rebuk-ing the self-righteous and self-satisfied, we need to remember that in Jesus' story the prodigal's father went out to the elder brother who had snubbed his father and broken his filial duty. We are in no position to judge even these. As we look at the total picture of what Jesus did and said, it is clear that Jesus did not view sexual misdemeanors as particularly heinous.

After Jesus spoke out against divorce and the necessity of maintain-ing a marriage, his disciples made a typical patriarchal statement: "If that is the state of affairs between husband and wife, then it is not advisable to marry." And Jesus replied: "Not everyone can accept what I said, but only those who to whom the ability to follow them is given." Jesus saw each individual within the context of what he or she was capable—in sexual matters as well as in the rest of life.

Jesus directly challenges the *lex talonis* (an eye for an eye and a tooth for a tooth), saying: "But I say this to you: offer the wicked man no resis-tance."[6] In the same passage in the Sermon on the Mount Jesus chal-lenges the Hebraic divorce law and Old Testament ideas about adultery, making oaths and hating one's enemy. By implication he is challenging all of the violent, vindictive punishments of the Old Testament. Jesus direct-ly questions these punishments in his treatment of the adulterous woman in the eighth chapter of John. Jesus knew the human heart and the Hebrew law and he knew that all were breakers of the law when the law is applied to our hearts, and so he said: "He who is without sin cast the first stone." When the accusers melted away, Jesus turned to the woman and asked her where her accusers were and then said: "Neither do I condemn you; go and sin no more." Jesus did not single out sexual offenses for special con-demnations. He saw all of us as failing in our duties toward God and our neighbor and therefore in no position to judge anyone else.

Jesus used human touch as sacramental of God's healing power.[7] He and his disciples often touched those who were sick or demon-possessed and they were healed. The mysterious depth and power of human touch is only beginning to be understood.[8] Jesus used touch to convey God's restoring power and God's spirit. The Church has continued to use touch as the outward sign of confirmation and of ordination to ministry through-out the ages. Touch became the symbol of Spirit-giving as food—bread and wine—became the symbol of Jesus' presence in Eucharist. In mutual sexual love touch can bring people to an ecstatic experience that connects them to the Divine.

Jesus was very much in touch with the natural world and its goodness. The only statement attributed to him in the Gospels that can be construed to devalue or downgrade sexuality was the statement about becoming a eunuch for the kingdom of heaven.[9] What did he mean by that statement? We believe that Jesus was talking to a particular man who was similar to the rich young ruler—except that this fellow was rich in sexual experience rather than in money. Jesus realized that this man was hooked on sexual adventure and that until he could control his sexual activity, he could not fully follow the way of Love. How fortunate that few people have taken this statement as literally as Origen did. Indeed the Church has wisely legislated that self-mutilation is not what Jesus meant and forbids this practice. However, the Church had at one time castrated boys when their voices were a perfect soprano to provide a magnificent choir for prelates.

Any emotion, any attachment, any sexual experience, any value, any practice that becomes more important to us than the way of Love and forgiveness that Jesus taught and lived, can become an idol and lead us away from the mark (the Greek word for sin, *hamartia*, means missing the mark). What practices keep us from hitting the target of life? What are the actions the Church has called sin? Even chastity, celibacy, honesty, "righteousness", courage, prudence, knowledge, spiritual gifts and ecstasies when placed ahead of Jesus' kind of love, can be sins. Indeed, these types of sins are often far more serious than the more obvious human failings. No wonder so many in the Church have failed to practice this kind of love; it requires daily dying and rising again. When men and women have succeeded in some small measure in living this way, they have been called saints.

SEXUALITY AND CHURCH HISTORY

We have already noted that in regard to women, some of Paul's writings and his downplaying of Jesus' resurrected appearances to the women are a step backward. We see the same movement away from Jesus' view of the naturalness of sexuality and from the ideas presented by *The Song of Songs*. Paul shows considerable emotion when the subject of sexual infractions occur. He was scandalized by the action of a man who was living with his stepmother. We are not told any of the circumstances such as the ages of the parties, or whether they intended to be married or considered themselves so. This was incest according to Levitical law, but not according to blood relationship. Indeed, many of the kings of Israel took over their fathers' harems. According to Leviticus 18:8 (Deuteronomy 23:1, 27:20), "You must not uncover the nakedness of your father's wife; it is your father's nakedness." It would seem that uncovering nakedness is equivalent to having sexual intercourse, and having it with the stepmother was like having sexual relations with the father.

We wonder if this concern for sexual morality not present in the teachings of Jesus were not a reaction to the sexual freedom in both Roman and Greek culture. Also Paul was living in a military society based on slavery. Slavery was not that much a part of Jewish society in Jesus' time. Many of his Church members in Corinth might well have been slaveholders. From the point of view of Jesus would not slavery have been a worse sin than illicit sexual acts? Paul was following the Hebrew law in condoning slavery and ignoring its effects upon human beings.[10] Lance Webb has written an excellent historical novel *Onesimus* that describes accurately the horrors of slavery in the Roman world. Could Paul's emphasis on sexual misdemeanors have been an unconscious reaction to his failure to recognize the vicious nature of slavery?

After Paul demands that the man who had relations with his stepmother be shunned and thrown out of the Christian community, he goes on in the sixth and seventh chapters of his first letter to the Corinthians to speak about other sexual relationships. His view of prostitution is clear: for him it is joining the body of Christ with that of a non-Christian prostitute. The idea of a Christian prostitute was unthinkable. Although many of his members at the church in Corinth were former prostitutes, his attitude toward prostitution was one of horror. He goes on to say that it is a good thing for a man not to touch a woman (I Cor. 7:1) and then: "But since fornication is such a danger, let each man have his own wife and each woman her own husband." (I Cor. 7:2.) He seems to imply that the real reason for marriage was not fellowship or even procreation, but to control the sexual urges so people would be less likely to sin sexually. Paul would have preferred that Christians remain unmarried as he was, but suggested that they get married; it was better to marry than to burn. This is hardly a recommendation for sexual mutuality and communion. Many Christian groups have taken literally the prohibition against any touching except in marriage and so inhibited the normal psychosexual development of individuals. Those who were brought up in a Jansenistic or Puritanical society know the disastrous psychological effects of this prohibition against touch—the very touch that Jesus used to heal.

In Paul's defense it should be remembered that he believed that the end of the world was imminent and along with it a time of chaos, turmoil and hardship. Bringing children into such a world was thoughtless and inconsiderate. Nonetheless, as we read through all of Paul, listening to him speaking of the flesh and marriage and fornication, we find him taking a step backward from Jesus' teaching about the naturalness of men, women, love, children, touch, and sexuality. Paul did write to the Galatians that there is "no difference between Jew and Greek, slave and free, male and female, but are all one under Jesus Christ." (Gal. 3:28.) However, his specific instructions do not bear out this statement. He said that the law no longer applied to those in Christ. This was true for Paul except when it involved his sexual attitudes. Paul also follows Hebrew law with regard to any homoerotic relationships. Paul did write the great ode to love in I Corinthians 13, but at times we fear that this love was more "spiritual" and less embodied than the love of which Jesus spoke. We wonder if Paul might have suffered from a negative mother complex and been unable to relate intimately with women. Some of these arguments about the evil of the flesh and sexuality and the place of women sound to us more like rationalizations arising from fear than sound, cogent reasoning. We are curious as to the nature of Paul's thorn in the flesh.

We are not suggesting that Paul did not make great contributions in his letters; however, there is a great gulf between Paul and Jesus. Let us not forget that St. Francis of Assisi preached the children's crusade and St. Teresa built her convents on the gold and silver seized from the Aztecs and Incas. Thank heavens that God can use imperfect people. We must be careful to keep this in mind and not deify anyone but Jesus of Nazareth.

As we now turn to the history of the Church's teaching on sexuality we find that the Church followed Paul's basic direction and then went further and further afield, further and further from Jesus' teaching of the equal value of women and the holiness of human touch and sexuality. In his book *Christianity, Social Tolerance and Homosexuality*, John Boswell traces the history of Christian attitudes toward sexuality from the New Testament to approximately 1200 A.D. With care and scholarship he clearly shows how the attitude of the Christian community changed during this time. His research deals specifically with the subject of homosexuality, but applies to the attitudes toward sexuality in general. He maintains that there was no Greek word for homosexuality as there was none for sexuality (just as in English until recent times). The Greek word usually translated as "homosexual" really means "homosexual prostitute"—quite a different meaning. According to Boswell the Church in the later years of the Roman Empire shared some of the tolerant attitudes of the Greek world. About the beginning of the thirteenth century a great change took place in the Western Church. A less tolerant attitude toward sexual acts developed and was written into the great medieval statements about Christianity and morality. These statements became the Canon law of the Church and people who broke the sexual laws were often put to death like the hapless women accused of witchcraft.

During the fourth century Ambrose of Milan wrote widely about the Christian life. In his discussion of the celibate life for women, there is not even the slightest suggestion that they sought this life because sexuality was evil.[11] The reason for celibacy was that few women could follow the way of Christ seriously and be married in that corrupt society. Through marriage they became playthings or slaves of men or they got lost in that pleasure-seeking world. Augustine did not share Ambrose's attitude as we have already seen. His morality, contaminated by gnosticism, led him to argue that even sexual relations *within* marriage could easily become venial sin and that all other sexual relationships were mortal sin.[12] Augustine himself may have needed to curb his sexual desire for his own salvation, but he went on to infer that everyone else needed to do so also and suggested that sexual pleasure itself was in most cases evil. Augustine became the major theologian for the next thousand years and gradually the ideas he espoused filtered into the Canon law of the Church and then into the secular law of the Western world.

We shall see later on when we look at clerical celibacy that churches of the Eastern Orthodox tradition followed the tradition of allowing priests and deacons to have one marriage. Only bishops were required to be celibate. This tradition came to a final statement in the Trullan Council in 680 C.E. and has been the law in all branches of the Greek, Abyssinian and Coptic Churches. Marriage was permissible if contracted before ordination. On the other hand, Pope Siricius in 385 C.E. lamented the dreadful immorality of the times and demanded absolute celibacy for all clergy. The Fifth Council of Carthage in 411 C.E. required all clergy to be separated from their wives and this was enforced by the Emperor Honorius. Even after the Trullan Council, which occurred before the Church was divided, the Western Church continued to fight for clerical celibacy and continues to do so right up to the present.[13]

Before taking a look at the history of the Western Church's attitude toward sexuality, we need to pause and look at the Greek Orthodox attitude toward this important subject in more depth. We find a much more lenient view of sexual offenses there than in the West. The Justinian Code of Byzantium contained few death penalties and was substantially more liberal in regulating sexual matters than the views developing in Rome. Of course, Orthodoxy had its celibate monastery, Mt. Athos, where no female of any species—not even a hen—was allowed. By and large, however, the clergy in the Greek Church followed the tradition of the apostles and were married. The ideas of the gnostics were more successfully combatted here than in the West.

One of the leading Gnostics, Basalides Saturninius, wrote that "marriage and generation are from Satan".[14]. Tatian, another Christian leader heavily influenced by gnosticism, called marriage "fornication and corruption".[15] Although the early Church fathers were fighting against these gnostic ideas, Augustine came close to incorporating several of them.

SEXUALITY IN THE WESTERN CHURCH

We turn now to the official attitude of the magisterium of the Roman Catholic Church toward sexuality in general. Most of the attitudes in Protestantism have a relatively short history and are so diverse that they do not give a coherent view of sexuality. Also, few of these churches have tried to spell out moral law with the care of Rome's nineteen-hundred-year-old tradition. Those unaware of this moral, legal and theological tradition will fail to identify one of the main sources of the negative view of sexuality which permeates so much of our Western civilization. In *Sexual Morality, a Catholic Perspective* Philip Keane, S.S. has provided a well-documented study and a careful critique of this view of this tradition from moral and theological standpoints:

"The Roman Catholic tradition has held that except for those sexually arousing thoughts oriented toward intercourse with a person's marriage partner, all thoughts that arouse sexual pleasure and are deliberately consented to are mortally sinful . . . Historical examination shows that the magisterium has consistently asserted the immorality of masturbation, premarital sexual intercourse, and other actions arousing venereal pleasure outside of marriage. This teaching holds that the matter involved in venereal pleasure outside of marriage is always a grave matter so that no one can in any way intend non-marital venereal pleasure, either as an end in itself or as a means to another end, without this pleasure being an objective, grave, moral evil."[16]

This teaching is based on the theory of natural law; to seek venereal pleasure outside of marriage is a sin against the nature of things, natural law. Even though Thomas Aquinas himself asserts that the morality of an action involves an object, an end, and the circumstances of the action, the general tenor of his writings views sexual actions as evil in themselves. Some manuals based on this approach refer to human genitals as the dishonest parts. Some seminaries provided paddles to tuck in seminarians' shirt-tails so that there would be no danger of self-stimulation. Women were not to wear patent leather shoes because they might reflect the unmentionable.

Fr. Keane points out that this tendency toward viewing an act as evil in itself needs to be carefully examined and that this view is being questioned by many modern Catholic moral theologians, even though the official position of the Church has not changed. Generations of Catholics were brought up fearing that if they masturbated and were hit by a truck on the way to confession they would languish in hell forever; mortal sin means being totally cut off from God, and that is hell. Pastorally this view was mitigated by the idea of full consent, which implied that mortal sin required sufficient reflection and an entirely free decision as well as an immoral action.

However, in popular Catholic thinking, according to Fr. Keane, seriously wrong, external sexual actions and mortal sin became virtually identified. Some men raised in this tradition told me that they were instructed on how many times they might shake the penis when urinating without being in danger of the grave mortal act of masturbation. This scholastic attitude formed much of Protestant thinking on sexuality but was not clearly formulated. When a law tries to cover all possible situations it usually becomes ridiculous. The Church did not condemn as mortal sins predatory wars, human violence, child labor, human slavery, the servitude of women, political tyranny, economic oppression and torture used in inquisitions; yet a purposefully sought sexual fantasy doomed one to hell. Jesus' teachings on love and forgiveness were somehow lost and forgotten.

Whatever happened in Western culture to make sexual acts the essence of moral wrongdoing? Even today when a person speaks of being immoral, the first thought that comes to most minds is some sexual wrongdoing. In their introduction to *The Fundamentals of Human Sexuality* Katchadourian and Lunde write:

> . . . sex figures predominently in an individual's moral and spiritual identity. At least in Western cultures, it is used as a moral yardstick more consistently than any other form of behavior, at both the personal and public levels. Many of us feel greater guilt and are often punished more severely for sexual transgressions than for other offenses. Common as sexual themes are in the mass media, the level of tolerance is nowhere near that for aggression and violence."[17]

Many suggestions have been offered and we are inclined to believe that all of them may have played a part in leading us to equate sin often with sexual sin:

1.   Syphillis and gonorrhea epidemics swept over Europe in the sixteenth and seventeenth centuries; these may have caused the sexual act to be closely associated with illness, disease, death and evil.

2.   Another theory suggests that as the age of mechanization began, the importance of logical programming and exact time and conscious will took precedence over spontaneity and sexuality. Sexuality seldom responds to logic and clock-time.

3.   John Boswell points to the break up of Medieval culture and values and the confusion about right and wrong which followed. In a fearful reaction to change, the Church and society became more rigid. Anyone different and nonconforming was condemned, heretics, usurers, Jews, as well as all those whose sexual acts were not entirely conventional. Sexuality

became for Medieval society the same sort of scapegoat that the Jews became for the Nazis.

4. Life in the Medieval world was uncertain and dangerous. The Black Death wiped out as much as half of some communities. This fear found a scapegoat in sexuality.

5. However, the most important influence was the gnostic attitude of Augustine. It combined with the above attitudes and was portrayed as natural law. These attitudes were then rendered permanent in Canon law. This view is being questioned, as we have noted, by many modern Roman Catholic thinkers; in many official statements of the non-Roman churches this attitude has been clearly rejected. The effect of this combination of attitudes towards sexuality on Western life and culture can hardly be exaggerated. How important that we listen to Jesus and try to understand what his ideas about sexuality may have been. When this negative view of sexuality becomes authoritative, natural law becomes unnatural law.[18]

A SHORT HISTORY OF MARRIAGE AND SEXUALITY

Some years ago the Episcopal Church considered revising its law concerning the marriage of divorced people. Morton was asked by a bishop to do a study on the history of marriage. He was quite surprised to find that marriage became a matter of concern to the Western Church only in the later Middle Ages. Up to that time marriage was a family and secular matter. The two people or the two families made the arrangements and carried them out. Theologically the man and woman getting married were the priest and priestess of the service and the minister or priest gave the blessing of the Church and later became the official witness of the Church and state.[19] In the state of Pennsylvania with its strong Quaker background the marriage license is so designed that legal marriage can take place with or without a minister because there are none among certain groups of Quakers. The signatures of two witnesses of the exchanged marriage vows are all that is necessary for a legal marriage. The vows mutually and solemnly made between two people form the essence of a wedding. Marriage has legitimacy and property ramifications and so the witnesses are required. It makes it easier for everyone to decide when a couple is actually married, when they get up before a church full of people and stammer out their vows. However, deciding when a couple in love is married in the sight of God is something like deciding when the fetus is imbued with human life.

Sometime during the twelfth or thirteenth centuries couples began to come to village priests to become betrothed, which was much the same as announcing an engagement today. At that time the banns were read and the couple went off to live together. They may well have been living together before this time, or the woman may have become pregnant. The betrothal took place at the church steps or porch. A second part of the wedding usually occurred after a child was born and the couple came for the blessing of their union. This could occur anytime, or not at all if the woman did not become pregnant. This division of time is represented in some traditional wedding ceremonies today. The betrothal takes place at the chancel steps; the marriage takes place at the altar rail.

Premarital sexual intercourse was common and accepted as natural in most places in that period. It was sanctified in the betrothal and blessed in the wedding. Social custom was able to accommodate a variety of arrangements very naturally. If no child were conceived or if the child was born and died, for example, the couple might separate if they so desired and nothing further was said. However, if the man died before the blessing of the wedding, the child was still considered legitimate. Erasmus, the great Renaissance scholar, is reported to have been born under these latter circumstances. The Church and society seemed to allow for something like a trial marriage. It should be noted, however, that promiscuity, although frequent, was never condoned by the Church.

In the Pennsylvania Dutch country old traditions linger on—the same customs as prevailed in the seventeenth century in the Palatinate in Germany. Many couples are married only after the bride has become pregnant. Part of this is the influence of the agrarian culture: a family without children could hardly survive. Most of Medieval Europe was agrarian and children were the only labor force. A woman who could bear no children was seldom claimed as a wife. No one understood that inability to conceive might be a male's failure.

One professor at the University of Notre Dame told us about a doctoral dissertation in which a comparison was made between the number of premarital pregnancies in 1650 and 1950. It was a very simple study: a random sample of parishes with a long history and with parish registers intact was selected. An examination was made of the marriages of couples and the birth and baptism of the first child in that marriage. In both 1650 and 1950 approximately twenty-five percent of the first children born in a family were conceived out of wedlock. Times have not changed as much as we may think, and contraception has not made a drastic difference.

As the Roman civilization collapsed and disintegrated, the only stable institution left in Western Europe was the Church; the only legal recourse was in the Church courts. Secular law and Canon law with its gnostic attitudes became indistinguishable. The Church courts were gradually brought under secular control, but the basic religious moral code was accepted as a matter of course as a part of the legal code. Even when separation between church and state finally evolved, the government and the legal profession were so accustomed to thinking of morality as a part of the law that legislation made the particular religious morality of the 13th century Canon law into secular law.

In addition may of the states of the United States of America began as theocratic states, dominated by a church and dedicated to a particular religious framework. They quite consciously legislated matters usually reserved for the religious realm. Much of the carefully worked out system of religious law in the Catholic Church was taken over unconsciously by Protestantism. Ultimately the legal attitude towards sexuality defined "natural" sexuality only as the insertion of the penis into the vagina for ejaculation, and other physical acts became "unnatural". "Crimes" against nature were treated with a kind of horror. Thus a code of "secular" laws developed that reflected one particular and narrow set of attitudes.

Most sociologists and psychologists of sexuality would say that anything a man and women do in private within a primary committed relationship is "normal" if it does neither of them nor anyone else any harm. But in many states in the U.S.A. many ordinary sexual practices are considered illegal. What is a matter of private sexual behavior has become instead a matter for public surveillance—to the extent that probably everyone of us could be convicted in some state or other for a misdemeanor or even a felony.[20] *The Wolfenden Report*, published in Great Britain, is one of the first comprehensive attempts to remove religious prejudices about sexual behavior from law. It has had a profound effect on all sexual legislation in the Western world.

During this process of changing morality and social custom into law, the patriarchal attitude toward women was also written into the law of most Western countries including the United States. The legal codes of many of its states followed suit. Changing this attitude required a constitutional amendment, the nineteenth, and that did not take place until 1921. Then women were given the same legal right to vote that former slaves had already won. A clear theology and anthropology of women such as we have tried to provide is needed to correct this attitude and bring a naturalness back to marriage and sexuality. We now offer our suggestions about the nature of committed, long-term relationships.

CHAPTER SIX

Sexuality, Love, Long Term
Committed Relationship, Marriage and Family

Placing these five concepts together as a chapter title would seem strange to people in many cultures. However, in the ideals of the Western world, these words are inextricably interconnected. The fact that few people live up to the ideal causes a lot of confusion.

First of all let us look at the interrelationship of these ideas and words. Then let us move on to the history of marriage in the Western world. When we begin to see some of the difficulties in modern marriage we wonder why people get married and we shall look at the many different reasons people have for getting married. This will bring us to the subject of sexuality, falling in love, and love, and how these can be integrated. We shall conclude looking at the family and its relationships and finally look at the importance of reconciliation in any family or committed relationship. In the next chapter we shall examine the nature of fulfilling sexuality.

Whatever else sexuality is, it is a driving biological and psychological desire, one that must be controlled in most societies, whether primitive or "civilized". And yet when sexuality is denied or repressed it can cause a host of psychological and physical problems. In addition, heterosexual sexuality (except in cases of artificial insemination) is the source of human offspring. Without the sexual act of intercourse the race would die out.

Throughout history some sort of family group has provided a channel for sexual drives and also a nurturing environment for the young that resulted from sexual union. Human children are helpless creatures for a long time after they are born, very different from most other animals. In order to survive and grow they need a stable group that can nurture them physically in their helplessness for many years. In addition to obtaining physical protection, children learn language from the nurturing group and with that achieve some of the unique attributes of humanness.

For hundreds of thousands of years the nurturing group probably centered around the mother and her family. We have no idea how long ago human beings became aware that sexual intercourse led to pregnancy. Until that time the mother and her child most likely were supported by her brother and the mother's clan. The mother's brothers took the place of the father. This situation most likely continued until the breakup of matrilinear society under the pressure of patriarchal power. The family as we know it now then developed, and the intimate group became the father and his wife (or wives), his parents and family. The anthropological evidence shows that we need these intimate groups if we are to be human.

Marriage and sexuality are obviously interrelated. Marriage is a social or legal commitment between a man and a woman for the procreation and raising of children and the legitimate channeling of the sexual drives. Marriage also creates the basic social unit. The nature of this commitment depends on the society; as we have seen, Old Testament patriarchy required women to remain faithful to their husbands while men had far more freedom. In the Christian *ideal* sexual experience is to be confined within the marriage relationship. For reasons we do not quite understand, the same ideal is also to be found in communist China, where extra-marital sex, divorce and all sexual relationships outside of marriage are strongly discouraged by the government and even punished severely.

The connection between sexuality and love is a relatively recent development. The relationship of love and sexuality is one of the main concerns of our Western world and is a mysterious subject of incredible power and diversity. The relationship between love and marriage is another recent development and another complex subject. We use the words committed relationship in the title of this chapter because long-term commitment between two people, whether in a purely mutual relationship or a legal marriage, seems to be the only way in which the deepest kind of caring and human development takes place.

Only one human institution needs as much prayer, sacrifice and divine support as celibacy—that of two people living together permanently and raising a family. To begin let us take a look at the various forms marriage has taken in Western history.

A SHORT HISTORY OF MARRIAGE

We have already discussed the matrilineal family situation in which marriage as we have come to know it was nonexistent. Lineage, name and property were carried through the mother. The impregnating male was about as significant as the male bee that impregnates the queen bee and about as expendable—in this family the maternal uncle fathers the children and becomes the male role model. Navajo Indian culture is still basically structured in this way. The idea of sexual relations with just one person is not even considered. Navajo women are not sexually deviant when they are promiscuous; they are living in accordance with their cultural tradition.

We have noted that polygamy and the devaluation of women that often goes with it are often found in patriarchal societies. Polygamy is also found where women greatly outnumber men in a social group. Likewise, polyandry, in which several men are permanently related to one woman, is often found where women are scarce. Mormon society is a perfect example of polygamy in these circumstances. Many more women than men were attracted to the faith, three to four women for every man. The logical alternatives to monogamy were either enforced celibacy for a large number of women (and consequently little increase in the membership of the church) or polygamy. Jung noted the same problem in Europe after World War I after so many men had been killed.

Even though polygamous marriage may be an adaptation to social reality, women are still devalued in it, as men are in polyandry. In Mormonism women can only enter heaven by being married—they have no eternal value except in relation to a husband. One observer involved socially with many Mormon women wrote to us that women in that culture still accept the dominance of men and seem naive in comparison with other women of the same educational background. Monogamy is really possible only when the natural chromosomal balance between males and females in maintained, *and* where this natural balance is reflected in a social structure where women and men are equally valued.

Marriage and sexual customs in the Western world have their roots in the cultures of Greece, Rome and Israel. In both ancient Greece or Israel the unmarried man was looked upon as peculiar, if not immoral. One of the great lawmakers of Greece, Solon, considered outlawing single people, and unmarried men were given fewer legal rights than married men. In the light of this it may seem paradoxical that homosexual relations were much accepted in classical Greece, but the homosexuality was seldom an exclusive relationship but rather an addition to marriage to an uneducated and subservient wife. Thus, many Greek men lived bisexual lives.

The prevailing attitude toward marriage in Israel also discouraged the single life; young men and women were married around the age of puberty. As we have noted before there were good reasons for this attitude toward marriage and child bearing: Israel was a small, sparsely settled country surrounded by great nations, and the Israelites needed as large a population as possible just to survive. Although women were given an inferior place in both Greek and Israeli cultures, they fared far better in Israel than Greece.

In Rome things were quite different. Although prior to the first and second centuries BC it was legal to sell, kill or mangle a wife or child, this attitude changed gradually and a point of view about the relations of men and women developed that has shaped the basic ideas of the modern Western world. In Rome there were three different kinds of marriage. The first type was known as *usus* or common-law marriage in modern legal parlance. Two people simply lived together for a year, and if they decided they wanted to be considered married, the union became a legal one. However, if the couple ever wanted a divorce, they simply dissolved the union themselves; no other legal party was involved. Two parishioners who had been prominent in Morton's first parish showed up fifteen years later to tell him that they had never been married. The woman had terminal cancer and they wanted to make it legal. The state law in California provided for this situation—a minister could marry a couple without a state license and record it only in the church records.

The second type of marriage was called *coemptio*. The marriage was ritualized and took place before witnesses; in the event of divorce, witnesses were again present. The last form of marriage, performed primarily among the nobility and the wealthy, was called *confarratio*. In addition to ten witnesses, a priest from the temple was also present. Dissolution of such a union again had to take place with witnesses and a priest. Men and women were viewed in almost every regard as equal, and a woman could even divorce her husband.

The Barbarian invasions and the collapse of the Western Roman

Empire ended the egalitarian view of women and marriage. Teutonic law and custom took its place and with it patriarchal attitudes toward women took over Western Europe. Women—whether wives or daughters—were viewed as property, and the father or other responsible male in the family could sell the daughter or give her into another man's hands along with a dowry. The giving of the wedding ring was originally the symbol that a contract had been made and part of the dowry had been delivered; the ring was given to the woman as evidence of this fact. When the rest of the property was provided, then the actual marriage was said to have taken place. The question, "Who giveth this woman to be married to this man?" was necessary legally to transfer the property rights of the father to the husband. The whole church stepped backward in accommodating itself to this barbarian attitude.

During the following centuries there were many different levels of marriage. Among prosperous burghers and landed gentry, arranged marriages were the usual custom. One of the most famous of these was that of William, Prince of Orange, age fourteen, and Mary Stuart, age twelve. From this marriage came the present lines of British kings and queens.

Then there was the trial marriage, a fascinating custom, called "sitting up" and "bundling" and many other colorful names in different European countries. With the parents' permission a young man was allowed to come and sleep in the daughter's bed. At first this was not sexual, but after seven or eight times it usually became so. Initially the couple tried to see if they could get along, and then the man needed to know for economic reasons that the woman could become pregnant before he married her.

In any case the purpose of marriage had little or nothing to do with love. It was a family business arrangement. As Dennis DeRougemont has shown clearly in his *Love in the Western World*, the idea of love as a basis for marriage is a fairly recent invention. In many European countries those of wealth had an official marriage, which had stability and provided the context for the desired number of children, and then one had no further sexual relationship with one's wife—the only safe way of guaranteeing no further offspring. Then the husband went out and sought sexual relationship elsewhere, with a mistress. We have no definitive statistics as to how frequent this practice was among the upper classes in Europe, but there is good evidence that it was quite common. In fact, the woman of the household often found it a blessing to be relieved of the necessity of bearing further children. Marriage was in some cases more a business relationship than a romantic one. Of course, in many marriages a deep and genuine relationship developed between the husband and wife, but it was incidental to the purpose of the marriage.

Then along came a new development—the idea that love should precede marriage and was its basic reason for being. In many of the arranged marriages the couple might not even have met before the wedding festivities. Henry VIII only knew one of his wives through a flattering portrait by a great artist of the day and was so shocked by the homeliness of his bride that he sent her right back home on her wedding day. The idea of love in marriage introduced a totally new dimension to the institution—that of the nuclear family, where the relationship between the couple takes precedence over economic, social, political or lineage concerns. And suddenly men and women began to relate on a more equal basis. The purpose of marriage became interaction, companionship, love and mutual growth *as well as* raising children and continuing the race.

Unfortunately, many nuclear marriages today are still quite patriarchal. Morton remembers life in a very patriarchal, nuclear household. He was born when his father was thirty-six, and his father was born to a man of fifty-one. Thus there were nearly ninety years between Morton and his grandfather. As far as the social attitudes in the house were concerned, Morton might as well have been born in the eighteen nineties. No one thought of questioning Morton's father's authority in the family. His mother was a very intelligent woman in a totally undemocratic organization. She learned quickly that frontal attack always failed, but tears were something that his father could not abide. And if she wept long enough and at the crucial moment, she could usually get her way. Even though both parents were well educated, there was no consideration of equality between male and female. There was a lot of sentimentality; but little real relationship.

Only when mutuality and honesty exist between husband and wife will there be mutuality and honesty between parents and children or among the children in a family. As far as we know the only kind of marriage that provides a real basis for equality, mutuality and honesty is a commitment made by a man and a woman who believe that genuine love (better expressed by Jesus of Nazareth than by any other person we know) is the central quality of the nature of our universe and is the essential characteristic of God, the Divine Lover. This commitment is made for the growth and salvation of both of them—and for the growth and salvation of the new souls this couple brings into the world. Any modern marriage made on any other

basis is likely to face almost insurmountable problems. The same truth applies to any extended or life-long intimate relationship, whether heterosexual
or homosexual. Such a relationship is a radical idea for most people and
working out this kind of relationship requires flexibility, patience, communication and being in touch with cosmic love.

WHY GET MARRIED AT ALL?

With all the problems, pain and suffering we find in marriage, why
do people continue to say "I do"? This was the very question that the
Disciples asked when Jesus told the Pharisees that Moses only gave permission for divorce because the people were so unteachable, and that anyone
who divorced his wife and married another is guilty of adultery. As we have
noted before, the Disciples replied: "If that is how it is between husband
and wife, it is not advisable to get married." (Matthew 19:3-11) The Disciples'
fear is mirrored today among those who refer to marriage as "holy deadlock".
Why do people get married today? There are many reasons. The order of
importance of these reasons will vary in different people.

Few if any of us are totally conscious and one of the first reasons for
getting married is the unconscious pressure of the collective within us and
upon us. We don't know why we get married. We come to a certain age
and nearly everyone is getting married and a deep collective pressure drives
us toward marriage. If people are living in an enlightened collective marriage, life in the collective can be tolerable or even satisfying. However,
few collectives are enlightened, as Flannery O'Connor pictures so clearly
in her story "Parker's Back," a picture of marriage of two people totally caught
up in the collective attitudes of lower class Southern society. People can
grow and develop where real love is the focus of the culture and religion
of the collective. But where this is not the case marriage can become the
endurance contest or tragedy that much literature portrays.

A second reason for marriage is the desire to have children and to raise
them. This instinct is very strong. Barbara attests to the fact that even in
her fifties the drive for more children was at certain times almost overpower-
ing. She said that it was an utterly irrational, instinctual urge that made
no sense at all and went against all her conscious attitudes. This same desire
is found in some men as well as in women—particularly the desire to have
sons and carry on the family name! Some lesbians will seek artificial in-

semination because this drive to bear children is so strong even though the idea of sexual intercourse with a male is repugnant to them.

A third reason for getting married is often unconscious. Many of us fear that no one would really want us—if they knew all of us. Many people marry in order to show themselves that they are in fact desirable. This unconscious desire to escape a bad self-image by marriage is usually disastrous.

The desire for companionship is a fourth reason for marriage and a very valid one. Companionship may in fact be the most important component in a marriage. As James Lynch shows in his book *The Broken Heart*, loneliness can cause not only psychological trauma, but physical illness and death. And then when some people are married they no longer have to look for a date. The world goes two by two. For real companionship two people need to like each other genuinely and have many interests in common in addition to physical attraction. Sometimes differences as well as similarities intrigue people in a relationship. Communication is absolutely essential if companionship is to continue and grow. Ann Landers' experimental design may leave something to be desired, but 90,000 women answered her question, "Would you be content to be held close and treated tenderly, and forget about 'the act'?" Seventy-two percent answered yes and forty percent of these were under forty.[1] When we come to the subject of love we shall see how important loving actions are to the development of companionship.

A fifth reason for tying the knot is sexual. Marriage provides a legitimate place for sexual activity and a social matrix in which the resulting children may be raised. People who think that marriage is the only way to get legal and religiously permissible sexual satisfaction, place physical need above relationship. The most ecstatic sexual relationship in the world cannot alone carry a marriage. The emphasis on sex in our culture and the resulting divorce statistics go hand in hand. Women who refuse to permit intercourse until after marriage may have a realistic view of many men; however, marriage for sex alone seldom succeeds.

SEXUALITY, FALLING IN LOVE, AND LOVE

And finally some people marry for love. And for loving. This word love is a slippery one that covers almost as many different experiences as the word sexuality. . . maybe even more, since it is used for scoring in tennis!

And yet one has to use the word "love", as Aldous Huxley has written with his usual incisiveness: "Of all the worn, smudged, dog's-eared words in our vocabulary, 'love' is surely the grubbiest, smelliest, slimiest. Bawled from a million pulpits, lasciviously crooned through hundreds of millions of loud-speakers, it has become an outrage to good taste and decent feeling, an obscenity which one hesitates to pronounce. And yet it has to be pronounced, for, after all, *Love* is the last word."[2]

Before we go further we need to distinguish, as in Morton's book *Caring*, between two quite different aspects of our caring for others: between falling in love and loving. However, some Christian theologians have declared that they are totally different; we believe, however, that they are distinguishable parts of one whole. We believe that falling in love may be necessary; it is at least a frequent precursor to loving and is an aspect of the most profound sexual love. When we fall in love we experience a projection: part of ourselves is projected and seen embodied in our lover. We feel whole because we feel in touch with our own soul. In *The Invisible Partners* John Sanford has pointed out that falling in love is a genuine way to be open to the Divine; we may sometimes think of our beloved as Divine. We wonder if people who have never allowed themselves to fall in love are truly capable of any other kind of loving. A deep desire to be close to or in union with the beloved is part of this ecstatic emotion. In this desire we can see the longing for union with the hidden parts of ourselves, with our souls, and with God.

However, in loving, which we see as a "call", the task is not so much what I can get, how whole I feel, but what I can *give*. As we open ourselves up to and find the Divine Lover, and as we allow that Love found at the heart and core of the experience of God to flow through us and out to other human beings, we sometimes experience compassion, caring and love for other human beings. The prayer attributed to Francis of Assisi pictures for us this kind of loving.

> O Divine Master, grant that I may not so much seek to be consoled
>   as to console,
> To be understood as to understand, to be loved as to love.
> For it is in giving that we receive,
> It is in pardoning that we are pardoned.
> And it is in dying that we are born to eternal life.

Scott Peck defines love in *The Road Less Travelled* as "the will to extend ourselves for the purpose of nurturing our own or another's spiritual growth."[3] We would change this definition only slightly by replacing "or" with "and". We believe that it is seldom, if ever, possible to nurture another's spiritual growth without nurturing our own; seldom do we genuinely nurture our own spiritual growth without providing spiritual stimulus to others. Jesus told his Disciples at the foot washing just before the Last Supper that the real sign of being his follower was that they were loving toward one another as he had loved them. The Christian spiritual growth of any human being has misfired if other people do not feel more loved because of the spiritual growth that person has experienced. When this kind of loving is present along with and as part of mutual sexual desire within a primary committed relationship, sexual experience can rise to the level of profound religious experience. Sexuality that is an integral part of this kind of loving can be a friend, not a foe, to spiritual development as Chavez-Garcia and Helminiak point out in their article "Sexuality and Spirituality" in the June 1985 issue of *The Journal of Pastoral Care*. After a wide ranging survey the authors conclude that it would be good to consider the possible value of genital stimulation toward personal and spiritual integration and growth. "First, bodily stimulation and sexual excitation have a healing effect as they result in relaxation, calming of the body and release of tension. Further, the intense experience of orgasm temporarily ruptures the world of ideas in which we generally live. It brings us back to awareness of our bodies, forgotten in our idea world. It opens us to the raw data of experience apart from preprocessed conceptualization and so allows the possibility of a new way of seeing and thinking about things. Experienced in honesty and love, it opens us anew to reality and its spiritual dimensions. Moreover, that intense physical experience also opens up the channels of the psyche. Feelings, memories, fears, dreams, fantasies, guilts, and hopes, all are released into reflexive awareness. This release of psychic materials fosters integration, wholeness, and spiritual growth. Said another way, the state of intense arousal that accompanies sexual experience allows one to focus on one thing. Distractions are gone; the mind stops flitting about. If one focuses on awareness itself, one can experience one's own spiritual reality. This appears to be the approach involved in Tantric sex.

It should be noted here that new openness to reality, release of channels of the psyche and focus of the mind are also effects of regular meditation. Like meditation, then, sexual experience can be considered a spiritual practice. Certainly, because of its intensity, genital experience binds people to one another even apart from the moment of the experience itself. It makes people long for one another and so draws them into continuing relationship. Their mutual affection, clarified expectations and practical responsibilities demand continual personal reassessment, change and growth. When a couple faces life together in honesty and love, supported by sexual intimacy, then the path of daily life becomes the path of spiritual perfection."[4]

FALLING IN LOVE[5]

Only with the advent of depth psychology has there appeared an adequate explanation of the process of falling in love. It is truly astounding that an emotional state so common and important to the human race should have been shrouded in mystery so long.

Depth psychology has come to three basic conclusions about human beings which relate to this powerful experience of being in love.

1.   All of us human beings have an unconscious aspect of our personalities, part of our psychological being of which we are unconscious at most times.

2.   In each of us, both in our bodies and our psyches, there is evidence of both masculine and feminine qualities. Males have vestigial breasts and female hormones; women's bodies contain physical remnants of male sexuality. The same bisexuality applies to our psyches. Most men have feminine psychic elements in the depth of their unconscious, and women have masculine qualities.

3.   One of the deepest desires of human beings, one of the strongest instincts (the primary preconscious urges), is to bridge the split between conscious and unconscious, to be whole, unitary, one, in touch with all of one's self, both masculine and feminine.

Falling in love is an outer, almost sacramental way of achieving this desired wholeness. Let's illustrate it in a diagram:

This pictures the inner woman (feminine qualities) in each man and the inner man (masculine qualities) within each woman. When we fall in love heterosexually we suddenly see our inner feminine in some woman or our inner masculine in some man. The arrows represent our capacity to project on others. We may even discover our inner contrasexual part for the first time by projecting it out upon a person of the opposite sex. When this happens we have fallen in love. We desire to be close to the other, to join in a psychological and physical union with him or her. In this way we are achieving a kind of ersatz union with ourselves. I asked a counselee who could only meet his beloved in church what he got from the experience. He answered with these revealing words: "When I am sitting next to her, I feel whole." Along with this kind of projection we usually experience strong sexual desire.

Projection in itself is neither immature nor wrong nor evil. The projection process actually enables us to discover parts of ourselves lost in the unconscious which we might not otherwise recognize as part of us. Also, projection can help us bridge the enormous gap which usually exists between two people. It brings two of us together so we can begin a relationship. The projection of our inner feminine or masculine sides (our ideal woman or man) is evil only when we truly believe that this ecstatic initial state is the norm for human relationships. As we begin to live with another person, we usually discover that the other person is quite different from the ideal person we have projected upon him or her. Ideal people do not exist.

LOVING

When we come to the disillusioning realization that the beloved is different than we thought or wanted, we usually do one of three things. We can call off the relationship and, if we have been married in the process, get a divorce; most people involved in multiple marriages and relationships fail to realize the difference between the inner image which we project on other people and reality. Instead of working out the nitty-gritty of human interactions, many people go on looking for the illusory ideal. Of course, there are impossible marital situations where divorce is a necessary solution. It is less damaging than the second alternative: destructive marital deadlock that wreaks havoc on the couple and their children. The third alternative is to is *get about the business of knowing the reality of ourselves and the other person and beginning the process of learning to truly love each other.* This is indeed a challenge which can last throughout life. Madeleine L'Engle has written profoundly about her personal marriage challenge in *The Irrational Season.*

This more whole and potentially more lasting relationship can be represented by the following diagram:

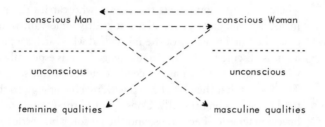

The broken lines with arrows at the end indicate an attempt on the part of each partner to understand and relate to the other person at that particular level: to the actual reality of the outer person, to the unconscious of the other person and to their own unconscious being. Perhaps when we make some headway in these relationships, it may be possible for people to relate on the unconscious level as well, from the unconscious of one to the unconscious of the other. Many people wonder if they will not lose the zest and life that comes with projection if they become thoroughly conscious. Fortunately or unfortunately we have never known any humans so conscious that they no longer projected onto other human beings. Total consciousness is an unattainable ideal. Sometimes we illustrate falling in love by interlocking our two hands and fingers; love can be represented by our two fists rotating and touching at all points.

The picture which we have presented of falling in love is, of course, oversimplified. Along with the lost or unknown masculine or feminine component of ourselves we may also project upon another person the image of the "holy", the beautiful, the self-sacrificial lover, the knight in shining armor, the all-caring parent, the damsel in distress or a thousand other variations. These other images can add and merge with our basic projection and greatly increase its power. A love affair is often a numinous experience. John Sanford has dealt with the whole subject of projection in human relationships in a thorough and creative way in his book *The Invisible*

Partners. In order to describe the important phenomena of projection and falling in love, let us turn to his description of the process:

> ...men, identified with their masculinity, typically project their feminine side onto women, and women, identified with their feminine nature, typically project their masculine side onto men. These projected psychic images are the Invisible Partners in every man-woman relationship, and greatly influence the relationship, for wherever projection occurs the person who carries the projected image is either greatly overvalued or greatly undervalued. In either case, the human reality of the individual who carries a projection for us is obscured by the projected image. This is especially the case with the anima and animus since these archetypes are so numinous. This means that they are charged with psychic energy, so that they tend to grip us emotionally. Consequently these projected images have a magnetic effect on us, and the person who carries a projection will tend to greatly attract or repel us, just as a magnet attracts or repels another metal. This leads to all kinds of complications in relationships...[6]
>
> If both a man and a woman project their positive images onto each other at the same time, we have that seemingly perfect state of relationship known as being in love, a state of mutual fascination. The two then declare that they are 'in love with each other' and are firmly convinced that they have now found the ultimate relationship...
>
> There is much to be said for falling in love. Most of us can probably remember the first time we were in love, and what unexpected and powerful emotions were released. To have the experience of falling in love is to become open to matters of the heart in a wonderful way. It can be the prelude to a valuable expansion of personality and emotional life. It is also an important experience because it brings the sexes together and initiates relationship. Whether this leads to happy or unhappy consequences, life is kept moving in this way. Perhaps, especially with young people, falling in love is a natural and beautiful experience, and a life that has not known this experience is no doubt impoverished.
>
> The fact is, however, that relationships founded exclusively on the being-in-love state can never last...being in love is a matter for the gods, not for human beings, and when human beings try to claim the prerogative of the gods and live in a state of 'in-loveness' (as differentiated from truly loving each other), there is a movement from the unconscious to break it up...[7]

These suggestions are verified by a recent survey by Jeanette and Robert Lauer published in the June 1985 *Psychology Today*. It shows that sexuality and in-loveness do not contribute to permanent relationships. They interviewed 351 couples, of whom 300 said they were happily married, in order to find out why they remained married. Both men and women agreed that sexual experience was important and that they had a common attitude toward it, but the sexual item was thirteenth in importance on a list of sixteen items for men and fifteenth for women. The first four items were the same: the partners were best friends, liked each other, viewed marriage as a long-term relationship, and saw it as sacred. Also important were that they had grown more interesting to each other, agreed on goals, put effort into the relationship, agreed on a philosophy of life and laughed together. They agreed about the importance of showing affection. Lucky are those who fall in love with people with whom they have these things in common, at least potentially.

The illusions that accompany any effort to enter into a long-term relationship based on in-loveness alone are aptly pictured in an an unpublished article by Donald T. Neblett, M.D. entitled "Choose You This Day." Although these words were written with marriage in mind, they apply equally to any attempt to create an intimate permanent relationship.

> I am convinced that man and woman make the same mistakes but in different ways. Both want the same thing out of marriage; i.e., to feel like the most important person in the world. That is the burden both put upon the other!
>
> The woman entering marriage is usually relationship oriented . . . she gives all to her husband. . . BUT the bottom line is: She gives all to him for what she can get for herself!!! She expects and desires to be the most important thing in his life. . . to possess his every thought and continually have his adoration, devotion, and love. . .
>
> The man entering marriage is usually conquering and achieving oriented. He married to add to his empire. . . a woman who is the necessary ingredient to make the proud gladiator a god! She is to adore, adulate, and elevate him to the highest pedestal. Since his universe is the world, she should appreciate all he is providing. . . Alas, he too wants to be the center of the universe and he expects her to help him achieve his ambitions by constantly feeding and fattening his ego. . .
>
> Thank God this arrangement never works. . .The fruits of such

marriages??? Her god tumbles. . . illusions give way to disillusionment
and she must search for completeness elsewhere. . .or yield to a life
of bitterness and hatred. . .

His empire crumbles when his #1 fan deserts his carefully prepared box seat for her. . .The myth has died. . .the painful lesson
has been learned—love only is life. . .

Man and woman have their choices. . .we are creatures of free
choice. . .but God confronts us continually with the fruit of the
choices we made in darkness. . .in ignorance of the meaning of
LIFE. . .He does not protect us from the pain and consequences of
our choices but lets the suffering reaped confront the choice again
. . .and we must face the choice of life versus death. . .be man
and woman.

The romantic ideal is that two people can come together in intimate
relationship and maintain the glow of falling-in-love permanently. This
illusory notion brings untold misery to thousands, probably even millions,
of couples who compare themselves and their relationships or marriages
to this inflated kind of expectation and find themselves wanting. Few people
look at relationship realistically before they embark on this "adventure".
Relationships that have not or cannot fall into the culturally approved bond
of marriage simply fall apart and are abandoned, but marriages are legal
institutions. Adolf Guggenbuhl-Craig calls this illusion of problem-free
marriage the "happy marriage" idea and describes our culture's unrealistic
expectations of marriage in *Marriage—Dead or Alive*:

> If one. . .were to dream up a social institution which would be
> unable to function in every single case and which was meant to
> torment its members, one would certainly invent the contemporary
> marriage and the institution of today's family. Two people of different
> sex, usually with extremely different images, fantasies, and myths,
> with differing strength and vitality, promise one another to be with
> each other night and day, so to speak, for a whole lifetime. Neither
> of them is supposed to spoil the other's experience, neither is sup-
> posed to control the other, both of them should develop all their
> potentials fully. This mighty oath is often declared, however, only
> because of an overwhelming sexual intoxication. Such an intoxica-
> tion is wonderful, but is it a solid groundwork for a lifetime together?
> It is well-known that most people get on each other's nerves even
> when they undertake only a fourteen-day trip together. After a few

days one may hardly even express himself anymore, and every little decision turns into a querulous wrestling match. The two marriage partners, however, promise to live their whole lives (thirty, forty, fifty, sixty years) together in the greatest physical, spiritual, and psychological intimacy. And this life-long commitment they make to each other in their youth![8]

There is, however, a more realistic, more grounded, and infinitely more satisfactory way to understand and to live out marriage or any other permanent intimate relationship. Some of the wisest words ever written about relationships are again found in *Marriage—Dead or Alive*:

> The life-long dialectical encounter between two partners, the bond of man and woman until death, can be understood as a special path for discovering the soul, as a special form of individuation. One of the essential features of this soteriological [salvation] pathway is the absence of avenues for escape. . .
>
> The word love includes a great diversity of phenomena, which perhaps have the same source but must nevertheless be distinguished from one another. Marriage is one of the soteriological pathways of love, but of a love that is not altogether identical with what is produced by the wanton youth Cupid. . .The love on which marriage rests transcends the 'personal relationship' and is more than merely relational.
>
> The modern marriage is possible only when this special soteriological pathway is desired and wished for. The collective, however, continues to herd people toward marrying for the sake of well-being. Many girls marry to evade the pressure of a career and to find someone who will take care of them. Only a few marriages can last 'until death' if marriage is understood as a welfare institution.
>
> . . .But people are continually being taught by psychiatrists, psychologists, marriage counselors, etc., that only happy marriages are good marriages, or that marriages *should* be happy. In fact, however, every path to salvation leads through Hell. Happiness in the sense that it is presented to married couples today belongs to well-being, not to salvation. Marriage above all is a soteriological institution, and this is why it is so filled with highs and lows; it consists of sacrifices, joys, *and* suffering. . .
>
> A marriage only works if one opens himself to exactly that which he would never ask for otherwise. Only through rubbing oneself sore and losing oneself is one able to learn about oneself, God and the

world. Like every soteriological pathway, that of marriage is hard and painful.

A writer who creates meaningful works does not want to become happy, he wants to be creative. Likewise married people can seldom enjoy happy, harmonious marriages, as psychologists would force it upon them and lead them to believe. The image of the 'happy marriage' causes great damage.

For those who are gifted for the soteriological pathway of marriage, it, like every such pathway, naturally offers not only trouble, work, and suffering, but the deepest kind of existential satisfaction. Dante did not get to Heaven without traversing Hell. And so also there seldom exist 'happy marriages'.[9]

We are reminded of the words of Carl Whitaker, the renowned psychiatrist and marriage counselor whose words in the *Family Therapy Networker* we have already quoted from: "The greatest ordeal in life is marriage—it is the central focus for enlightenment and the natural therapeutic process in the culture."[10] Again we emphasize that these statements apply to marriage and to any other long-term, intimate relationship.

One reason that marriage may be more difficult than most other intimate bonds is that children are usually introduced into the picture and the network of relationships increases in geometrical proportions. And precisely because marriage *is* hard work, *is* painful, *is* creative, *is* existentially satisfying, we personally can only find it a creative possibility as we cultivate our prayer life. It is out of our own prayer life that forty-two years of growth in relationship has come. When we have a first-class, full-throated disagreement about basic values (and we have some basically different values), our human reaction is to say to the other: Go stew in your own juice. But if we listen inwardly to the Risen Christ, we hear something like this: "Remember, you are not perfect yourself; if you wish to remain in fellowship with Love and follow me, go and make up and give love." Then we usually come to our senses and start making overtures to each other. We have also found the daily Eucharist a perfect vehicle for reconciliation. It is difficult to receive communion when we have unresolved acknowledged resentments or angers within us.

The declining spiritual life of our times is one of the major factors affecting marriage and other relationships. Another closely related influence is the rise in women's consciousness. Women are less and less satisfied with patriarchal marriages and will not take from men what they once endured.

Divorce statistics reveal a part of the picture. In 1920 approximately one out of seven marriages broke up in divorce; in 1940 one out of five; in 1960 one out of four; and in 1980 one out of three. Some studies show that the rate is far less among couples who are committed religiously in the same way. In an increasing secular culture, lifelong marriages or relationships become almost an impossibility. *Where individuals have not God, they usually become gods and goddesses.* Greek mythology clearly shows the problems that gods and goddesses had living with each other on Mt. Olympus. Individual divine beings seek their own will and pleasure; they seldom seek transformation and reconciliation. This may help to explain why enduring relations are not even valued where secularism is rampant. Secularism, like some humanistic psychology, has a tendency to deify the human psyche.

LIVING WITH DIFFERENT VALUES

Value clarification, the study of the importance of values to us all, has shown that human beings have widely differing values. In addition we need to remind ourselves that men and women often expect different things from marriage and relationships. Basic value differences need to be dealt with day after day. For example, Barbara's number one priority is her family—husband, children, grandchildren. For Morton, the family takes priority when they *need* him, and he gives to them first whenever family need is expressed. But there are also other people whom he has come to know in depth whom he feels have legitimate demands upon his time, energy and person when these demands do not conflict with those of his family. And so we make compromises.

Barbara feels that she must first show love, concern and be helpful to her husband, children and grandchildren and that she needs to be kind and considerate to each human being with whom she comes in contact each day. To her Christian love is shown, for example, by being quiet and not awakening the person in the next hotel room, by staying and listening to the problems of the clerk in the store, the nurse in the doctor's office or the hairdresser. She wishes to be of help to these people in any way she is able. She does not feel called, however, to long-term, intensive counseling. She accepts each individual encounter each day as a God-given responsibility and an opportunity to show love and concern to others. She does not feel it part of her duty to take on other people in the same way that she has taken on her family. She is very good at short-term counseling and believes that those who need her will cross her path if she is meant to be concerned with them.

Morton believes that those whom God puts in his life (he does not wish to seek out people any more than Barbara) need to be dealt with in depth as long as the family needs are cared for first. He tries to always discern whether the people that seem to be put into his life are really "his bundle" or whether he needs to refer them on to others. One can handle very few people when one counsels in depth.

Barbara needs companionship, sometimes alone with her husband, and sometimes in light social settings. Morton is more of a loner and enjoys his own solitude. It has been helpful for us to articulate these differences and deal with them. We would say that we have as good a marriage as any that we know, but ours is certainly not perfectly harmonious at all times. Major conflicts have arisen, but often as they are resolved they have brought us closer together and forced growth upon us both.

We cannot, however, overstress the husband's responsibility to wife and children and the wife's to husband and children in this age of professional women. Both parents need to give children the nurturing and love they need for growth and development of their personalities; both need to share their goods and their lives with them so that they all feel partners in a common enterprise. Such giving is seldom possible when father and mother are not giving the same kind of nurturing to each other. As children become more mature they will want to share with parents in return. It came as a surprise to us several years ago that our grown children (presently forty, thirty-seven and thirty-two) still want our time and attention and need to be considered, but in a different way than when they were at home. However, they still need to be first in our lives before any friends or counselees. Both of us had lost a mother in early adulthood and did not realize that family bonds continued on in depth as long as we live. Having children is really a responsibility, a joyful, difficult, loving and life-long undertaking. Our children have also come to our support. We will never forget their care for us during the months when Barbara was in the hospital after a serious accident five years ago. We have many friends with aged parents and we imagine our dependence upon our children may well become greater as age inevitably creeps upon us.

When Morton was first interested in going into the priesthood, George McKinley, an old family friend, and rector of the parish in which he grew up, gave him what seemed at the time the strangest advice: "For heaven's sake, don't do it unless you can't help it." We would say that same thing of marriage or any intimate, long-term relationship. People shouldn't do it unless they can't help it. Of course, without real relationships we hardly touch the core and meaning of life. We are caught between the rock and the hard place: either we do not enter deeply into intimacy with another or else we struggle through conflicts and growth. If more of us dealt honestly with the problems of our relationships, there would be much less misery in the world.

As a parish priest, Morton listened for twenty-six years to the fortunes and misfortunes of his parishioners. In his last parish he had approximately 750 families. He found very few families totally free of major problems. And the ones we both thought were the most ideal often had the worst problems: they were just carefully and skillfully covered up. Often the children of these families went out looking for ideal partners and ideal relationship situations. Of course they could not find them; the cover-up had extended to the children as well as to the outer world. Bishop Carmen was a wise pastor and he once told the story of the most perfect wife and mother that he had ever known. She had three sons, all of whom went through multiple marriages looking for someone as perfect as mother. Imperfect parents may be better training for an imperfect world—imperfection, of course, with communication and honesty and love.

One of the most interesting things we discovered in counseling male students at the University of Notre Dame was that they were more devastated by the fear that they might be incapable of loving than by the fear that no one might love them. Many of them truly feared that they were incapable of allowing themselves to love and so might be cut off from the very meaning of life itself. Women, usually, have less fear of their capacity to love than men, but we also found this fear among some women. People who have never let themselves go in infatuation may never be able truly to learn to love. Thomas Tyrrel has made this point with clarity and eloquence in his book *Urgent Longings: Reflections on the Experience of Infatuation, Human Intimacy, and Contemplative Love.*

We need training in the art of love as Morton has detailed in *Caring: How Can We Love One Another?*. Infatuation is good and is to be judiciously encouraged. However, when infatuation passes immediately into sexual expression, particularly among adolescents, it can become an end in itself and genuine love that builds upon relationship has no chance to develop.

The goal is love that builds on infatuation and retains some of its zest, but moves beyond it to the very doorway of heaven. We then continue to try to love by Divine prerogative, through difficulties and angers. Any relationship that does not acknowledge these difficult aspects of togetherness may well explode and dissolve. As we live together, both of us with good will, both under God, there can be a basic harmony, but both people need to have the same basic commitment to the relationship and to the Holy. The Roman Catholic Church still exercises the right to grant an ecclesiastical annulment in a marriage where only one partner has a Christian commitment. Most relationships can best grow where there is a mutual response to the same Divine Lover. Such a marriage or relationship, such love, becomes not only a call, but a work of salvation.

Finally, speaking as a former parish priest and a minister's spouse, we offer three suggestions to Christian congregations. One, each congregation needs to provide some basic courses that center around the belief that sexuality is good—courses that contain the facts and findings of good researchers such as Masters and Johnson. Second, every truly Christian parish will offer classes in communication and listening. In these husbands and wives, children and parents, brothers and sisters, friends and lovers can learn the art of listening and communication without which genuine love is not possible. And third, the congregation needs to provide a solid framework that supports husband and wife and children in the difficult task of marriage and family life. It needs to support and encourage all those relationships that move beyond infatuation to genuine love. Seldom can any two people who are not devoted to the same Lord of Love produce a relationship that is creative, transforming and eternally meaningful. However, we believe that it is important that an enthusiastic spouse does not try to convert the other spouse to his or her way of experiencing the religious aspect of life. Two very different people can have their individual beliefs and practices and respect each other's without trying to influence the other spouse. Nothing is harder to endure than one who is sure he or she has found the right path or correct religious answer.

RELATIONSHIP IN THE FAMILY

Just as much frustration and discontent in marriage and sexual relationship arise from lack of response to the other person, so malaise in the family relationship often arises from lack of attentiveness and real caring. We remember the story of the Iowa farmer who had been married for twenty years, whose wife was constantly complaining, "But darling, you never tell me that you love me." And he would look grimly at her and go on. But on one particular Sunday when she aired her usual complaint—after a dinner of fricasseed chicken complete with dumplings—the farmer rose to his full height, looked at his wife, and said, "My dear, when I married you twenty years ago, I told you I loved you. If it changes, I'll let you know." The tragedy is that this attitude prevails in more homes than we would care to think. Sexuality within relationships like this usually becomes a perfunctory duty and a release of physiological tension or dries up like an old well. When Morton tells this story at a conference it invariably provokes laughter in mixed audiences and even in male ones. The laughter acknowledges the reality of what is.

Morton will never forget the day many years ago when his seventeen-year-old daughter was driving him to some hospital calls after a long day. Suddenly at the corner of Mountain and Royal Oaks in Monrovia she said out of the blue, "When are you going to start treating my mother like a human being?" Although it stung at the time, this statement is something he came to be grateful for; he knew that it was true. He came home and we talked. We realized that Morton had indeed been taking Barbara for granted. We decided right then and there that we would create a structure that would ensure more consideration and attentiveness. One of the things that we decided was to have a date, a dinner and evening out, once a week. That was twenty-five years ago and we doubt if we have missed more than half a dozen weeks in all the years that have passed. It makes all the difference in the world having a set, definite time that we know is for each other.

Another plan we made was to refuse to be out away from each other in the evening more than two evenings in a week. A parish can gobble a person up with evening commitments if one is not careful. Whenever work becomes a first priority rather than a secondary one and is not consciously controlled it can eat away at family relations. One successful businessman was asked how one could sustain a real family relationship and be truly successful in business. He replied candidly that it was impossible. Such a perspective is ridiculous within the Christian framework. If love is part of the ultimate nature of things, then love within one's most intimate relationships becomes a holy matter, a matter of religious commitment.

This involves communication and communication involves time together. How easily in our egotism and self-centeredness we do take for granted those we love the most.

Another way of being attentive in loving is to show specific acts of kindness, to bring appropriate gifts on occasion, to listen carefully, and to provide uncluttered time *alone* with the loved one. We also need to remember that touch is sacramental. How many families openly display affection by touching? James Lynch has shown the psychological and physical results of isolation in his ground-breaking book, *The Broken Heart*. Touch is a form of communication that gets below the conscious threshold and speaks to the depth of human beings. Verbal communication goes only so deep. Are we perhaps afraid of touch, which often reveals so much of us in a culture that often turns us away from the depth of ourselves? Few things are more important than being able to touch those we love and to distinguish between touch that ends in affection and touch that leads to full sexual expression. Morton has described the importance of this kind of concern and love in greater detail in his book *Caring*. This book is an attempt to explain what we have learned about caring for each other in our forty-two years of relationship.

RECONCILIATION

In every honest long-term intimacy we human beings trespass against each other. We engender anger and cause hurt feelings. Any interest in sexuality usually disappears under these conditions. If it doesn't it is one-sided or it becomes a duty. When people are at odds the life goes out of sexuality. If this attitude persists a real rift occurs. We have discovered both in our own lives and in listening to others that most situations can be forgiven. We have known well a family where there was divorce and then remarriage, then unfaithfulness, alcoholism and a scandal. Yet because of the essential good will of both people reconciliation occurred and a truly fine relationship developed.

What makes it possible for such reconciliation to take place? There are many factors, but the essential one is the conviction that reconciliation is a moral and religious obligation, that without it we are going against the grain of the universe; we are out of sync with the loving reality at the heart and center of all being when we remain unreconciled. Forgiveness and reconciliation are at the heart of the Christian message about life, even if Christians don't always put first priority on them. During the blitz on London during World War II Charles Williams wrote a little book entitled *The Forgiveness of Sins*[11] in which he speaks to those suffering from this catastrophe around him. He states that there are three kinds of forgiveness: things that need not be forgiven (there was only misunderstanding), things that ought to be forgiven (ordinary human trespasses) and things that can't be forgiven like the destruction of the blitz. The true follower of the risen Jesus bears the intolerable burden of forgiving them all. He then goes on to describe how we can live up to this high calling.

Instead of giving a dissertation on how we forgive, Morton will tell a story from his own life. It is a story he has told in other contexts, but one that applies here. "It is my children and my wife who have taught me more about reconciliation and forgiveness than any others, but particularly my younger son. We realized that something was wrong as he had not yet learned to read as he entered into the sixth grade. Barbara and I talked the matter over when we realized that his school was going on split, half-time sessions. We decided that there was nothing wrong with his genes and so we sought out the best advice we could find and were directed to an excellent remedial school. He wanted to go to a private school but didn't like the one we selected as some children present had rather obvious problems. Because it was an excellent school, the first thing they did was to administer a full battery of psychological tests. We had a clinic at the church and I did most of the interpretation of the tests for those who came to our clinic. We received a call from the school and the psychologist wanted to talk with us. I found myself in the unusual position of sitting on the other side of the table with the psychologist asking me: 'Do you have any idea what is wrong with this child?' I was a little annoyed with this question and answer game and wanted to say that his problem was a little innate orneriness, but I was too wise to make such a response and so groaned that I didn't have any idea. And then he dropped the bombshell!!: 'The problem with this child is that he doesn't think that you, his father, love or really care for him.'

"I protested vigorously that whenever I tried to show him love, warmth and affection, he pushed me away. The psychologist continued. 'Why do you think he pushes you away?' I was getting more and more uncomfortable and replied that I didn't have the foggiest notion of why he did. The psychologist went on relentlessly, 'He is testing you to see how much you really do love him.' 'At eleven years of age?' I responded with unbelief. 'Even at eleven,' he answered.

"I decided right on the spot that I was going to love that child if it killed me, and sometimes it takes this kind of determination in order to work for reconciliation. And it did kill part of me, an egocentric part. We went horseback riding together. We spent time at anything that he seemed to like to do. Even though I have the manual dexterity of a palsied hippopotamus, I tried to do woodworking with him and other manual activities he enjoyed. The real turn around, however, came one day in a motel on the ocean front at Laguna Beach. I came into his room one morning and asked over the noise of the blaring television: 'Johnnie, how would you like to go swimming with me?'

"Then, as only an eleven-year-old can say it, he replied, 'Nah. . . . I'd rather watch television.'

"In the past when I got this kind of response I would leave feeling rejected to spend my time doing something I would rather have done anyway, but after the revelation in the psychologist's office I thought to myself: 'Perhaps he is only testing me; I'll keep my sense of humor and try to engage him.' In a very *playful* way (and the playful attitude was absolutely essential) I capered over to the TV and turned it off. He came over and turned it back on. In a period of fifteen minutes we tussled around the room, out toward the door, down the stairs, around the corner, out on the walkway and into the ocean.

"Do you know what that child said to me as we emerged from the first wave? He blew the water out of his nose and exclaimed, 'Father, I wondered how long it would take you to do this.'

"I now knew that the psychologist was right; he did want to relate to me. The old pattern was broken and our relation improved. His Iowa tests went up three years in six months' time and he began to learn to read. Don't think, however, that everything was smooth sailing from that moment on. On a trip to Europe when he was fourteen every bit of patience in me was tested and sometimes I failed. Another climactic situation occurred when he was nineteen and going to college in Arizona. It was Christmas and the family had gathered at our daughter's home in Phoenix. I had just finished a busy teaching schedule at Notre Dame. We were sitting around the pool and out of the blue he spoke these words very calmly and deliberately: 'Father, you know, I have never liked you very well.' That was not what my jaded ego needed at that moment, but I remembered what the headmaster of a school told parents to do when their children said that they did not like them. I replied, 'John I don't blame you; there are many times that I don't like me very well either.'

"From that moment things between us moved to a new level. He knew that I could even accept his criticism and rejection. A couple of years later John picked me up at the airport and drove me to a conference I was giving on the centrality of love. He decided to stay for part of the conference. I told the story of Laguna Beach; I wanted to hear his response. As we drove out to spend the night at the beach house of a friend, John spoke up: 'Father, did I actually say that?' I quietly assured him that he had.

"The next morning as we were breakfasting, John started up the conversation: 'Father, I remember when I made up my mind that I would never ask you for anything again in my life.' I knew that we were hitting pay dirt and asked him to go on. 'I was seven years old. You had been reading *The Tales of Sherlock Holmes* to my brother and me.' He remembered the name of the literature that I had been reading them. 'My brother was away for several days on a camping trip, but I wanted you to read aloud to me anyway, and so I brought you the book and asked you to read. You said that you were too busy. I brought you the book the next night and you again said that you were too busy. The same thing happened on the third night, and I quite consciously made up my mind that I would never ask *you* for anything else again in my life.'

"I had been unconscious of how sensitive and needing of my love and attention this son of mine was. I hadn't thought to say, 'John, bring me another book and we'll come back to this one when your brother returns.' My cold refusal had struck at him as effectively as if I had wielded a club. Only vaguely did I remember the incident. Still another level of relationship developed. However, it was adversity that finally brought us into real relationship.

"On a freighter trip my wife was run over by a container straddler on the docks of Yokohama. After her condition stabilized we brought her back to Los Angeles to the doctors and hospital we knew. We did not know if she would recover or if she would walk again. I wanted to be close enough to the hospital so I could go in daily to spend time with Barbara and have Eucharist and the laying on of hands for healing. My son John lived not too far from the hospital in a one-bedroom apartment. He invited me to stay with him. He worked nights and I typed and went to the hospital during the day, and so we kept the bed warm most of the time. I was there when he came home from working nights at the Hyatt Regency, and I was there when he awoke, and we talked about all sorts of things. I did most of the shopping, did the washing, and kept the place clean and neat. We became good friends.

"Several months later Barbara was released from the hospital and we went out to a friend's house to continue her convalescence. When I packed up my things to leave his apartment, John handed me a card. I opened it. On the front of it were two iguanas facing each other; one of them was weeping iguana tears. On the inside were printed these words: 'Iguana miss you.' And then he wrote: 'It seems strange how we were forced together. You have become truly my best friend. I love you more than I ever imagined. I can truly see why all those kids have always looked up to you. I only hope that we can continue to spend time together. I hope all goes well with Mother's recovery, and if you need my help, you know that I am here.' Nineteen years had passed from the original injury and fifteen years I had worked at reconciliation. But the years that the locust had eaten were restored. We have continued on in a growing relationship and grown closer."

Recently when Barbara and I were walking through a climax forest of Coast Redwoods we talked about the incredible patience of these trees that grow to such enormous size. Reconciliation, forgiveness and love require the same patience. This patience will be an essential element of any intimate relationship and truly adequate sexuality. Lovingly reaching out to others and forgiving others are necessary if we are to achieve growing intimacy and depth in any full bond between human beings.

CHAPTER SEVEN

The Varieties of Heterosexualities

Truly satisfying marriages and satisfactory sexuality go hand in hand. But before we can go on to the nature of fulfilling sexuality, we need to look at the wide differences of expression in heterosexual relationships. The words sexual intercourse cover a range of activities so diverse that they are hardly meaningful unless we know the circumstances under which the relationship has taken place. These words cover everything from brutal, destructive violence to a union of two people so complete and ecstatic that it can be a symbol of the human union with the Divine Lover. Sex, like making money, can be valuable or destructive. One person makes money by making slaves of people (economically or legally) and only to build up his or her power; another makes money in order to provide jobs for needy people. One person sings to give pleasure to others; another for the adulation, power and money the singer receives. Heterosexual intercourse may occur within any of the following contexts:

1.   The physical union of man and woman can be the ultimate, ecstatic sacramental expression of the love that two committed people bear for one another. For some people, such an expression may be a window into heaven. Sexual relationship of this kind is usually the result of a long-term commitment in which communication has developed between two people on all levels, from simple warmth and affection to more and more total com-

145

munication. Masters and Johnson in *The Pleasure Bond* emphasize that sexual satisfaction is as much psychological as physical and that sexual relations are a form of communication which can seldom if ever reach their full potential unless that communication extends to other areas of partners' lives. We shall deal with the relationship of love and sexuality in greater depth later.

2.   Sexual intercourse can also be the truly blissful expression of two people meeting and merging for the moment. This can occur when, consciously or unconsciously, the people are caught up in the very generative, creative process at the heart of the universe. In his story, "The Sword and the Doll" in *The Seed and the Sower* Laurens van der Post describes such an encounter of a man and a woman meeting in the jungle of Malaysia, escaping from the Japanese invasion. Their encounter is the finest description of the kind of ecstatic sexual union we know. Such an experience can be holy, but in ordinary human experience genuine sexual joy is more likely to grow as two people in a committed relationship learn to communicate in depth with one another. However, such a committed relationship can begin with the experience of ecstatic union. Shakespeare describes this kind of love in *Romeo and Juliet*. It can happen to people of any age. It often happens between an older person and a younger one as portrayed in the Venus and Adonis myth and in the book and film *The Summer of '42*. It can also occur between members of the same sex as Jung describes in "The Love Problem of the Student" in *Civilization in Transition* to which we refer as we discuss homosexualities and bisexualities. Marguerite Yourcenar has described such a relationship in *Hadrian's Memoirs*.

3.   Sexual life may be a duty which one or both partners give to one another in spite of their fears, hang-ups or personal wishes about sex. Such people miss much of the joy in life and much of the meaning of love as well as much sexual pleasure.

4.   Some people may enter into the sexual union merely because they wish children. If this is the desire of both people then the sexual relation may grow beyond mere duty to real love and caring. If the decision to have children is not mutual then sexual relationships can be only burdensome duty.

In the April 1985 issue of *Discover* Jared Diamond summarizes what we know and *what we don't know* about the biology of sex. One of the most puzzling aspects of human sexuality is that unlike in all other mammals (even those most like us), ovulation is concealed, so that human sexual intercourse is not necessarily related to conception. Whatever else this means for human beings, it may imply that sexuality has other meanings than reproduction. Diamond goes on to plead for a better understanding of this biological reality by the Church: "In these days of growing human overpopulation, one of the most paradoxical tragedies, in my view, is the Roman Catholic Church's insistence that copulation has conception as its only natural purpose, and that the rhythm method is the only proper means of birth control. These claims would be valid for gorillas and most other mammals, but not for us. In no other species besides man has the purpose of copulation become so unrelated to conception, or the rhythm method so unsuited for contraception."[1]

5. In patriarchal society, particularly where polygamy is still permitted, the sexual relationships are permanent. However, the sexual needs of women are denied, ignored, or considered unimportant. As we have already noted, meaningful mutual sexual relationships can develop even in such relationships, but this is the exception to the rule. For centuries women have been seen as inferior and have simply not had the sexual freedom of men. Among certain African tribes some women state that they prefer polygamy since they have others with whom they share the work load. The idea of sexual fulfillment or loving, mutual sharing is hardly considered.

6. Human beings can engage in sexuality just for the orgasmic pleasure of sexuality with little concern for relationship or communication between the people involved. The basic desire in this kind of sex is release of sexual tension. This kind of relationship may continue for a time if it meets the needs of both parties, or it may be a casual sexual encounter, even a one-night stand. When sex is experienced before relationship it can often short-circuit any possibility of relationship and even take the place of relationship. In *Love and Will* Rollo May describes sexual relationships that are nearly as casual as a handshake and mean as little. If sex is indeed closely related to love and relationship (and there can be no real love without relationship), then casual sex may be a misuse of sex whether the pleasure is freely given or paid for.

7. One person can obtain power over another either by sexual attractiveness, psychological persuasion or social control over another's life. When sexual relations occur under these circumstances and there is little free choice on the part of the powerless one, then the one with power uses

the other person just as much as if he or she were an owner of slaves. Prostitution itself is slavery with a time limit. Incest is particularly dangerous just because parents have such power over their children and the children have so little freedom of choice. For many women, the patriarchal social system can be little better than slavery. Even today many women are at the mercy of their husbands because they are more or less completely dependent on them economically.

8.   Sex can be a brutal act of aggression and violence. Rape is nearly always a devastating, demoralizing and traumatic experience. Susan Brownmiller has described the full range of forced sexual experience in her definitive book *Against Our Will: Men, Women and Rape*. Her study covers the violent heterosexuality in slavery, war, and in prison, as well as homosexual prison rape and the rape found in the police blotter. This study shows that rape is not so much a crime of lust as of violence and power. Sexual expression in which one person has some form of power over the other, differs only in degree from sexual violence and rape. Sexual experience can be seen as a continuum which has at one end sex in the context of equal and mutual relationship and at the other end has violent rape. When sexuality is confused with power and violence it becomes demonic.[2] In *Civilization and Its Discontents*, Freud suggests that all sexual intercourse involves an element of violence. It would seem to us that the less this element of violence is present in sexual relations the nearer sexuality approaches its more developed meaning. It is interesting how little attention has been given to the subject of rape by the major schools of psychology.

THE MEANING OF SEXUAL FULFILLMENT

Over the last forty years both of us have listened to a great many men and women who have had problems with the sexual aspect of their relationships. We have heard directly from individuals about most of the complaints and failures discussed in manuals on sexual dysfunction. We have listened to stories of infidelity, premature ejaculation, lack of response on the part of both women and men. The one major complaint that we discovered, for which our reading had not prepared us, was the complaint on the part of women that they were not given enough *loving*, sexual attention by their husbands. They wanted affection and loving concern that comes to a climax in sexual union; sex for sexual release alone was not enough. Getting into bed and getting it done fast was certainly not what they wanted. This data would seem to go against many of our preconceived notions, the old wives' tales and the men's locker room talk. The fact remains that over the many years we've spent listening to people who had the confidence in us to share their lives, this has been the number one sexual complaint. It is safe to say that the overwhelming percentage of husbands have not been warm enough or comfortable enough with all of themselves, their total being, to deal with and respond to the whole woman. The result is that we have many basically unsatisfied, unfulfilled women and when this is the case we have unfulfilled men as well. There are many women who find sexual intercourse a necessary evil, but the number of these is certainly diminishing as women come to accept themselves more totally.

We would suggest that the basic feminine urge for sexuality may be even stronger and more persistent than the masculine urge. The female certainly has greater orgasmic capacity than the male. And whereas the male peaks sexually somewhere in his late teens or early twenties and then gradually levels off, the woman's capacity for orgasmic releases continues to build and grow. We have sometimes thought that God may have got things a little bit mixed up in the whole business of male and female sexuality because the sexual high point for males in our society occurs when they are not permitted much expression of it, while women peak in their late twenties, thirties, forties or even fifties, even after conception is virtually impossible and when men have lost much of their sexual drive.

It appears to us that aside from the biological instinctual reasons for this imbalance, the more highly developed affective nature of most women may be responsible for continued sexual-emotional development. Many men seem to grow more and more out of touch with their feelings as they grow older. Certainly the culture fosters this discrepancy between men and women. Once a woman has overcome her basic fear (if indeed she has any) of sexuality, her desire for warmth and affection as well as orgasmic sex seems much deeper than many men's desire or capacity. We need to remind ourselves that many of our sexual inhibitions have been religiously and culturally induced. We have talked with some very mature women who have told us (and we have seldom heard this statement from men) that sexual play and orgasm with someone they truly love has many qualities of a profound religious experience. They sense the nearness and presence of God and of the Holy in sexual ecstasy.

What do we mean by fulfilling and meaningful sexuality? Obviously it means that both people are capable of achieving orgasmic release on occasions, but this is not necessary in every sexual encounter. There are some groups who have taught that sexual intercourse without orgasm was more meaningful and satisfying than orgasmic sex. Satisfactory sexuality means comfortable freedom with another person to explore and give affection to any part of one's partner's body and the freedom to enjoy the same from the other. It is the freedom to say what is pleasant and what is not pleasant, what is pleasurable and what is not pleasurable. Emotions are hybrid creatures; they are a combination of inner thoughts and feelings along with physical response. Satisfying sexuality is emotional and physical play. Just as there are few people who entirely overcome their authority problems, just so we have found very few people totally devoid of sexual inhibitions. One man who had less sexual inhibitions than any other met an untimely end at the hands of prostitutes. In a world as mixed up and confused as our own it may be healthy to have some authority problems and sexual fears.

The statement that women as a whole are not interested in sex is simply an old wives' tale. We need to remember that we are just emerging from the Victorian era in which any mention of sexuality was taboo and masturbation (playing with one's self!) was viewed as leading to total physical and emotional disaster. In that age women were conditioned to be asexual. The proper lady never referred to sweat or any other bodily function, let alone sexuality. Women simply submitted to sex. Interestingly enough, one of the instruments of "liberation" for women, sexually speaking, was the sexual manual. The first sexual manuals were written in the early 1920s by men. Up until that time it was considered indecent in the Western world even to describe the subject. And there was little objective knowledge or data until the Masters and Johnson studies in the 1960s. And now we have Dr. Ruth answering questions on cable television nightly, questions like, "How can I overcome premature ejaculation?" Barbara went to say good night to our sixteen-year-old grandson and heard through his radio the unmistakable voice of Dr. Ruth.

How ironic that women and men have been brought up in a patriarchal society to believe that women had little sexual interest when women are really more earthy—closer to the earth—than men; women really have much deeper need for sexuality and it seems to provide a deeper and more long-lasting kind of satisfaction than for men. However, often a woman needs much longer to get aroused than does a man. Before this was known few women were given the time to become interested and involved in the sexual act. It was over before the woman had begun to respond. Many women need manual stimulation before intercourse and some find that orgasm during coitus is more satisfactory if they have received an orgasm manually before intercourse.

Few men realize how differently men and women are raised in our society. We have already described Barbara's sexual education and the fact that ten years ago things were not so very different. The freedom to discuss sexuality has certainly improved, but still we find that few young people (even the well-educated ones) have correct and adequate information on sexuality, contraception, venereal disease, sexual play and genital intercourse. Even when they have adequate information, few sexual partners have the freedom to discuss with each other their sexual desires, fears and experiences. We speak from the experience of listening to hundreds of young and older people in all parts of this country with all kinds of backgrounds. Where people are not comfortable with their own bodies and their sexual desires, fantasies and responses (and we have shown how many religious groups discourage this kind of comfort), it is difficult for people to have the freedom to find mutual, satisfying sexuality that is a sacrament of love even in marriage.

A story illustrates the sad lack of sexual information in a specific segment of the public. During the 1960s Barbara worked in a planned parenthood clinic in a Hispanic community in Southern California. The clinic had seldom been very busy, but one day people interested in visiting the clinic were lined up all the way down the street. They came for birth control information and counseling. The nurses and clinicians were so curious that they asked the women what had happened. The cause of the lengthy line was the Pope's declaration against birth control. Many of these women had not clearly understood that there was such a thing as contraception and then they suddenly discovered that there was something they could do to prevent further births. As we have already indicated, this lack of information extends to all levels of the social spectrum.

TREATING SEXUAL INADEQUACY

The sex manuals created a sexual revolution, a revolution for which Freud's thinking had paved the way as it gradually percolated through the general populace. These manuals were written to provide people with enough information so that they could enjoy adequate and satisfying sexual fulfillment. Anything that got in the way of the free and mutual enjoyment of sexuality was labeled sexual inadequacy. These manuals proposed quite different theories about sexuality and so provided quite different solutions for dealing with sexual problems. Four theories can be clearly distinguished from one another: the drive model, the analytic model, the behavioral model and the response model. The drive model suggests that we need to release the latent sexual drive by proper technique; great emphasis is placed upon learning skills of exciting and releasing the other partner. The analytic model teaches that the most serious sexual dysfunction arises from pleasure anxiety—that people are afraid to enjoy their sexual feelings because so much of human sexuality is tied into the Oedipal conflict. Such feelings are often contaminated with incestual fears. The therapist tries to help people to be released from their deep-seated fears in order to allow them to enjoy their sexuality. The basic implicit point of view of the Hite Report is behavioristic in orientation. By working to free ourselves from our conditioning we can allow sexuality to flow more freely. For many women this involves consciousness raising as well as behavioral modification.

Each of these points of view contains important insights, but they are at odds with one another in many areas. Along with the Berkeley Sex Therapy Group we have come to see the response model which they propose as the most adequate; not only does it appear to have the greatest success in treating dysfunction, but it is able to integrate the insights of these other points of view. The very first sex manual was written by two doctors and assumed the response model. The authors maintained that the cause of sexual problems was neglect and the therapy was extended foreplay and a concern, a sense of responsibility for the other partner. In premarital counseling and in counseling people with sexual problems we have often suggested that those coming to us read a little paperback by Oliver M. Butterfield, *Sexual Harmony in Marriage*. It was one of the early sexual manuals and was given to us by Barbara's doctor before we were married in the early 1940s. In one edition or another it has sold more than a million copies and has been revised to stay up to date. It contains clear, simple diagrams and descriptions of genital functioning and sexual foreplay and intercourse.[3]

According to the response model the major cause of sexual problems is that we have viewed sex in the bedroom as an arena for performance. Many people have tried to participate in sex, in sexual techniques, without total response to the other person. And sometimes when the "performance" failed or wasn't fully appreciated by the other partner, many of the participants went looking for a different arena and a different gladiator. Such an attitude overlooks creativity and commitment. Masters and Johnson, with whom the response model therapists have much in common, point out:

> But for sexual swinger and sexual conservative alike, at the heart of the wish for sexual newness or change is a stereotyped concept of sex which omits any idea of sex as a medium where the feelings and needs of two individuals take on the mood of time, place and circumstance and are communicated clearly and without exploitation of either partner by the other. The idea that sex functions naturally when it is 'lived' instead of 'performed' seems to escape many people. That sex can be 'lived' in marriage or in a deep and continuing commitment seems to have escaped almost everyone.[4]

What do these sex therapists suggest for couples who have lived together for years without permitting themselves to *enjoy* each other emotionally and physically as sexual partners? The Berkeley Sex Therapy Group has had remarkable success in the treatment of sexual malfunctioning. They advise individuals to get to know their own body and the body of their partner. They need to become comfortable with themselves and with the other person, to enjoy both, to feel warmth and caring flowing through the person to each other with no expectation of orgasm—then often orgasm comes of its own accord. Stroking exercises are encouraged—where men and women learn what is pleasurable and unpleasurable for each other. Sexuality in any people is still almost totally unconscious and unrelated to the total life pattern—but that can be changed.

One of the most important factors in a partner's sexual relationship is communication—the ability to say what they feel and what they need. Many men and women are so uncomfortable communicating about sex that they cannot say to one another, "That feels uncomfortable," or "Your stroking feels mechanical," or "Please touch me here or rub me there." Many partners feel that they are *supposed* to like everything and anything that their mate does. But until we begin to communicate honestly and openly, there is little possibility of a total sexual response between two people. Women need to know that men do not know automatically what feels good to their partners. Men also have no inborn knowledge of what

is best for the woman. When sexual functioning became less purely instinctual and further removed from conception, this instinctual ability was
lost. Women and men tend to believe that if someone loves them they will
know what is satisfying to them. This idea is a myth, cheats both men and
women and gets in the way of genuine communication. Good sex is the
result of deep caring, genuine loving, freedom from inhibitions and good
communication. The Berkeley Group have shown that many people diag-
nosed with the sexual dysfunctions of impotence and frigidity have usually
overcome these blocks by becoming more response-oriented and less
performance-oriented.[5]

What are the problems most frequently found among those men and
women in a marriage or long-time-committed relationship? Most people
with developed ego strength will not divulge their sexual problems until
they find someone whom they can trust. This person may be a doctor,
minister, psychologist, marriage and family therapist, or social worker. Each
of these professionals should be equipped with enough knowledge to speak
to the individual about their problems *without judgment* and either deal
with the problem or refer the person to a sex therapist who is properly
trained. We have found that the greatest number of problems lie in the
following areas:

1.   Even among the most sophisticated people there is an incredible
lack of ability to talk about sexual matters. Few people have the confidence
in themselves to express what they feel and wish in sexual play. This probably more than anything else hampers open and free sexual expression.
Most people in our culture find it easier to act sexually than to talk intimately about it.

2.   For the male the inability to obtain a firm erection and to sustain
it and then come to orgasm is a real blow to masculine identity as well
as making impossible the full sexual act. In such a situation a woman's sexual
needs are not fulfilled. Sometimes a fear of his partner makes a man impotent. With another woman who does not set off this fear within him, he
may be quite adequate sexually. Aging males sometimes need stimulation
of the penis before they respond and are able to have sexual intercourse.

3.   Some women are unable to respond to sexual stimulation and
achieve no orgasmic response. This has little or nothing to do with their
capacity to conceive. They may even be more attractive to some men if

they fail to respond. Women often need a great deal of affection and manual stimulation to become orgasmic. Some women enjoy intercourse but do not become orgasmic.

4.   One common male problem tied to fear and anger with women is premature ejaculation, in which the male ejaculates either before entrance into the vagina or almost immediately upon entering. Obviously this provides very little sexual satisfaction for the woman and is a source of humiliation for many males. Getting at the roots of one's fears and finding a partner with whom they can communicate and share their feelings helps many men with this problem. Nothing is worse for the male or female with difficulty in responding sexually than *sarcasm or ridicule*. These can put an end to sexual function as effectively as a knife.

5.   Sometimes sexual relationships simply cease within a committed relationship or marriage and often along with their cessation there is diminished expression of affection. This can be caused by many things, but almost always goes along with breakdown in communication.

6.   Most men and many women find that they sometimes have fantasies of sexual relations with people other than their sexual partner. Those who keep track of their dreams will discover that dreams sometime have us involved with others than our partners. We are not responsible for our dreams and sexual fantasies. We need to deal with them. However, sharing them, particularly during love making can be deflating and even damaging to the other person's sexual functioning. Out of kindness some things should not be shared. Guggenbuhl-Craig in *Marriage—Dead or Alive* deals with the importance and use of sexual fantasy.

7.   Sexual infidelity on the part of either or both partners can be extremely destructive to the sexual relationship of either or both people. Indeed it has been the one basic reason for obtaining divorce in many Christian churches over the ages. It often becomes the conflict that cannot be tolerated and causes not only sexual problems but dissolution of the relationship itself. However, disagreement about money and general lack of communication are more often grounds of divorce than infidelity. Infidelity should never be taken lightly. It is also important that neither spouse rush home to tell the all-loving partner about an escapade in order to reduce his or her own guilt. This can destroy the other partner's self-esteem. St. Catherine of Genoa is a model of a Christian wife who not only took back

her unfaithful husband, but also continued through her life and after her husband's death to take an interest in and show responsibility for the child of his affair. The frequency of sexual infidelity is far greater than most people believed before the work of Kinsey and his associates.

8.   The majority of men and women experience moments when their bisexual nature reexpresses itself in either dream, fantasy, desire or action. This can cause consternation to men and women brought up in a society where one homosexual act or occasional interest in a member of the same sex makes one a "homosexual". Unrealistic fears of homosexuality can inhibit the sexual functioning of both sexes. We shall discuss this matter further in a later chapter.

9.   There are physical difficulties that make complete sexual union impossible. Early in parish life a young man who had been recently married came to Morton because of incipient stomach ulcers and tension. As they talked he revealed that he had not been able to have sexual intercourse with his wife. His wife's hymen was so thick and strong that he could not penetrate it. They had not followed Morton's premarital instruction to see a doctor for a physical examination before marriage. Often physical difficulties interfere with sexual funtioning and many people are so uncomfortable about their sexuality that they do not seek out medical advice. Good medical advice is essential where it appears that physical problems are present.

10.   One real problem for couples desirous of having children is the inability of either partner to have them. This can cause great tension, particularly when one blames the other for the problem. Excellent clinics dealing with the problem in sterility are to be found in most medical centers. Couples who adopt a child often find that pregnancy results soon after as fear of being childless subsides.

11.   In a later chapter we shall discuss the paraphilia, the less common forms of sexual gratification. The presence of fetishism, sadism, bestiality, or any other similar paraphilia, can cause great guilt and pain and keep one or both partners from adequate sexual functioning.

When things go wrong in sexual relations it is most important to find trustworthy, competent people to talk with about the full range of the committed bond. "General" problems can directly affect the sexual relationship. It has been demonstrated that when two people are truly committed to each other, working out of sexual hang-ups is much easier. A relationship has two strikes against it when either partner believes that the other may walk out on them. A sense of permanency, of commitment is almost essential if two people are to deal with their sexual failures. The Berkeley Sex Therapy Group maintains that they can bring to sexual satisfaction 85% of the partners who come to them with sexual problems— but the partners must be committed to each other on a long-term basis in order for the success rate to hold true.[6] When the attempts of two people to deal openly and honestly with their sexual difficulties are not successful, then some kind of outside advice and therapy is certainly indicated for such stumbling blocks as premature ejaculation, impotence, frigidity, or a view of sex as evil or as only a duty.

Ironically some people maintain that because the sex manuals revealed and dealt with the double standard and put women in touch with their sexuality to a greater extent than many of them had been before, they inadvertently contributed to impotence in men. Some men now feel that they have to "perform" to please liberated women. Masters and Johnson have this to say on the subject:

> In rightfully assuming a 'full voting partnership' in the sexual relationship, however, women must be careful to avoid making the same kind of mistake men have made for a long time. The mistake can be found in the remark of a wife who said in no uncertain terms that she was just as 'entitled' to sexual satisfaction as her husband was. To be entitled to something means to have the right to claim it and expect that it will be provided. No matter how gently she may let him know, this wife is in effect saying to her husband: 'I should be enjoying intercourse more than I am, and I would like you to do something about it.'
>
> Unfortunately, the coin is counterfeit. In a continuing relationship sex-as-service rarely leads to sustained pleasure and is very unlikely to bring a woman the fulfillment she desires. It is not different for the man. Contrary to one of the most widespread of all sex misconceptions, the fact is that sex-as-service has failed to reward most men with the erotic gratification they anticipated.[7]

One suggestion we would make to virtually every man and woman in a committed intimate relationship is that they pick out a good marriage manual and read it *out loud* together. Actually reading to each other breaks the taboos of talking about the specifics of sex with which many of us have been raised. However, we have already shown that the sex manuals propose quite different theories about sexuality and we need to read them critically and test their assumptions against what seems right to us. We need to get over the attitude ingrained in most of us from grade school on that because something was written in a book it is true. In addition, although sex manuals have done women a service through promulgating more information, they have been almost entirely written by men and are therefore biased in many respects. Nat Lehrman quotes Virginia Johnson to this effect in his authorized explanation and simplification of their findings in *Masters and Johnson Explained*.

We have read dozens of sex manuals together and we have found the most adequate and least sexually biased to be: *Sexual Harmony in Marriage*, to which we have already alluded, *Masters and Johnson Explained* by Nat Lehrman and *The Pleasure Bond: A New Look at Sex and Commitment* by William H. Masters and Virginia E. Johnson. We would warn the readers about many of the manuals that sail under the Christian banner: we have found many of them the most sexually biased and generally imbalanced of any that we read.

We would also suggest that for many couples it might be helpful to take a sex therapy course. These courses are particularly valuable and often required for counselors, therapists and other helping professionals. There are dozens of short courses available (one or two days)—particularly in California. Both of us were very appreciative of the course that we took although it dealt largely with improving the sexual relations of the committed couple and did not deal with the wider range of sexual problems that plague so many.

CHAPTER EIGHT

Sexuality, Love and Celibacy

It may appear strange to find a chapter on celibacy in a book on the sacrament of sexuality. However, when we consider the important role that celibacy and monasticism have played in many of the world religions and the controversy that rages around the subject in Christendom today, the subject must be dealt with. It may seem even stranger to have a married priest and his wife write on the subject of celibacy—no stranger, however, than celibates writing on marriage, love and sexuality. We believe that religious celibacy is an important institution and a symbol of religious commitment even if we do not see it as necessary for priesthood in the Christian Church.

Frankly, the whole question of the relationship of sexuality, love and celibacy is one of the most difficult subjects we have ever dealt with. We have worked closely with celibate nuns, brothers and priests for the last sixteen years and we have heard their stories. We have come to the conclusion that until celibate men and women come to terms with the realities of love and sexuality in the context of their singular lifestyles (whether lived in individual or communal apostolic endeavors), they will not be able to deal creatively with the vast majority of people who are wrestling with problems of intimacy, love and sexuality. We repeat again that sexuality is a unique and universal human component; undealt with, it hampers our ability to function as total human beings and also interferes with our serving and ministering to others. What celibacy means to someone and how he or she is going to live it out will depend upon each person's unique developmental history, upon that person's understanding of the dynamics of love, sexuality and relationship, and upon their personal relationship with God.

One thing is certain, however, and every single book we have read on the subject of celibacy (and we have read dozens of them) agree: attempts to deny love in order to make celibacy easier result in a diminished capacity for ministry and an inability to communicate on the deepest and most significant levels with other people. We don't know the exact figures, but a very large number of celibates have left the ranks of ministry during the last twenty years. In addition, there are far fewer new vocations to celibate priesthood and religious orders than there were twenty-five years ago. Empty convents and lack of celibate clergy attest to this reality. In his book *Priest in the United States: Reflections on a Survey* Andrew Greeley analyzes the reasons that priests are leaving. Three reasons stand out: unhappiness resulting from the loneliness of the lifestyle, the desire to get married and the failure of their theological framework to sustain the celibate lifestyle.

The significance of these factors varies according to the individual. For example, the third of these reasons proved to be crucial for one of the wisest people we have known who switched from celibacy to marriage. This man was a priest, a member of a religious order and a professor of psychology. He told us that the moment that his confidence in Thomistic theology crumbled, his rationale for celibacy was gone and he could no longer make the sacrifices that celibacy entailed. Within several years he was married. There must be a solid theological base for celibacy if it is to be lived creatively.

One possibility for reducing the loneliness of the celibate lifestyle is what we call creative commitment—long-range commitment of affection and companionship between two people, both of whom are committed to celibacy. Two very gifted and dedicated celibates, a priest and a nun, had known each other for many years and finally made a formal commitment to each other. They made this commitment in a church with a priest officiating. Their vow was to be lifelong companions with no genital contact. These two achieved a much deeper relationship than many people in successful marriages where genital expression is expected. They both realized that they could not work effectively within the Roman Catholic Church except under these conditions and their commitment to the Church was such that they were willing to make this sacrifice.

Human beings are able to live without genital contact, but they are not able to live creatively without communication, love, affection and touch. Celibates who attempt to be equally committed to all people and/or avoid selective intimate relationships tend to become inhuman. We need a base of intimacy from which to go out to others. Some of the great Greek Orthodox spiritual leaders quoted in the *Philokalia* were celibates and yet so close to one another that some observers said that they were as one person. This bonding was seen as a great capacity for love. It is simply impossible to have forty-one intimate relationships. Father Donald Goergen has written wisely on this subject in his book *The Sexual Celibate*:

> My own opinion is that celibate people choose to forego genital love. This is not because we now transfer a negative attitude toward genitality. Genital love is beautiful and enjoyable. But celibate love is not genital love. Nor is celibacy primarily genital abstinence. Someone may well abstain from genital love and still not be celibate. The life of a celibate involves concentration on forms of loving other than genital. Genital love requires commitment to physical presence with another person...
>
> Genitality will be satisfied only in exclusivity, marriage, superficiality, promiscuity, or by transcending genitality as a need. Only the latter is compatible with the celibate life.[1]

Goergen's point of view is that there are many levels of sexuality and one can sacrifice genital love and still remain in touch with and express other levels of love and sexuality. We would agree with this view of sexuality as the permeating element in all close human relationships. It recognizes genital love as good and a need. The celibate makes a *conscious sacrifice of this need* in order to serve others in a special way. Without *conscious* sacrifice we are likely to fall short of our commitment or repress our sexuality.

Father Andrew M. Greeley, best-selling author and professor of sociology at the University of Arizona, has written a most enlightening article entitled "Do Priests Fall in Love? Of Course They Do." The article appeared in the March 26, 1983 issue of *TV Guide* as a commentary on and response to the TV presentation of *The Thorn Birds*, the best-selling novel about forbidden love. Father Greeley says:

> Many Catholics want to have sexless priests. Well, they can't have them. The pretense of some Catholic laity, even good and sympathetic and sensitive laity, that priests are not humans like other

humans is cruel and unjust. The diversion of sexual energies into the service of others (sublimation is the technical psychoanalytic term) does not mean the denial (repression) of these energies. You can no more have sexless priests than you can have married men who never find other women attractive. A man who never found another woman sexually appealing wouldn't find his wife sexually appealing either. A priest who did not react strongly to women wouldn't react strongly to anything.

Do priests fall in love, as Ralph does with Meggie? Of course they do. Men fall in love with women; that's the way the species is designed. Married men and women also fall in love with other people, and some do so often in their lives. But such romantic responses no more necessarily drive a priest to violate his vows than they necessarily drive a married person to violate his or her fidelity.

Both fidelity and celibacy are difficult, chancy, risky commitments. So what? That's the nature of the human condition...

As a half-hour's reading of Catholic history will reveal, those Catholics who wish to pretend that priests are immune from temptation and sin will have a hard time with Alexander VI, who fathered children not only as a cardinal but even as a Pope. And those Catholics who are horrified at the thought that the hands that touch the Eucharist might also touch the body of a woman might ponder the fact that St. Peter, the first Pope, from one Catholic theological perspective (others say Peter was an apostle and his successor Linus was the first Pope), was a married man who touched both the Eucharist and the body of his wife...

But *The Thorn Birds* is not mainly about an adulterous priest. It is about a harsh, insensitive, ambitious priest who is saved, if he is saved at all, by the humanization he experiences in his love for Meggie. The love is sinful, all right, though not nearly as sinful as his crass and cruel ambition. But it also breaks through Ralph de Bricassart's smooth arrogance and brings him into the human race. The God who draws straight with crooked lines uses this illicit love to attract Ralph to Himself (Herself, if you wish).

If Ralph makes it to happiness—and I think he does—Meggie will be the reason. In the providence of a tricky, persistent, irresistibly loving God, Meggie, sinner or not, becomes for Ralph, grace, sacrament, salvation.

The Thorn Birds is not about an uncontrollably passionate priest who will stop at nothing to find power and pleasure. It is about an implacably passionate God who will stop at nothing in the pursuit of creatures with whom He/She has fallen in love.[2]

As we have indicated earlier celibacy may be interpreted in many ways, as refraining from touching one's own genitals in masturbation, as avoiding warm embraces, as denying oneself the experience of physical excitement, as avoiding sexual intercourse. However, there is no doubt that the relationship of Meggie and Ralph was a breaking of any celibate vow. If that was sin, and it was certainly a breaking of a vow, it is comforting to realize that God can bring transformation even into such a situation.

CELIBACY IN THE CHRISTIAN CHURCH

One of the most telling cross-cultural examples of celibacy is found in the classic Hindu text, the *Ramayana*—comparable in authority to the first five books of the Bible in the Judaeo-Christian tradition. This majestic epic tells the story of a king and his wife who are separated by an evil creature who steals her away. The king goes through all sorts of adventures in order to get her back. Many of the dramas and dances of Hindus from India to Thailand to Bali dramatize various parts of these adventures. Finally the king is victorious and the couple is united; they are the ideal king and queen, both in their personal lives and in their rule over their kingdom. Their marriage and relationship are ecstatically happy. However, as the king ages he comes to the realization that he and his wife must part. He leaves her to enter into a life of solitude since he believes that he can only achieve his religious potential and realize his identity with Brahma as he cuts himself off from the illusions of this transitory world. His emotions of love for his wife keep him bound to this world, and so he must leave her.

This is not the Christian reason for celibacy. In its official statements, Christianity never views the world as a snare or illusion, and never states that only the spiritual world is real. This view is similar to the gnosticism with which the early Christian fathers battled. People who make an easy transition from Christian practice to the lifestyle of Hinduism or Buddhism are naive. They don't understand the basic philosophical differences between East and West. Celibacy in Christianity is not a withdrawal from an evil or illusory physical world, although there are many Christian authors whose writings are tainted with this point of view. (We are embarrassed, for example, by Ignatius of Loyola's view of women as snares of evil that is found in his *Spiritual Exercises*.)

Three quite different views about celibacy and priesthood are found in the Christian Church. The first is the ancient tradition of the Greek

Orthodox Church. It continued the practice of the Apostles and the first clergy. Jesus would have been hard put to find twelve celibate young men to be his followers in Judea in the first century of our era. In the Trullan Councils held in Constantinople in 680 and 692 C.E. it was agreed that clergy could be married if they were married before ordination. Bishops, however, were to be chosen from celibate clergy or widowed clergy; if married they had to separate from their wives. Controversy rages as to whether this was an ecumenical council or whether Pope Agatho endorsed its decrees. Pope Sergius I refused to agree to sign the canons of this fifth council of Constantinople in 692. However, in the earliest days bishops as well as priests and deacons could be married. Bishop Synesius of Cyrene, one of the greatest thinkers of the fifth century, was married and elected bishop by popular acclamation. The Church was largely a Greek speaking church in its early days, even in Rome up into the third century. The Roman Church gradually developed the view that all priests within the Roman Rite were to be celibate. The third view developed in the Protestant churches where compulsory celibacy was rejected for all clergy.

The Irish Church flourished from the sixth through the ninth centuries, the very time that the light of Christianity was dimmest on the continent. Ireland was the only place in the West where one could learn Greek and missionaries went out from Ireland to England and Scotland to Iona and Lindisfarne and to the most barbaric sections of Northern Europe successfully bringing the Christian message. Most of these missionaries were monks, but at home most of the clergy in parishes were married. Some ties remained between the Greek Church and these islands.

The history of how compulsory celibacy came to be the discipline of the Roman Catholic Church is a long and controversial subject. Henry C. Lea's somewhat polemic history of *Sacredotal Celibacy in the Christian Church* was first published in Philadelphia in 1867. The fourth edition of this work was republished during the Second Vatican Council in 1966. This is still one of the most easily available studies of the subject, but needs to be checked with other sources.[3]

Living under the threat of persecutions for its first three hundred years kept the Church on its toes and pruned of curious bystanders. With the edict of Milan in 312 C.E. Constantine removed the torture, terror and martyrdom to which the earliest Christians were subject. The Church came out of the catacombs. Gradually it was not only tolerated, but became the religious foundation of a new Empire. People were then attracted to the

Church not through conviction, in spite of the price they might have to pay, but to curry favor with the leaders of the state— one of the real tragedies in the history of Christianity. The Church began to accommodate itself to a corrupt and sensuous world.

Many Christians felt that they could not live the life of apostolic Christianity and stay in the world: many of them fled into deserts, particularly in Egypt. There they lived solitary lives as anchorites or formed communities in which they made vows of poverty, chastity and obedience. Great religious and spiritual vitality was found among these desert fathers, men like St. Anthony who was a friend and supporter of the bulwark of Orthodoxy, St. Athanasius. The monastic tradition continued on through the Orthodox churches in Asia Minor, Greece and the Balkan area. It remains little changed today on the holy mountain of Mt. Athos and has influenced the monastic life in Russia.

However, the celibate life was never considered necessary for the ordinary priest. Few Western Europeans or Americans realize that the civilization that was Rome continued and flourished in Byzantium until it was finally destroyed by the Ottoman Turks in 1451. Up until the end, Byzantium was a sophisticated culture with a stable government and a high level of civilization, with libraries and universities. It never experienced the dark ages through which all of Western Europe was subjected after the barbarian invasions.

In the Western Church under the direction of the Popes in Rome the view that celibacy was an inherent part of priesthood gradually developed. There were many reasons for this development. Although the invasions of the Goths and Vandals and Franks spelled the end of the brilliant Roman culture in the West, these invaders did not wish to destroy the civilization, but rather to take it over. Much of Italy, North Africa and Spain was reconquered by the Byzantine Emperor Justinian around 550 C.E. Ravenna with its magnificent Byzantine mosaics became the seat of government in Italy. The total collapse of the West in the Dark Ages did not occur until shortly after this and many of the great cities of Europe remained. Early in the seventh century the Moslem religion arose in Arabia and swept away all of North Africa. Islam has few laws against piracy; the Mediterranean was infested with pirates and became unsailable. Trade ceased and the civilization of Europe collapsed. The city of Aquileia at the head of the Adriatic had been a marble beauty of 300,000 people; it soon became a wasteland. Dozens, maybe hundreds of cities not quite as large or spectacular disintegrated in the period between 600 and 1000 C.E. when a new civilization began to arise.

The idea of the monastic community was introduced into the West by St. Benedict, whose wise and sensible Rule provided a way of life in the midst of the growing chaos. One wonders if real Christianity would have survived in the West without the monasteries as centers of religious life, learning and culture. Family life in that dissolving culture became problematic and tenuous. It took all of one's energies to survive. Lawless nobles and roaming bands of warriors controlled the countryside. Europe was swept by one plague after another. Bringing children into such a world was difficult to justify morally. Many of the most intelligent men and women retired to monasteries and convents not only to find fellowship in following Christ but also because these were safe refuges in a disintegrating world. Under these conditions it is little wonder that celibacy became a dominant idea in the Western Church. Augustine, whose ideas about marriage and sexuality we have already examined, became *the* theologian of the Western Roman Church.

Another element affected attitudes about celibacy—the problem of selling Church benefices, ordination and ecclesiastic preferment (simony) and the arrangement to have one's children inherit these benefices (nepotism). The safest and most solid jobs and properties were in the Church. In fact, the Church became the only vestige of government in many places. Clergy found ways to augment what Church properties and income they had. They also wanted to pass these on to their children (legitimate or not) and relatives. Celibacy was seen as a way to reduce the problems of nepotism and simony. In addition to all this, in 1051 the Western and Eastern churches split apart. Eastern practices were considered anathema in the West and the Eastern custom of marriage among clergy became suspect along with everything else in Eastern Orthodoxy.

It is no wonder that this struggling church opted for compulsory celibacy for all clergy. We can trace the increasing pressure by the Papacy for the acceptance of this policy and the resistance it created. A series of Synods and Councils enacted the most stringent rules. Clergy, "from Bishops to subdeacons were ordered to remove women, concubines and other suspicious women from their houses at once, and to remain separate from their consorts forever. Not only were women to be turned adrift on the world, but the children born of such unions were pronounced slaves."[4] Peter Damiani put pressure on several Popes who enacted legislation on this subject.

Hildebrand, later Gregory VII, authorized the laity to withdraw allegiance from any clergy who did not follow the rule of celibacy. The Bishops were most fierce in their opposition as these rules threatened their independence and prestige. War followed and an anti-pope was elected, but the papacy won the battle and established its position in the very significant Fourth Lateran Council in 1215.

The matter of celibacy was considered a matter of discipline and not of doctrine until the Council of Trent. At that time the rule of celibacy was practically elevated to the rank of dogma. And yet there was no attempt to condemn the Eastern Church or to enforce the rules on married clergy of the Eastern Rites in communion with Rome. The recent decline in vocations in the Roman Catholic Church has caused some real concern about the practicality of compulsory celibacy. At a conference on community held in the summer of 1985, Basil Cardinal Hume, archbishop of England, stated that if the distribution of the sacraments was given top priority it might well be necessary to ordain some carefully selected married men to the priesthood.

A third view of celibacy is that which has become the common practice in the Protestant churches. Married clergy became the norm and real doubt was cast upon the celibate lifestyle. Someone has said that celibacy was obligatory in Rome and marriage became almost compulsory in most Reformed denominations. Indeed, when the Church of England separated from Rome in 1549 only 10% of the clergy remained loyal to Rome and most of the remaining 90% brought forth their wives or married their concubines.

In the Second Vatican Council in "The Decree on Ministry and Life of Priests" Pope Paul VI and the Council make clear that celibacy is not necessary to priesthood and that the Roman position is one of discipline and not doctrine or dogma.

> With respect to the priestly life, the Church has always held in especially high regard perfect and perpetual continence on behalf of the kingdom of heaven. . . It is not, indeed, demanded by the very nature of the priesthood, as is evident from the practice of the primitive Church and from the tradition of the Eastern Churches. In these Churches, in addition to all bishops and those others who by a gift of grace choose to observe celibacy, there also exist married priests of outstanding merit.

> While this most sacred Synod recommends ecclesiastical celibacy, it in no way intends to change that different discipline which lawfully prevails in Eastern Churches. It lovingly exhorts all those who have received the priesthood after marriage to persevere in their sacred vocation, and to continue to spend their lives fully and generously for the flock committed to them.[5]

Nearly all the reformers attacked the institution of celibacy. As early as 1520 Luther attacked compulsory celibacy as the work of the devil and in the Diet of Augsburg in 1530 said that celibacy as a requirement for ministry was "popish innovation against the eternal word of God". In section VI. xiii and xiii of his Institutes Calvin denounced compulsory celibacy for the clergy, writing "The first place of insane audacity belongs to celibacy." Article 24 of the Presbyterian Westminster Catechism confirms Calvin's idea. Zwingli also condemned celibacy for the clergy and article 32 of the well-known 39 *Articles of Religion of the Anglican Church* does the same. A real reaction had set in to the idea of celibacy as a requirement for ordination; this was probably one of the practical reasons for the success of the Reformation.

THE VALUES OF CELIBACY

Some of our closest friends are celibate priests, brothers and nuns. We have come to appreciate them and their ministry greatly. As a married priest and coworker with many celibates we see the importance of the celibate lifestyle as long as it is not made the norm for all priesthood. Through years of reading and reflecting we have come to see six important contributions of committed celibacy.

First of all, celibacy frees people for service—there is no doubt about it. There are places that we could never have ministered as our children were growing up. The health of the spouse in a clerical marriage may limit service as well. And as one of our children once remarked to us: "It is fine if you want to take the vow of poverty for yourselves, but you don't have to take it for me." If a couple wants to live in poverty, that is their decision, but to bring up children in that condition when their friends are much better off than they may be quite unfair and may even scar them. Unfortunately or fortunately, clerical jobs are no longer as prestigious or as remunerative as they were in the Middle Ages and raising a family on a clergyman's salary is no easy task. Indeed, one nun who married once remarked to Barbara, "I never knew what poverty was until I left the order and was out on my own teaching school." Many married clergy live a very marginal existence financially. In the Episcopal church there is a humorous and tragic prayer known as the vestryman's prayer concerning ministers: "Lord, you keep them humble and we'll keep them poor."

There are many places where married priests cannot go, situations they cannot take care of. They do not have the freedom for total service that is possible for celibates. The issue ultimately has more to do with children than with marriage itself. Children are to a large extent shaped and given security by the love and attention and care that parents give them. Morton has said many times that if he had one thing to do over in his life he would have spent more time with his children when they were growing up and less time with the parish. Although childless marriage is certainly a legitimate vocation, it is not possible in a church that prohibits contraception.

Some years ago we visited the nuns of St. Scholastica's convent in Chittagong, Bangladesh. They taught us much and we have become good friends. We saw the absolute necessity of celibacy for service in that poverty-stricken culture. The work that they were doing, taking in and educating orphans, children who would have otherwise died, would have been impossible there if these women had not accepted the celibate lifestyle. They could not have been married, had children, grubbed for a living and done the work that they were doing. They quite consciously sacrificed their sexuality for a greater good. Sexuality, in spite of some current voices to the contrary, is not the final good, and like everything else, it needs to be subordinated to the great good, love and Love. What we experienced among these nuns in Bangladesh is the same kind of service for which Mother Teresa of Calcutta is so admired. Again her service would be practically unthinkable except in the celibate lifestyle.

Related to this lack of children is the lack of entanglements in the celibate lifestyle. On a number of occasions in the Gospels Jesus made comments that indicate the kind of total commitment expected in single discipleship—but in all such Biblical passages, you will notice that references to total commitment never include children or wives. The nature of Jesus' call is seen in Mark 3:31-35 (Good News Bible):

Then Jesus' mother and brothers arrived. They stood outside the house and sent in a message, asking for him. A crowd was sitting around Jesus, and they said to him, 'Look, your mother and your brothers and sisters are outside, and they want you.'

Jesus answered, 'Who is my mother? Who are my brothers?' He looked at the people sitting around him and said, 'Look! Here are my mother and my brothers! Whoever does what God wants him to do is my brother, my sister, my mother.'

Again in Mark 6:7-10 (Good News Bible) Jesus asks the Disciples to lead a lifestyle no one with a family could possibly manage:

He called the twelve disciples together and sent them out two by two. He gave them authority over the evil spirits and ordered them, 'Don't take anything with you on the trip except a walking stick— no bread, no beggar's bag, no money in your pockets. Wear sandals, but don't carry an extra shirt.'

Certainly one could not take a small child on such a trip even if one could take a wife. This passage became one of the central texts justifying celibacy and the radical lifestyle of many of the religious orders in much of Christendom.

Other passages stress the importance of total commitment to Jesus and the Kingdom:

As they went on their way, a certain man said to Jesus, 'I will follow you wherever you go.' Jesus said to him, 'Foxes have holes, and birds have nests, but the Son of Man has no place to lie down and rest.' He said to another man, 'Follow me.' But he said, 'Sir, first let me go and bury my father.' Jesus said, 'Let the dead bury their dead. You go and preach the Kingdom of God.' Another man said, 'I will follow you, sir; but first let me go and say good-bye to my family.' Jesus said to him, 'Anyone who starts to plow and then keeps looking back is of no use for the Kingdom of God.' Luke 9:57-62 (Good News Bible)

These are radical statements and such following of Christ almost requires celibacy, but Jesus also counsels love and concern. We believe that once two people are in committed relationship and have children that their Christian priorities need to shift. If children are sacrificed for outsiders, something is wrong with one's Christian priorities. We have tried to listen to God in the depth of our prayer and quiet, and we have come to the conclusion that we genuinely lose certain freedoms when we are married and have children. We become part of an integral unit and community when we are married and if we fail in obligations to this unity, we can damage ourselves, our children and the community. Other priorities can take precedence over getting married and having children. Celibacy and monasticism witness to this truth.

It is important to remember that Jesus was speaking to a society in which celibacy was unthinkable and obedience to parents was unquestioned. He had to be very incisive to get his message about dedication to the Kingdom across to his hearers. On the other hand, no major religious leader of humankind has stressed the value of children and women (and therefore of family) more than Jesus of Nazareth. He was adamant on the subject of divorce. We see a genuine balance in his teaching about discipleship and marriage. Our first concern is to serve the kingdom whether we do it by sacrificing the joys and problems of sexuality and family life or whether we serve through our marriage, our relationship to our children, our ministering, and our financial help to others.

We see celibacy as a sacrifice of one valuable part of life for another more valuable. How important it is to see celibacy as a sacrifice of a valuable way of life rather than as getting rid of an undesirable and tainted aspect of life (the gnostic view). People who make this sacrifice consciously and willingly can often minister in a unique way to people caught in the darkness of the world. Baron von Hugel was brought out of inner confusion and chaos by the great French spiritual director, Abbe Huvelin. He said that only a person who had made the celibate sacrifice could have helped him in the depths of his own struggle. Only one who had sacrificed his own natural desire and shown that such a sacrifice was possible could have broken through into the depth of him. We were talking to a very conscious and mature woman who was a member of a celibate order and asked her how she could live the celibate lifestyle and she replied: "I can do it only as I make my vow fresh each morning as I get up."

Fourth, we think that celibacy can be a definite call to a primary friendship with God shared with others with the same commitment. Within the family we need to deal with people where they are and seldom will all members have the same kind of commitment to God. It seems far better to us for one to remain unmarried than to get married and not live fully in the faithfulness, intimacies and relatedness of family life.

The importance of this parental involvement is evident in the recent emphasis on parental bonding with the newborn child. This has come to be appreciated by many physicians and psychologists. A baby needs from the very beginning to have a sense of unique attachment and closeness to both the father and the mother. Our most recent grandchild was born on St. Bartholomew's day in 1981. Our son, like many fathers nowadays, took courses along with his wife and coached his wife through the labor and delivery in a hospital room that looked like a well-appointed bedroom in a home. After the birth, he slept there that night with the baby on his chest. We are coming back to what primitives knew instinctually and what much of our Western civilization has lost touch with. This closeness takes time, and as the children grow the demands on a parent increase. These demands will often take precedence over relationship with those who share the parents' religious commitments. Real bonds are needed in celibate friendships in God and in true family life. Both are witnesses to the love of God.

We believe that there is a fifth legitimate reason for celibacy for some people. Human beings are very different in the way that they experience reality and respond to it. Jung's theory of psychological types has been translated into a readily usable instrument known as the Myers-Briggs Type Indicator. Some human beings are far more introverted and solitary than others. For some introverted intuitives and thinkers the more cloistered and contemplative celibate lifestyle may be the most meaningful and satisfactory way of life. Certain extroverted sensation or introverted feeling types may find community life and service and fellowship truly meaningful. Some types who are very independent may have to make great sacrifices to live the celibate existence.[6]

Related to type, but involving other factors, some people prefer group life rather than the one-to-one relationship of a nuclear family. Celibate community can provide some extroverts with something of the group experience and freedom of an extended family without the responsibilities and insularity of the nuclear family. Group living and sharing can foster education, growth and development of the individual, and offers a truly satisfactory alternative to the responsibilities and difficulties of marriage. This may be particularly true when people have experienced family life as a place of tension, pain and hardship. Being celibate (vowing no genital love) often saves community life from degeneration and much interpersonal tension.

And last of all, Christian religious celibacy can be an outward and visible sign, a sacrament of one's devotion to Christ and one's openness to all people. In his book, *Celibacy, Prayer and Friendship—A Making-Sense-Out-of-Life Approach* Christopher Kiesling characterizes celibacy as an ultimate dying and rising again, as an extension of true poverty. He sees it as a symbolic living of the kind of life that Jesus lived. Of course our vocation is to live our lives as truly as Christ lived his, and not to imitate Jesus of Nazareth slavishly. Celibacy can be a sign of radical discipleship, not only a sign of sacrifice. Real marriage and genuine celibacy are both signs of different kind of Christian commitment and we need both. Both options include vows taken and lived to the fullest.

As we reflect on all these values of celibacy we come to see this lifestyle as a particular gift of God or charism. The early Church believed that different Christians were differently endowed with spiritual gifts, with special abilities to serve God and each other. The Church, the Body of Christ, was made up of people with these different gifts. This is not the place to discuss in detail the nature of these gifts. Some of the most important passages on the nature of these different kinds of giftedness are: Romans 12.6 ff, I Corinthians 12-13, Ephesians 4:7 ff, I Peter 4:10. These passages point out gifts of healing and miracles, the gifts of tongues, prophecy and interpretation of tongues, the gifts of wisdom and knowledge, the gift of being open to revelation. And then there are the more prosaic gifts of preaching, serving, administering, teaching, encouraging, evangelizing and pastoring. In I Corinthians 7:7 Paul adds the gift of sexual continence or celibacy. We see celibacy as such a special gift and it is as difficult to make a person a healthy celibate without God's charism as it is to make a person who is tone deaf a great singer. God may well grant the gift of celibacy if we ask for it, but the celibate lifestyle is nearly impossible without God giving the charism of continence.[7]

THE DANGERS OF CELIBACY

In our years at the University of Notre Dame we came to know many celibate clergy and religious, both men and women, from many different orders. Indeed we found closer Christian fellowship within these Roman

Catholic communities than almost anywhere else in our experience. In addition to the values of celibacy, we also observed several real dangers.

The question of obedience that often goes along with celibacy in religious orders is a sticky one indeed. A woman religious was considering leaving her community. Like many others who had trouble with their communities or with celibacy, she came and talked with us because she knew we saw celibacy as a real vocation and yet were married; thus we would exert no pressure either way. She reported that when she told her superiors in the community of her doubts and questions about remaining in the order, they replied to her, "Who are you to think that you know better what you should do for yourself than we do?" This kind of attitude about running others' lives can become very dangerous and inflating for any human being, and may be as damaging for those in authority as for those upon whom the authority is inflicted.

We have observed in some religious orders that the demand for complete obedience can result in an abandonment of responsibility on the part of those under authority. This can keep adult men and women childish. One of our friends was a superior in an order and then eventually married. She told us that she didn't even know what colors she liked or what ego strength it took to live in the world. Another was so out of tune with the ways of the world that he didn't even know how to start keeping a checkbook or what steps to start making in order to finance a family home. Religious orders must be careful not to abuse authority and keep people from ego development in order to maintain dependence upon the order. Another demonic misuse of authority was reported by some who left their orders in the days before Vatican II. Some of the superiors believed that if the religious did not have enough suffering within them, it was their duty to provide it through oppressive tasks and disciplines.

Opting for celibacy can also be a way of avoiding sexuality, marriage and children because of fear or anger directed toward the opposite sex or because of traumatic childhood experiences. The fact that a person had a drunken and abusive father, a dominating and possessive mother, or an incestuous relationship with a parent or sibling, and is therefore literally scared to death of physical or genital contact, is not a call to celibacy. A desire to avoid childbearing due to having seen a mother physically destroyed by having to cope with a continuous stream of children is also not a celibate vocation. Childbearing can be a deeply instinctual need, stronger even than the desire for sexual experience. Some women members of orders told us that the maternity ward was off limits for them when they were working in hospitals because it might arouse their maternal instincts.

Such psychological problems and instinctual desires should be faced and dealt with *before* a permanent celibate vow. People who have had serious psychological problems or have strong sexual or parental desires can make excellent and dedicated celibate followers of Christ if they are conscious of their problems and desires and make deliberate, informed conscious choices. Likewise, people who have a homoerotic orientation can make excellent celibate servants of God. We know few places where a man or woman with strong homosexual tendencies can find a more acceptable context for service in society than celibate ministry. On the other hand, if people are trying to avoid their sexuality or childbearing desires, real problems may arise. Repressed instinctuality can emerge explosively in inappropriate ways.

Many people have entered the celibate service of God and the Church within the Roman communion because they wanted to serve the Church, without even considering what celibacy entailed. Far from facing the sacrifice they were making, they directed their attention away from what it meant to give up sexual expression permanently. In our experience the most successful celibate priests and religious are those who did not decide on the celibate life until they had tasted the world and knew something of their sexuality; they were clearly conscious of the sacrifice they were making. Statistics bear out our observation: the younger the person who entered into total commitment to the celibate life, the higher the percentage of those leaving their vocations after the more liberal view of Vatican II permeated the Church structure. The minor seminaries in which young men began their celibate life as freshmen in high school have largely been abandoned. The objective studies of James Michael Lee showed that this kind of training produced immature and repressed adults as well as a huge percentage of people leaving their orders.

This brings us to the question of how old a person should be in order to make a lifelong commitment to celibacy. At what age can we decide what we wish to do with the rest of our lives? The two of us have been through five professions together, and we may have several more as we hope to live another twenty or twenty-five years. And to make a decision, sometimes we have to try something out. If it works and we like it for ten years, fine; we can always commit ourselves to another five or ten years. The Benedictine Community at Pecos provides first of all a three-month commitment, then six months followed by a year and then a three-year term of service for those who come to the abbey. They also provide for permanent vows for those who find this to be their way of life. And at Pecos no condemnation or rejection is leveled at those who try celibacy and community life and find that it is not for them.

The idea that we have to continue in the same kind of occupation forever is a bad idea vocationally speaking. This is quite different from making a commitment to the risen Christ so that we can grow in depth and intimacy of relationship or in making a commitment to one person for the same reason. The form that commitment should take may change over the years. Different ways of serving may enrich not only the individual but the Church as well. If the Roman Catholic Church insists upon celibacy for priesthood, perhaps diocesan priests could be asked to make five- or ten-year vows of celibacy and service that can be renewed or not renewed at the end of that period.

In our experience celibacy without close relationships both with individuals and within a group demands a sacrifice almost beyond human endurance. As long as the Church requires celibacy for service, it has a moral obligation toward its priests and religious to provide them with opportunities where they can find genuine fellowship with other celibates and establish reasonable guidelines as to how far intimacy should go in relationship to the same or the opposite sex. Many communities provide little in the way of closeness or direction and the average diocesan rectory with several priests is often one of the loneliest places in the world. Close relationships between committed celibates and noncelibates can be *very dangerous*, because they may have very different hopes and aims regarding the eventual outcome of the relationship. *This is particularly true of priests and noncelibate women.* We have known many women who have fallen in love with priests and were never able to break their attachments. These relationships gave real support to the priests, but led to unfulfilled women.

Relationship means communication. Vincent Dwyer in his *Genesis II* program has tried to deal with the problem of clerical loneliness by providing groups in which real communication can take place. The matter of communication is so vital and important that we can hardly overestimate its influence and significance in marriage, committed relationships, mature sexuality and celibacy. In his book *The Broken Heart* James Lynch, professor of psychiatry at the University of Maryland Medical School, shows the effect of loneliness upon physical health. Where there is little companionship, relationship and touch, people become much more susceptible to disease. People who live alone with little physical or emotional contact have a death rate in every major disease category in each age group at least 100 percent greater and sometimes 1000 percent greater than those living with others. We have come to the conclusion through the years that relating to other human beings in depth is important not only for our religious health, but also for our psychic and physical health. And a relationship that is upbuilding and healing will be one in which some level of love is shared. So, without genuine interrelationship with other human beings, celibacy requires an heroic stance that is beyond most people and can be destructive if forced upon them.

Another very bad reason for celibacy is to ensure a cheap labor supply. If the priest living alone in a rectory had a wife and children, what he is given as compensation would not keep them all alive, let alone put the children through college. It is much less expensive to use monks and nuns who usually live a life of poverty as well as celibacy than people—even those living very modestly—who live singly or in families in the world. Many nuns with whom we have talked felt that the work they did could have been done just as well by married people, but would have been much more expensive. Celibacy for economic reasons is simply immoral. Even the laborer in the church is worth his or her hire.

When celibacy is practiced because sexuality is perceived as evil, it can become demonic and repressive. A host of moral and psychological problems arise. If, however, celibacy is seen essentially as a sacrifice of something good for a greater good, then it can lead to transcendence. This principle has wide applications. Honesty is an important virtue, but when honesty is viewed as more important than charity and love, it can be hurtful. And when chastity (and celibacy) becomes a higher virtue than genuine loving care, it can actually become destructive. When our sexuality is seen as a good part of life that is sacrificed for something higher or better— loving service or coming closer to the center of being (which is Love), it is not only legitimate, but can be a great and magnificent lifestyle. We believe that celibacy may require a special charism and can be a truly noble profession; however, as long as sex is seen as evil and celibacy is seen as a way of avoiding this evil, celibacy may itself become evil. We wonder if there are enough people with this charism to provide adequate ministers for the entire Church.

If either marriage or celibacy is to work, human beings need to come to some modicum of inner wholeness, come into touch with their own inner contrasexual side. If this does not occur in a marriage one partner is likely to live through the other, rather than developing his or her own inner wholeness and autonomy. Coming to this kind of inner wholeness may be even more important for celibates so that they do not fall into harmful transferences with those with whom they work. This is not the place to discuss the whole matter of individuation and growing toward wholeness. Morton has dealt with this at length in *Christo-Psychology*. In his book *Spiritual Pilgrims, Carl Jung and Teresa of Avila* Father John Welch has shown the many similarities between the psychological way of Jung and the religious psychology of Teresa. Both show that we first deal with our shadows. Then we must deal with our contrasexual natures. We need to deal with all of ourselves. We need a spiritual director with whom to discuss the many difficult issues that raise their heads as we deal with all the strange things we find within. We need a peer group in which we can let down our hair and have understanding and fellowship. We need to have healthy relationships of real intimacy with both men and women.

In his book *The Illness That We Are: A Jungian Critique of Christianity*, John Dourley writes wisely about the inner meaning of celibacy. He is both a Jungian analyst and also a celibate priest:

> The point is that a Christianity which may have rightly need to restrain the sexual excesses of the society in which it first appeared, and indeed excesses in any historical period, may have come to see sexuality itself as somehow peripheral to life, and so conceived of the possibility of healthy life, even or especially the life of spiritual perfection, without it. In some external and merely physical sense the sexual dimension of life could perhaps be considered peripheral, and so dispensable for a 'higher' goal, though this is a dubious proposition at best. But in the light of Jung's exploration of human interiority, the reality of sexuality is neither dispensable nor peripheral to the life of the soul and to spiritual maturation. For Jung, individuation cannot take place without an intense relationship to the contrasexual. Thus the question is not *whether* the sexual will be faced in the pursuit of spiritual and human growth, but *where*. If it is sacrificed in its external manifestations, this can be healthy only if the sacrifice intensifies the inner relationship. Otherwise such spiritual heroics, though they may win a 'supernatural' crown, can only make natural humans sick.[8]

The recent decline in vocations in the Roman Catholic Church has caused some real concern about the practicality of compulsory celibacy. We have already noted the bold statement Basil Cardinal Hume, Archbishop of England, made in the summer of 1985 on married clergy.

A wise abbot told us that men have a tendency to become a little strange when they have no contact with women; women have the same tendency but seem to survive better. Barbara noted when she was hostess in our home for groups of celibate men that it was just as if she were not present; she often felt like a nonbeing. Of course, these men were taught this way of dealing with sexuality in many religious orders in the days before Vatican II.

And finally, without vital prayer lives, without a vital relationship with the loving God, both celibacy and marriage tend to become thinner and thinner. The essential reason for celibacy is to promote relationship with God and service for God; it loses its meaning when it is not integrated into a lively, continuing experience of the loving Other. When celibacy is divorced from prayer it can actually result in cold, unreal people and can cause a lingering resentment and bitterness. In other words, for people to maintain a healthy, vital, creative celibacy or a truly meaningful marriage, they have to maintain living relationship with the One whom they are serving, who constantly reaffirms the importance of love and gives us the strength to continue on growing in our human vocation.

CHAPTER NINE

Homosexualities, Bisexualities, Psychology and Religion[1]

A number of years ago Morton was asked to participate in a panel discussion on the subject of homosexuality aired on a television station in Los Angeles. His role was to speak as a clergyman who had done a considerable amount of counseling with homosexuals. Other people on the panel included a lawyer, a psychiatrist, and a judge. Even before the panel went on the air, the panelists had embarked on a heated discussion, but only a few moments into the actual show, the judge had a cerebral hemorrhage, was rushed to the emergency room, and later died in the hospital. Although this incident was a painfully flamboyant one, it has become representative, for us, of the extreme emotional reactions generated by discussions of homosexuality.

The incident is also significant to us because, before the judge was stricken, the moderator asked Morton a memorable question: "What is the Church's moral attitude toward homosexuality?" Morton gave an inarticulate reply, and only later, after discussing the question with a psychiatrist friend, did he realize the reason for his bumbling response. The friend said, "Of course you have difficulty giving an answer to that question. Homosexuality is no more a matter of morals than the peptic ulcer."

More recently, when Morton was asked to give lectures on the subject of religion and sexuality, we—Barbara and Morton together—began once again to read the literature and to ponder the Christian Church's reactions to the issue. As we tried to fit homosexuality into the total Christian world view, we found that first of all we were appalled at the conventional "Christian" attitude, and then overwhelmed by the complexity of the subject of homosexuality itself. We discovered a morass of different ideas on the subject coming from many different sources.

First there was the popular attitude, and next the legal and social viewpoint (which is closely allied to the popular attitude). Then there were the viewpoints of physical medicine and of psychology. In addition, we discovered many different attitudes toward homosexuality in the literature of comparative religions and in the history of philosophy. And we found still another view of the subject in the expressions emanating from the "gay" world.

To find some order in the confusion, it is important to begin by defining what we are talking about, and then to consider some actual facts. First we must look at the various medical and psychological attitudes and try to see historically how the current ideas about homosexuality came into being; this will necessitate a discussion of the Church's thinking about this subject. Then we will examine the Church's overall attitude toward sickness and psychological variation, and see how this attitude applies to the homosexual. This will bring us to the question of the Christian valuation of love and relationship. And we will conclude by looking at what the Church's attitude and action need to be, based on the teaching and practice of Jesus. In presenting this historical survey we are not presenting our own view which will appear later. We are trying to present as clearly and forcibly as possible the view of those who view homosexual and bisexual acts and attitudes as immoral and pathological. We are not presenting straw effigies to be demolished.

WHAT ARE HOMOSEXUALITIES

Before we even begin we need to look at the language we use. When a word is used to describe a certain set of behaviors, we often think that these behaviors are similar. But the most important fact discovered by Alan Bell and his associates at the Institute for Sex Research at Indiana University was that there are no more common patterns among people with homosexual orientations than there are those with heterosexual inclinations. Kinsey had started to collect these hard data on homosexuality before his death. After a lapse of a decade his former associate, Alan Bell, continued Kinsey's researches in the late 1960's, and he has presented an exhaustive study of the subject in two books, *Homosexualities* and *Sexual Preference: Its Development in Men and Women*. Excellent information on the subject, in other words, is now available, and it indicates that homosexual behaviors vary widely.

It is also dangerous linguistic practice to refer to a person or a group of people by only one aspect of their lives and personalities. To label people as cripples, homosexuals, glasses wearers, blacks or pipesmokers suggests that the people in that group have a common identity. It tells little more about a person to call that individual a homosexual than it does to call him or her a heterosexual. It is important for people with homosexual or heterosexual experience or feelings to realize that simply because of occasional actions or even some persistent feelings that they are not therefore "homosexual" or "heterosexual"—one's sexual orientation is not necessarily the unchangeable and essential characteristic of their lives. Labeling ourselves or others in this way can get us stuck in a dangerous mind set. We must, therefore, try to avoid this use of language.

Homosexualities are the sexual desires and/or actions on the part of one individual toward a member of the same sex. Indeed the Greek word simply means "same sex." "Sexuality", furthermore, includes a full range of physical and emotional forms of expression. Homosexualities, therefore, are empowered with the full energy of the reproductive instinct; they fall into the same category with regard to their potency as the drive for food and self-preservation. They have deep unconscious roots and take the same heroic strength to control as heterosexual desires. Homosexual desires can be expressed in dreams, fantasies, or acts of bodily contact: there are as many variations of physical gratification of the homosexual urge as there are of heterosexual desire. The more common ones are mutual masturbation in various ways, fellatio, cunnilingus and sodomy.[2] These desires, on the other hand, may also be latent—consciously known, but suppressed and sublimated. Some celibates possess homosexual desires of this sort. The desires may also be unconscious and repressed, and therefore they sometimes become expressed in the form of a neurosis because of the unconscious conflict generated within the personality. Some of the rebellious teen-age males of our society who are involved in violence, for example, are probably overcompensating for their unconscious homosexual feelings. There is also probably a relation between unconscious homosexuality and voyeurism, exhibitionism and transvestism. Like the heterosexual act, the homosexual act may be the result of mutual consent and affection, or, if it is purely sensual, it may be a one night stand, the result of seduction, violence or compulsion; it is sometimes associated with sado-masochism. Homosexuality, then, contains the full repertoire of sexual expression, but it happens to be directed toward the same sex rather than the opposite one. We have already detailed seven different levels of sexual expression in Chapter 6, and only one of those levels is not generally present in homosexual experience: having children. (Some women with homosexual preferences, however, have had artificial insemination in order to have children, and some engage in heterosexual intercourse for the same purpose.) But because of popular and legal condemnation, the totally dedicated and loving homosexual relationships are usually unknown or ignored.

There are few subjects about which there is more general prejudice and lack of information; comparable in intensity are the violence of race prejudice and the popular attitudes toward mental illness and mental institutions that existed at the turn of the century. Yet homosexuality is far from rare. Margaret Mead has pointed out that almost all cultures of the world show some evidence of homosexual practice and that in a number of these cultures homosexual orientation earns a person honor and veneration. Mircea Eliade in his definitive book *Shamanism* showed that many of the shamans, both male and female, have this orientation; we have already discussed this aspect of the American sand painter, Hosteen Klah. And an exhaustive cross-cultural study concludes that 64% of the 76 societies investigated permitted homosexuality. In the other 36% of the societies, although homosexual actions were prohibited and punished with varying degrees of severity, they were still clandestinely present. Zoologists, finally, tell us that many non-human mammals indulge in acts of homosexual play, although none remain exclusively homosexual in practice.[3]

We have already mentioned the Kinsey data, but we should repeat it in this context: somewhere between 3-16 percent of the questioned males reported exclusive homosexual behavior, but many of these had been married and had previously experienced heterosexual activity. Only 1 to 3 percent of the women claimed to be exclusively homosexual in sexual activity. Among males, 9 to 32 percent had as much homosexual experience as heterosexual; among women this percentage varied from 4 to 11. And according to Kinsey, less than 50 percent of the men could claim no homosexual experience, and slightly less than 60 percent of the women.

In order to provide some way of dealing with all these variations of practice, we will look at five different groups: those who have decided on exclusive homosexual preference and activity (just as the majority have decided upon exclusive heterosexual activity); people whose orientation is bisexual, who have nearly equal homosexual and heterosexual activity; those whose activity is predominantly heterosexual, but have occasional bisexual activity; those who have some desires for the same sex but who have had no homosexual experience; and last, those who have some homosexual desire, but are totally unaware of it. Only the first group can be considered "homosexuals"; the others would be better called "bisexuals", although it is wiser to speak of *people* who have an exclusive sexual preference, coupled with a sexual activity with the same sex, from those whose sexual desire and active preferences extend to both sexes.

One of the most tragic and unfair old wives' tales is that one or several homosexual acts makes a person "homosexual", and that such a person can henceforth obtain satisfaction only from this kind of sex behavior. Great numbers of men and some women feel that this is their situation. This is particularly the case for the more sensitive and gentle men and for the more assertive and dominant women. It is the basic idea used by heterosexual groups in order to outlaw any homosexual behavior. As we shall see, this can disrupt any genuinely emotional relationship between men— though women are wiser about maintaining affectionate relationships among themselves despite taboos. And the same idea is used, ironically, by some homosexual ("gay") groups in recruiting people to their lifestyle who have had minimal homosexual activity but who are not truly "homosexual".

Three stories speak to the ridiculous nature of this prejudice. A young man of sixteen was referred to Morton by the courts for counseling. His mother had remarried several years before. When the boy was fifteen it was revealed that the stepfather had been having sexual relations with the boy several times a week over a two-year period. The mother divorced her husband and the sexual activity ceased. However, the teenager was having serious inner conflicts. As he and Morton talked it became apparent that although he had submitted to the affectionate and sexual advances of the stepfather, he was entirely heterosexual in preference. Having a chance to talk the whole situation over frankly with him relieved him of his fears and conflicts; he finished school and college, married happily and had children. Even more significant was the case of a man of twenty who came to know a man slightly older who convinced him that he was a "homo-sexual". They lived together for nineteen years before he gradually came to realize that he had heterosexual desires also and that they were really stronger than those he had been acting upon. He and his friend separated. He married and has had a very satisfactory heterosexual relationship and heterosexual sex life. Indeed one person has reported that not infrequently at "gay" parties, where both men and women are present, as the liquor flows freely the guests can be observed making sexual plays for the *opposite sex*. And the converse situation is sometimes seen in similar heterosexual events.

We have already referred to Kinsey's scale, showing that only a relatively small portion of the total populace is entirely either homosexually or heterosexually inclined. William Stayton has commented wisely on what society does to the large number of people who do not fall at either end of the scale.

> Nevertheless, all people, regardless of their place on the scale, are literally forced by our culture and mores to declare either a "0" or a "6" position in the diagram to which I have referred earlier, as a way of life. The result is that when a person *does* feel some physical attraction for a person of the same sex she/he is understandably up-tight about expressing any type of affection for that person for fear of being put down or criticized or of being caught in a socially unac-ceptable pattern. Some may even feel threatened by the mere fact that they *have* attractions for the same sex, and will repress any need or desire for a meaningful relationship with their own gender. Others, who do not repress, and who have some homosexual experience may wrongly believe that they belong in the "6" category and *cannot* develop any heterosexual relationships. The outcome is that a per-son limits his own self acceptance, her own happiness, and/or his ability to develop meaningful relationships. (It should be noted that an understanding of the homosexual and heterosexual components of one's personality does not mean one must act upon those needs through genital expression; such expression would always be in the realm of choice.)[4]

While a small proportion of homosexuals do have bodily characteristics of the opposite sex and some occasionally affect the mannerisms or clothes of the opposite sex, the great majority have no outer physical characteristics that identify them with their sexual predilections. Indeed, many feminine-appearing men are exclusively and enthusiastically heterosexual. The great majority of homosexuals—many of the best adjusted—pass through society without heterosexuals even knowing about their sexual preference. It is a small percentage of identifiable homosexuals who create most of the prejudice, since the popular attitude has until recent years forced the adjusted homosexual to hide his variation.

The laws in England, West Germany and the United States have expressed the popular horror of homosexualities. Sentences ranging from fines to life imprisonment are on the statute books for many American states for the punishment of one homosexual act. Some people are actually imprisoned under these laws. If people commit murder, their friends will probably come to visit them in jail; but if they are in jail for homosexuality, they may find themselves completely shunned by their heterosexual friends.

As with heterosexual people, the object of the homosexual's affection may vary from an adult of the same age to either an older adult, a younger adult, or a child. The actual sexual expression may take place in a fleeting and casual encounter in which the only important factor is sexual release. Or the homosexual act may be merely one aspect of a relationship characterized by commitment, affection, devotion, as well as sexuality, which may even have the quality of the kind of romantic love between the sexes that we discussed in an earlier chapter. In fact, it is almost as meaningless to speak of homosexuality without defining its particular variation as it would be to refer to all heterosexual relationships as if there were no differences between the long-time committed love of a man and a woman involving all levels of sharing and the rape of a young woman by an older man. The value of a relationship will depend upon the mutuality, communication and love expressed within the relationship; this applies to the bond between two people whether they be of different sexes or the same sex.

THE DYNAMICS OF HOMOSEXUAL AND BISEXUAL LOVE

In an earlier chapter we described the insights that depth psychology has provided to help us understand falling in love, the strong erotic bond. Do these same considerations apply to the love between people of the same sex? Can people of the same sex fall in love? One of the most significant aspects of the person with exclusive homosexual desires is that the male has identified sexually with his anima, the feminine aspect of his personality, and the female with the masculine aspect of her psyche, the animus. As we have just noted our society almost forces us to either a full identification with one aspect or another of our inner being. Thus the masculine sexual aspect of the homosexual male will tend to drop into the unconscious, and the feminine sexual aspect of the homosexual woman will disappear out of touch into the unconscious.

The following diagrams explain the dynamic forces at work.

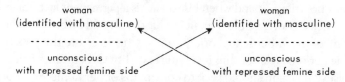

The same forces operate here as with heterosexual love, we explained earlier. There is the same desire for wholeness, the same projection of the unconscious feminine upon a woman, and the same erotic energy released. Exactly the same dynamics take place when the male has identified sexually with a feminine model and his masculinity has dropped into his unconscious. His way of psychosexual wholeness will be to project this unconscious masculinity out upon a man.

Everything that we have said about heterosexual love and its dangers applies here as well. This kind of love is stormy and needs to develop a genuine caring and communication before this tumultuous excitement of in-loveness can become a truly full loving relationship. The pressure of society and children to turn heterosexual infatuation into the more stable kind is notoriously lacking in success, and it is all the more difficult for homosexual relationships, which are discouraged by society, to make this transition. All of these aspects of homosexual love have been described in many places by some of civilization's greatest thinkers and artists. Plato speaks of Socrates' attraction to Charmides, Michaelangelo wrote sonnets to his male beloved, and some of the Shakespearean sonnets are written to the dark-haired youth. In her book *Memoirs of Hadrian*, Marguerite Yourcenar has described the love of the Emperor Hadrian for Antinous. In *Christianity, Social Tolerance and Homosexuality*, John Boswell has provided translations of poems and other writing relating to erotic attachments in medieval monasteries. The poetry of C.P. Cavafy also expresses these themes.

Realizing that reality is both/and rather than either/or is difficult for human beings. The statistics point out that a large number of people who are capable of romantic attraction, sexual love and even deep relations with both sexes. But apart from the literature mentioned above, little is written specifically on this subject; nonetheless, it is important for those who would listen to others and help them upon their psychological, spiritual journeys to understand the conflicts and fears raised by society's condemnation of these feelings and actions so they can be dealt with. Philip Keane, to whom we have referred before, is one of the few to refer to the problem. In *Sexual Morality* he writes: "If and when bisexuality is a permanent fact, the bisexual person who is not capable of perfect chastity should be counseled to control one of his or her sexual orientations, so as to create the possibility of a stable personal relationship involving sexuality. Other things being equal, the bisexual person should seek to control his or her homosexual orientation. Marriage for bisexuals would seem inadvisable until clear controls over the bisexual's homosexual drive has been established." In a footnote to this passage, however, Keane goes on, "If a bisexual person is able to develop a stable sexual orientation only by moving toward homosexuality, this would seem to be preferable to remaining in a state of bisexuality."[5] Although Keane states that much less is known about bisexual adaptations, he concludes that it is better to opt for one exclusive position or the other, and often gay literature states the same point of view. For him it is better to live the exclusive homosexual way of life than remain in a state of tension between the two. We think that this either/or position shows little understanding of the bisexual person's dilemma. If people can contain their sexual actions to one sex, it is easier for them. But many people find that they cannot (and should not) try to stamp out all bisexual feelings.

The same sort of diagram as we have sketched above also applies to the bisexual and bierotic interest and lifestyle. Here both men and women are consciously androgynous; they identify with elements of both the masculine and feminine, but other aspects of each have fallen into the unconscious. Thus people with this orientation will be most attracted to people of a similar androgynous nature, but they can also fall in love with and relate in depth to the same or the opposite physical sex.

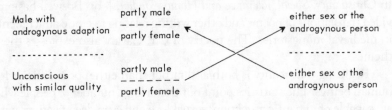

Jung writes of this situation in a chapter "The Love Problem of a Student" in *Civilization in Transition*:

> Homosexual relations between students of either sex are by no means uncommon. So far as I can judge of this phenomenon, I would say that these relationships are less common with us, and on the continent generally, than in certain other countries where boy and girl college students live in strict segregation. I am speaking here not of pathological homosexuals who are incapable of real friendship and meet with little sympathy among normal individuals, but of more or less normal youngsters who enjoy such a rapturous friendship that they also express their feelings in sexual form. With them it is not just a matter of mutual masturbation, which in all school and college life is the order of the day among the younger age group, but of a higher and more spiritual form, which deserves the name "friendship" in the classical sense of the word. When such a friendship exists between an older man and a younger its educative significance is undeniable. A slightly homosexual teacher, for example, often owes his brilliant educational gifts to his homosexual disposition. The homosexual relation between an older and a younger man can thus be of advantage of both sides and have a lasting value. An indispensable condition for the value of such a relation is the steadfastness of the friendship and their loyalty to it. But only too often this condition is lacking.[6]

Jung goes on to say that such experiences do not impede heterosexual development. Whatever else we can say about sexuality, we can affirm that it is much more varied and fluid than most of us have been taught to believe. How important to know this and to be open, without condemnation, to whatever people tell us about themselves.

A very gifted psychologist with three children came to see Morton. He was divorced. He had had strong homosexual desires as well as heterosexual ones. He was a deeply religious person. He had had many torrid heterosexual affairs in which he played something of the Don Juan. These affairs helped to allay his fears of his homosexual feelings. When he came to see Morton he was in middle life and had never told anyone of his inner sexual conflicts; reading what Morton had written in *Prophetic Ministry* on homosexualities had given him the courage to share his story. His relief at being readmitted into the human race was very moving. One of the few studies of bisexuality is Dr. Fred Klein's *The Bisexual Option, A Concept of*

One-Hundred Percent Intimacy. The author presents statistics showing the frequency of this sexual adaptation as well as many case studies.[7]

Certainly those with conscious bisexual desires pose real problems for their spouses when and if they get married or enter a long time relationship and many of their relationships do end early. But these problems are probably not much greater than those of men who find that their anima attractions move to other women, or of women like Bizet's Carmen whose passionate love moves from man to man. Romantic love, in other words, is transitory; however, the path of truly committed caring is a path of growth and salvation in no matter what kind of relationship—but one of great existential satisfaction.

SEVERAL WAYS OF LOOKING AT HOMOSEXUALITY

The popular approach of our culture, which condemns all homosexual behavior and sees no distinctions, is only one of several different value judgments directed toward homosexuality. This popular attitude concludes that individuals involved in homosexual acts perversely desire to participate in such behavior and are purposefully defying the social conventions—they could change if would just try. Along with this attitude goes the belief that they *must* be changed, and since the perversity lies in the will, it is only through punishment that they can be brought to change. But there is no shred of evidence supporting this point of view. Indeed, because of the social sanctions against homosexualities, many people with such inclinations *have* desired and tried to change, but without success. Still this negative attitude remains the basis of most of the legal statutes in this country. I have yet to find one homosexual person, however, whose basic pattern was changed by legal punishment. Instead, punitive imprisonment simply places the individual in a situation that is more favorable to the unsavory forms of the homosexualities.

The view of physical medicine involves a second judgment, accepted by many of this profession, that homosexuality is either a physical, glandular, or brain-wired predisposition about which little or nothing can be done. Homosexuality, according to this theory, is either an anomaly like left-handedness or an extra toe, or a physiological or psychic defect like color blindness or a club foot. Of course, if this were true then there would be little point in punishing homosexuals, except to protect the public who are offended by this particular human variation or to limit the practices of this variation to those among whom these practices are not offensive.

With the studies and theories of Freud a new phase in the discussion of all sexual variations arose. Freud made the hypothesis that human beings are essentially bisexual and capable of reacting sexually to either the opposite or the same sex. Nothing in his analytic experience gave him reason to doubt this hypothesis. He believed that changing the homosexual was seldom achieved, although younger people without a strong psychic predisposition might be changed more often than older people. He felt that through analysis, however, a homosexual person could adjust to his or her situation.

Although Jung usually put more emphasis upon the psychic inheritance than did Freud, Jung seemed to stress the *environmental* causes of this variant behavior as well. In what can be gleaned from his scattered references, he saw male homosexualities as the result of a mother complex, of an identification with the feminine psychic framework usually induced by closeness to one's own mother. His conclusions suggest that this early predisposing factor must be present in order for extensive homosexual feelings and behavior to develop as a result of seduction. In fact, one of Morton's friends, a psychiatrist whose practice is basically Jungian, has argued that the term "homosexual" fails to describe the actual fact; the expression for male homosexualities, he feels, should be "ascendancy of the feminine." And female homosexualities would be understood as a female identification with the father or the masculine, an "ascendancy of the masculine". In any case, Jung would undoubtedly see psychic inheritance as at least one factor in the development of these sexual attitudes.

In modern psychoanalytic theory, as we have pointed out in an earlier chapter, homosexuality is sometimes seen as one stage in the development toward full heterosexuality. The individual is drawn first to the same sex because he relates to the known more easily than to the unknown. The person then remains in this polymorphously perverse stage. Homosexualities, then, in this third view are a sickness in that they are a fixation at an immature stage of development, although this is using the term "sickness" in a loose way. The sickness described is due more to the inability to participate in heterosexual experience than to the presence of the homosexual feelings or acts themselves.

According to the various schools of depth psychology, altering this personality variation is extremely difficult; it requires that individuals change their identification with an essential part of their psychic role. This may be possible where motivation is very great, and where insight and ego strength are also present; but even under the best circumstances it requires exceptional effort on the part of both analyst and patient. Condemning one who backs away from this kind of effort hardly makes sense—unless all of us who do not exert the greatest effort toward the full development of our own personality are also ready to accept condemnation.

Still another psychiatric viewpoint was expressed by the late Dr. Blanche Baker, who counseled many people with a homosexual orientation and worked with the Mattachine Society educationally. She once stated in a radio interview: "I feel that a homosexual is, first of all, a human being. Now that may seem to be a rather elementary statement, but I very much believe in the individual adjustment problem, and I think that homosexuality may have many different kinds of causes, and each individual case needs to be studied and interpreted on its own merits. I do not look upon homosexuality as a neurotic problem, but more a basic personality pattern reaction. Just as some people prefer blondes and other prefer brunettes, I think that the fact that a given person may prefer the love of the same sex is his personal business. Now, this does not mean that homosexuals may not become neurotic—I think that they often do, because society is so hostile to them and their own families do not understand them, so they are subject to a great many pressures and a great deal of unhappiness."[8] Our own view lies close to this, with the difference that it is a generally Jungian approach (about which we shall say more later).

Finally, there is a certain segment of the homosexual society which expresses the views, in articles and novels, that the homosexual adaptation is superior to the heterosexual—a final, crowning mutation. The heterosexual world, from this perspective, is to be looked down on. But there is little objective evidence to support the position that the homosexual is more advanced than heterosexuals or is psychologically superior to them. People with this attitude, furthermore, often proselytize among people who have bisexual feelings, an activity that is as offensive as the heterosexual pressure that is more commonly placed on people.

And after all these explanations we still find ourselves asking what really causes the development of the exclusive homosexual orientation or the permanent bisexual orientation in human beings. But we might as well ask: What causes the development of the heterosexual orientation? *Nature produces all three.* According to the best knowledge at this time, there are no convincing or generally accepted answers. Undoubtedly there is a genetic factor in people who are exclusively homosexual or heterosexual. The evidence does not suggest, however, that this is the case in people with a bisexual orientation. It seems that good relationships with a strong parental figure of the same sex often have an influence that turns people toward an exclusive heterosexual orientation, and that negative relationships with the parent of the same sex and very strong attractions to an unconsciously seductive parent of the opposite sex seem to push people toward a bisexual or homosexual preference. But there appear to be no absolute answers.

ONE GOOD QUESTION

In this sketchy survey, we have ignored one good question that deserves to be asked: Is homosexuality a sickness? Certainly it is not a physical disability in the ordinary sense of the word, and psychologically there seems to be no direct connection between homosexuality and mental illness. Dr. Evelyn Hooker, one of the leading experts on homosexuality, has made careful studies of both homosexuals and heterosexuals. With her years of work on the subject, most of it under a federal grant, Dr. Hooker had access to a sufficient number of individuals living a stable homosexual lifestyle for comparative study, and she also worked with groups of people with a basic heterosexual orientation, selected at random. Using the best testing tools available—the Rorschach, the MMPI and the T.A.T., which can pick out the psychotic and neurotic personality with considerable accuracy— she was unable to distinguish those who preferred homosexual behavior from those with a heterosexual pattern. No significant variations were found, other than a slightly higher rating in general intelligence for people with the homosexual lifestyle. Apparently homosexuals as a group are no more psychotic or neurotic, and probably no more immature than their heterosexual brothers and sisters. Dr. Hooker's conclusions are similar to those of Dr. Baker; her basic observation is that there is no easy understanding of this sexual problem.

It is true that those with a homosexual disposition may be immature, and if they are unconscious of their bisexual desires, they may manifest neurotic symptoms. Perhaps because of the difficulty of their situation, they may seek psychological help more often than heterosexuals, and that is why their immaturity is rather well-known. Still the best-adjusted homosexuals would rarely be seen in a psychiatrist's office. The American Psychiatric Association formally voted within the last several years to accept Dr. Hooker's view and no longer list homosexuality as a sickness. And, in any case, if we define sickness as the inability or unwillingness to conform to society's regulations, then many others besides those with the homosexual way of life—including many religious groups, such as the Christians of the first centuries of our era—would come under this designation.

People with strong homosexual desires are subject to more sexual tension than are those who follow the cultural norm, in part simply because they are often placed in situations that are analogous to a dormitory of chorus girls in which a group of heterosexually active males have been housed. And just as there are sick people with heterosexual adaptations, these are sick people with homosexual patterns. They usually have little control over their sexual impulses (certainly they are likely to express them in an antisocial way); these are the homosexuals who tend to clash with the predominant social group, either because of their lack of control or through a deliberate, rebellious flaunting of their difference before the public eye. Many people assume that all people with homosexual needs are like this, which is just as logical as thinking that, based only on what we read in the newspapers, all heterosexuals are rapists.

It is questionable, therefore, whether objective studies can evaluate homosexuality entirely in terms of sickness, any more than they can look at it solely as a problem of prostitution or perversity. Neither evaluation takes into account the full scope of the complexities surrounding homosexuality. At the present writing not enough is known about the origin of homosexual behavior to decide whether it is hormonal, brain-wired, a psychic predisposition, socially induced, or a learned way of acting. It appears to be a complex combination of all these factors.

THE ORIGIN OF THESE ATTITUDES IN OUR CULTURE

The Judeo-Christian attitude toward homosexual behavior during the last six centuries has been one of violent condemnation of any homosexual act. This is quite different from the attitude of the Great Mother cults of Asia Minor, of shamanism, and of other religious groups. The Christian

Church took over and expanded the old Judaic laws against homosexual behavior that are found in Leviticus 18:22 and in 20:13 and in Deuteronomy 23:17, and that represent the essential attitude expressed by Paul in Romans 1:25ff, I Corinthians 6:9-10, and I Timothy 1:10. The same disapproval of the practice has also been understood to be expressed in the story of Sodom in Genesis 19:5, and in a similar story in Judges 19:22. The penalty for homosexual acts in the older Jewish code was death, and although there is a question as to how frequently it was invoked, the disapproval was as vehement as it was for nearly every other sexual variation from bestiality to adultery (for the female) and even to the nearly universal practice of masturbation.[9]

But there is nothing specifically in the teachings of Christ to encourage us to continue the violence of this rejection;[10] yet it appears that many leaders of the Christian church took over the Jewish attitude without re-examination. One reason for this Jewish rejection was the fear that population growth would be deterred if the male semen were not put to productive use. Another reason was the common practice of female and male homosexual prostitution in the Mother cult religions of the Near East and the fact that anything to do with these religions was rejected, whether it was the sacred groves or mediumship or divination or interpretation of dreams by the foreign priests. In no place was homosexual activity viewed as a sickness or affliction over which the individual might have little or no control; it was viewed purely in moral terms.

As Christianity developed in the Graeco-Roman world, one of the greatest difficulties was in teaching the control of the instinctive life. Lack of control led to lack of containment and so to a lack of psychological growth and of a conscious direction of the personality, and this led to a lack of mature spirituality. Christianity, therefore, stood for control and direction; early in the Church great emphasis was laid especially upon sexual control, and gradually the attitude that sex was not quite nice crept into Christian thought, even though there was little basis for this in the teachings of Jesus. Finally, particularly in the writing of Augustine, the view that sexual expression was only permissible for reproduction came to predominate. From the point of view of "natural law", only sexual relationships that lead to reproduction were natural. All other acts—masturbation or any action between two partners of the opposite sex, such as oral intercourse or sodomy, let alone homosexual acts—were unnatural, against nature, against God, etc. This same attitude still dominates our secular legal statutes today.

There is little reason to go into the unsavory history of the Church's attempt to stamp out homosexuality through law, punishment and persecution. John Boswell has written a definitive study of this subject in his book, *Christianity, Social Tolerance, and Homosexuality*,[11] published in 1980. This Yale professor of history maintains that the early Church's official attitude toward homosexual behavior was not as violently antagonistic as the popular Christian attitude of the thirteenth century which Aquinas redacted into dogma. The same age burned witches and heretics, fought infidels and banished usurers. Boswell also maintains that the Greek language had no word for homosexual, and that many of the New Testament words translated as "homosexual" actually refer to a male prostitute. Boswell's work is a fine piece of scholarship, and it should be studied by anyone dealing with the subject of homosexualities in the Church.

It is certainly open to question whether the moral laws of late Christian heritage have a place in our legal structure when they refer to a practice that may be a sickness or an involuntary affliction or merely a preference of taste rather than a moral problem. If this is true, then by the same logic we should also have laws against tuberculosis and the peptic ulcer. (Samuel Butler's *Erewhon* contains a grimly satirical picture of such an imaginary culture, which puts the sick in prison and gives treatment to the criminal.) It is hard to calculate the effect of legislation against sexual behavior. In homosexually inclined individuals who are struggling with their own nature, these laws can raise up rebellious attitudes toward society and so bring forth the most negative aspects of the homosexualities. And all essentially bi-sexual individuals are also viewed, from this restrictive legal standpoint, as "homosexuals"; this has surely caused some with a homosexual lifestyle to select it out of rebellion against such laws.

A real difficulty emerges as we try to develop a Biblical morality that represents the Old Testament, Jesus, and some of his interpreters in the New Testament. Jews need to interpret the Old Testament and do so through the *Mishna* and the *Talmud*. Jesus exhibits two attitudes toward old Testament law: one, that it is to be set aside; and the other, that not a marking of the Hebrew text is to be changed. As we read the New Testament and deal with the risen Jesus in prayer and meditation, it seems to us that the only law of Jesus (and he as the incarnation is for Christians the most comprehensive moral revelation) is the law of love—the love ethic—which is constantly being brought to bear on whatever sexual mores are dominant in a given culture, country or period. As a Christian, one cannot pick and choose amid the many regulations of the Old Testament except on the basis of Jesus' attitude. Jesus is the Christian *Mishna* and *Talmud*. To accept the Old Testament's condemnation of homosexualities as a direct statement from God is questionable unless at the same time we accept the Old Testament's approval of slavery and polygamy, and its relegation of women to the status of mere property. An overturning of these Old Testament attitudes is implicit in Jesus' teaching, but only recently has this been accepted by the Christian churches (and some of them have not accepted Jesus' teaching yet).

This is not to suggest that homosexual behavior or premarital sexual activity is or should be the norm of society. It is as offensive when gays try to make their lifestyle the norm as it is when heterosexual people try to force everyone into *their* mold. The best social ideals remain justice and Christian charity, which view all people in and through the infinite love and mercy of the dying and rising Jesus.

> It is worth remembering that along with Jews—communists, gypsies, the disabled, and homosexuals went into the ovens of Auschwitz. . . . We believe the Spirit is inviting humanity to a homecoming banquet where Arab and Jew, male and female, Russian and American, white and people of color, gay and straight will sit down at table together with our Lord, in mutual acceptance and peace. The church of Christ is called to embody such reconciliation now.[12]

Why is there such horror of homosexualities in the culture today? One factor today is the AIDS epidemic, but there is more to it than that. It appears that the distaste for sexuality in general has been focused on this one expression of it. It seems that after repressing the bisexual nature of human beings, our society has come to fear that men and women will be more attracted to the homosexual way of life than to the heterosexual; what is denied expression tends to become overvalued, and at the same time to be feared inordinately. In societies where there is little attempt to discourage homosexual activity, cultural studies show that most young males and females pass through a homosexual phase to a heterosexual adjustment, and that only about one percent remain in a homosexual lifestyle. In societies with violent antagonism to homosexuality somewhere between six and ten percent remain in a homosexual adaptation. Many societies, in fact, provide initiation rites to help the male make this transition from the feminine identification with the mother to a masculine one, while our society offers almost no help in this area. Instead, our society has repressed homoerotic desire, and this has created a fear that young men and women will be lured into homosexual activity if homosexual practice in any form is permitted. In part this is the kind of ordinary fear that most of us have for the unknown, for anything that is strange or different. But in the main it is a *neurotic* fear in that it is not realistic, since there is little evidence that persons who are not already predisposed to homosexuality will be attracted to that sexual expression. Indeed the very fear of our society may push some people in the direction of the homosexualities.

THE CHRISTIAN ATTITUDE TOWARD SICKNESS

Christianity's attitude toward sickness and most abberrant behavior has been quite different from that of many religious groups. Most of the religious communities in the ancient world, from the pagan to the Jewish, viewed sickness as a visitation of the gods; indeed, we still find this attitude in many places in the world. The sick individual, from such a viewpoint, is the tainted one, to be avoided and shunned as a moral leper. Christians, on the other hand, at first understood sickness of mind and body to be the result of some evil force in the universe—the destructive, the uncreative breaking out in human beings. Their task, instead of condemning or avoiding the sick, was to bring them the healing available both through the Holy Spirit and through medicine. Within the Christian framework, there was no judgment placed upon the sick.

But as Teutonic pagan ideas filtered into the Church during the Dark Ages, the Western Church forgot the basic teaching of Christ on sickness and adopted instead the idea that sickness is a punishment from God; virtue consists of simply enduring this punishment. Thus, if enduring sickness is a virtue, the Church has no reason to take it away. But this is sheer nonsense in the light of Christ's teaching. The clear task of the disciple of Christ is to preach, to teach, and to heal—to defeat the forces of evil in every way. If the homosexualities, then, are seen as a physical illness, there is no reason for the Church to condemn or avoid it, but every reason for it to come forward to offer help and understanding. When the pagan emperor Julian made fun of Christians for caring for the cripples, the sick and the poor, he left no doubt about the kind of concern they showed. A true Christianity would offer the same concern for the homosexualities if it were consistent and prejudices were well in hand.[13]

If, on the other hand, homosexualities are a psychic illness, then the importance of acceptance and concern is even greater. Jesus evidently had considerable success in healing the mentally ill. He *never* condemned those in that condition. We have seen, however, that modern psychiatry no longer views homosexualities as mental illness.

If in Jungian terminology the homosexualities are seen as an incomplete detachment from one's contrasexual side, the feminine in the male and the masculine in the female, it is important to be conscious of this condition on the path to wholeness. Some people may wish to work at creating a greater detachment from their contrasexual side and so be freer from their sexual desires for the same sex. Other people may discover that this contrasexual side is so much a part of the very fabric of their personalities that they would be reduced to rubble if they tried to remove these attachments. These people need to be helped to integrate their desires for the same sex in the most meaningful and loving way that is possible. As we shall see in a few pages, Jung does not view either a deep relationship to one's own contrasexual side or its expression of the homosexualities as necessarily negative.

To view these contrasexual feelings as demons possessing us goes against the facts that point to our bisexual natures. To try to exorcise these contrasexual feelings is to strike at the very structure of the psyche and does violence to the soul, mind and body of people; and if it were to succeed, could even inhibit a person's capacity to love at all. We remember at this point the importance of love in the teachings of Jesus. Fortunately most attempts at trying to exorcise these feelings are unsuccessful and either bring an added sense of guilt upon the person treated in this way or cause duplicity as the person hides true feelings from the person trying to exorcise them.

The same thing is true if homosexualities are merely a fixation at a lower level of maturity. Very few people are spurred by hate and contempt to grow and develop toward maturity; love and acceptance again offer the only route to healing, even though these can be confrontative at times. This is one reason for the emphasis on love in Christian practice and on loving concern in psychotherapy. The attitude of rejection is common in most churches and in most of society, Church and society end up collaborating to exacerbate the problem of homosexuality rather than solving it.

Even if homosexualities are essentially a moral problem—although, as we have noted, it is hard to find objective evidence for this that does not raise doubts about the "morality" of most of us, if the same observations still hold true. One does not change people by rejecting them and refusing to view them as valuable. Seldom is anyone transformed by judgement. Acceptance and love provide the tools for moral transformation, and so the church's attitude can hardly be supported even on this ground. Jung has pointed out that, although the church often treats a doubter as contemptuously as an estranged wife, non-believers are actually changed only when the church becomes secure enough not to be threatened by them but rather to meet them with loving concern and interest. Likewise, when the church is no longer threatened by the actions or rebellion of those adopting a homosexual way of life, it may be able to offer them acceptance and help.

But if homosexual desires and actions are neither sick nor immoral but are mere variations of nature, the attitude of Western society and the Church is cruel indeed. Whether the homosexual condition is psychic or physical or a little of each, whether it originates more in the environment or from heredity, people with homosexual inclinations are not responsible for these factors, and there is little they can do to change them. This being the case, homosexual people are being judged morally for feelings over which they have as little control as they have over the color of their hair. Or, if it is only the actions that are objectionable, is it possible to deny people an expression of themselves that is so large a part of other people's lives, simply because the constitution of these people is such that homosexual actions are their way of expressing their sexual desire? The fact that the sex drive is directed toward non-heterosexual expressions in no way diminishes the power of the drive itself; among heterosexual people only a few particularly gifted individuals are able to suppress and sublimate their sexual expression completely. A very astute and honest heterosexual man once said that a man and woman can remain friends only so long; the same essential truth applies to all but the most disciplined homosexually-oriented people, once they realize that a mutual sexual feeling exists between them.

If, then, homosexualities are merely a variant type of personality (and this is our position), the performing of homosexual actions is hardly a moral question if these actions are not exercised with force, or upon those who have no right to consent, or in a way that is dangerous to health, or in the open violation of public decency—rules that apply to heterosexual acts as well. In these circumstances it would seem that the task of the Church and society is to offer people with a homosexual preference understanding, helping them to change their sexual preference if they wish, to find a meaningful relationship, or to control or sublimate their desires, or to abstain from sexual activity altogether, as individual circumstances dictate. Homosexuals would thus be encouraged and helped not to use sex as an avoidance of relationship, but as a part of an abiding and meaningful one. And this brings us to the matter of relationship and love.

RELATIONSHIP AND LOVE IN CHRISTIANITY

We have already seen that Christianity has always placed a high value upon human relationship. One of the basic themes of the New Testament is that we cannot love God if we do not love our brothers and sisters. The experience of caring for others, of love, of agape (to use the Greek word for the most self-giving form of love), is one way in which we are given genuine access to the realm of the spirit. This is not accomplished by thinking or acting logically, but by something quite different. Unless our experience of God is related to human caring, even our experiences of the spirit may be confused and deluded. Love gives access to God and to another dimension of reality. This is the basic teaching of Jesus, of Paul, of John (particularly in the first Epistle), of St. Francis, St. Catherine of Siena, Martin Luther King and Mother Teresa.

It was undoubtedly this that made the philosophy of Plato so influential in the basic thinking of the very early Church. Plato's main concern is with the world of forms—the eternal, unchanging realities that lie behind the transitory things of this world. He claims that human beings reach this realm not through intellect or self-directed imagination, but rather through what he calls "divine madness"—the experience of the dream (a cathartic kind of madness), of prophecy, of artistic madness, and of the madness of love itself. A knowledge of the eternal realm is given, according to Plato, in each of these experiences. In the *Symposium* and particularly in the *Phaedrus*, Plato makes this very clear. Paul Friedlander in his book *Plato* and Joseph Pieper in his discussion of Plato, *Love and Inspiration*, both emphasize this.[14]

Love as we have already indicated, is a very mysterious force, and one with strange consequences. But the Western Church has more or less forgotten about the importance of the strange and the mysterious; for several centuries now it has had its thinking determined, not by the Platonic understanding, but by the rationalism of Aristotle and Descartes, with their emphasis on reason and the mind. Consequently the Church has become almost antagonistic to the irrational aspects of religious experience. Those who speak in tongues, have visions, and dream dreams come in for a rejection comparable to that inflicted upon people with homosexual inclinations. Where reason is enthroned as ultimate, all the divine madnesses— all the nonrational religious encounters that are so central to the thinking of Plato and so foreign to that of Aristotle—are inevitably devalued, love included.

We must re-discover, in our time, the truth that when a man and woman have come to a deep abiding relationship of love in which physically, emotionally, and spiritually their lives are blended together into a harmony of closeness and yet distinction, there is expressed in reality that mystical union which exists between Christ and the Church. Most modern churches romanticize marriage but fail to see what it can become in honesty and reality. And when we look at these facts, we must also realize that the love Plato speaks about includes love between men and men, and between women and women, and that this can give the same access to new levels of spiritual reality as we have seen in some examples of heterosexual love. In the deep commitment and sharing of lives that we call love, another dimension of reality does open up. There are people who have experienced this breakthrough through homosexual love and spoken of it in our own time. We may not like to face the facts, but in spite of the condemnation of much of the Christian Church, they appear to be the religious facts.

Dr. C. G. Jung has given an interesting support to this thesis in a profound passage in which he discusses the positive side of a mother complex, which in his mind is related to homosexual activity. He wrote:

> Since a 'mother-complex' is a concept borrowed from psychopathology, it is always associated with the idea of injury and illness. But if we take the concept out of its narrow psychopathological setting and give it a wider connotation, we can see that it has positive effects as well. Thus a man with a mother-complex may have a finely differentiated Eros instead of, or in addition to, homosexuality. (Something of this sort is suggested by Plato in his *Symposium*.) This gives him a great capacity for friendship, which often creates ties of aston-

ishing tenderness between men and may even rescue friendship between the sexes from the limbo of the impossible. He may have good
taste and an aesthetic sense which are fostered by the presence of
a feminine streak. Then he may be supremely gifted as a teacher
because of his almost feminine insight and tact. He is likely to have
a feeling for history, and to be conservative in the best sense and
cherish the values of the past. Often he is endowed with a wealth
of religious feelings, which help to bring the ecclesia spiritualis into
reality; and a spiritual receptivity which makes him responsive to
revelation.[15]

Although to many with homosexual fears the problem of their sexuality
may, for good reason, be a grave concern, Jung points out that homosexual
feelings are often just a peripheral aspect of a whole personality development that is far from totally negative. Many of the people with homosexual
and bisexual inclinations, active and latent, whom we have counseled have
found in this passage from Jung's works a penetrating description of themselves and a source of hope for dealing with their own personality problems
as well as providing an understanding of their religious interest and
experience.

    In another context Jung also shows that there is far more involved in
homosexualities than simply a pathological problem. In discussing the
general question of therapy he wrote:

> The growing youth must be able to free himself from the anima
> fascination of his mother. There are exceptions, notably artists, where
> the problem often takes a different turn; also homosexuality, which
> is usually characterized by identity with the anima. In view of the
> recognized frequency of this phenomenon, its interpretation as a
> pathological perversion is very dubious. The psychological findings
> show that it is rather a matter of incomplete detachment from the
> hermaphroditic archetype, coupled with a distinct resistance to
> identity with the role of a one-sided sexual being. Such a disposition
> should not be adjudged negative in all circumstances, in so far as
> it preserves the archetype of the Original Man, which a one-sided
> sexual being has, up to a point, lost.[16]

    One of Jung's basic ideas is that the male is given access to the un-
conscious through the anima or feminine aspect of his personality. Through

the anima, therefore, men can be given access to the realms of archetypal powers and the divine itself. And through the animus, the masculine element in the woman's psyche, the woman is given the ability to differentiate the contents of the unconscious and so come to a clearer understanding of her experience. We have observed that men in touch with their feminine sides, their animas, are indeed often deeply moved by spiritual considerations. It seems unfortunate that those with a natural openness to the spiritual domain should be condemned because of one aspect of their personalities, by churches and synagogues which claim to value openness to the Spirit. (We have perceived that women on the whole are more open to religious attitudes and understandings, and that being in touch with the animus does not have usually the same religious effect upon them as the contrasexual configuration does for men.)

As one studies the whole subject of homosexualities objectively and dispassionately, it is difficult to come up with the totally negative reaction to it that is found in the popular culture. It is true that there are outer manifestations among certain rebellious and sick people with homosexual lifestyles that give rise, quite understandably, to society's prejudices, but these troubled individuals are not an adequate sample of the homosexual population, nor do they represent the essential quality of this sexual variation. Rebellious and sick people are found among those with a heterosexual orientation as well.

THE CHURCH'S ROLE

There are three areas in which the Church needs to be involved as far as ministry to people with homosexual or bisexual behavior is concerned —educational, legal and pastoral. All blind prejudice is a bad thing, so the Church needs to provide a means for groups of people to speak out in an enlightened way on the subject of homosexualities, bisexualities and heterosexualities. Just as the Church has taken a stand against discrimination against minorities, it needs to speak out against unjust sexual discrimination—wherever it occurs. But this will only happen when priests, ministers, pastoral counselors, lay people and all concerned people find the ability to take a stand in spite of whatever prejudices exist in their congregations.

We must realize, however, that taking such a stand is not easy. It may demand that some ministers fight an uphill battle—perhaps even losing their jobs. Or it may cause tensions among Church members themselves. The furor surrounding Proposition 14 on equal housing opportunities for racial minorities on the California ballot in 1964 showed us how heated emotions can be when prejudice is pinched. And for their part, people with homosexual inclinations need to learn, as much as possible, to understand the fears many people have of homosexualities, fears which cause prejudice and blind hatred.

The Church also should shoulder the burden of helping families to assist sons, brothers and fathers to make an adaptation to a male identity, when this is indicated, and to help daughters to a feminine identity. Sometimes this process requires education about psychosexual growth; sometimes it means establishing initiation rites for young men and women so they have a stronger feeling of identity with their masculinity and femininity. A strong, healthy family life is probably the greatest way to foster healthy sexual adaptations, both male and female, but if a father or mother figure, or a strong male or female identity, is lacking at home, the Church may on occasion step in and fill this gap. Currently many young men and women with homosexual feelings can find entirely unbiased people to talk freely with only in homosexual groups—not in the Church or in the family. Churches need to provide a setting where fears, doubts, anxieties, hopes and longings can be expressed without censure or judgment.

We have already shown that the common belief that one homosexual act makes a permanent homosexual adaptation is fallacious. This notion is an old wives' tale with no foundation in fact. It comes as a great relief to people who have had homosexual feelings—or who have even performed homosexual acts—to discover, within a sympathetic context, that these feelings and acts do not necessarily make them one-sided beings. Human beings are basically bisexual; rarely do we find people who are totally homosexual or totally heterosexual. The continuum along which our sexual feelings are found is a multipointed one. (Perhaps the loneliest of all people are those who are consciously aware of their bisexual nature—and almost all of us have some bisexual attitudes—since most of our society's individuals and groups, both homosexual and heterosexual, negate the existence of bisexuality and press people to see things in black-and-white terms only.)

With regard to the area of the law, the Church needs to be actively engaged in working toward the repeal of those laws against homosexual acts (and certain heterosexual acts) that are unrealistic and un-Christian. If certain homosexual acts damage other members of society, then, of course, this damage must be defined legally. But if we are dealing with what can only be termed private morality among consenting adults, then the law should not punish these "offenses". And, if we view homosexualities either as mere variations or as a kind of disease, how absurd it is to have laws against them! The American Bar Association, the Woolfenden Report in England, and the Church of England have all taken stands that say no legal sanctions should be brought against mutually consenting adults. Indeed, English law has actually been changed because of this. Can the Church in America do less?

What, then, should be punishable by law? Lack of public control where indecency and public nuisance become issues, or where acts are physically damaging, or use of force (i.e., rape), or the practice of promulgating homosexual or heterosexual practice among children and teenagers should certainly be illegal. And it goes without saying, of course, that in fighting bad laws, the Church should be sure that it isn't fostering or aiding variant heterosexual or homosexual behavior to become the norm.

Perhaps the most important thing of all is for the Church to remember the words of the Gospel: "Judge not, lest you be judged." Each person, regardless of his or her sexual adaptation, must be treated as a person in the pastoral ministry of the Church. The homosexualities are never singled out for condemnation in the sayings of Jesus. How, then, can the Church be less tolerant than Jesus is in its attitudes?

Our own basic belief is that the homosexualities are not a matter of morality, and that using moral judgment in this area only creates a greater problem. We repeat once again that it is not clear whether homosexuality is basically psychological or physiological, and it certainly depends on our definition of sickness whether we regard the homosexualities as an illness or simply as a variation in sexual adaptation.

The Church must, then, offer counseling services for people who are confused about their sexual orientation or who wish to explore the possibility of making a different adaptation. Even if one concludes that homosexualities express a state of being caught in an arrested development, then still it is incumbent on the Church to provide loving acceptance and help. Condemnatory action and judgmental attitudes seldom move anyone beyond where he or she is; they merely enforce a paralysis at the current stage of development.

In addition, if the Church is to be truly helpful it must have clergy, religious and lay persons who are secure in their own sexual identities, who are dealing with their own sexual problems; and who can bring a true objectivity to a situation that is often distorted, muddled and hard to deal with.

Even the most deliberately conscious and sincere person can make mistakes. We have certainly made our mistakes. This is particularly true of clergy who are trained as experts in intellectual theology rather than as pastors. In his autobiography, *Some Day I'll Find You*, the well-known British clergyman, H.A. Williams, tells of how his attitudes on homosexual lifestyle changed.

> A young man of about twenty-five called on me one morning and told me that he had made his confession to me the previous day. He asked me whether I would have given him absolution had I known what he was now going to tell me—that all the time he had no intention whatever of discontinuing to sleep with his boyfriend of the same age. The answer to his enquiry seemed to me quite clear. The books said that homosexual practices were wrong. If the young man had no intention at all of amendment of life in this respect, then he could not be given absolution. And that is what I told him. I now only hope that he disregarded everything I said. I had given no consideration whatever to the delicate, complicated, vulnerable humanity not only of my penitent but also of his friend, nor had I taken into account the fact the real genuine love, God's greatest gift making us only a little lower than the angels, can find expression in an infinite variety of way, including those which any particular culture may find unacceptable.[17]

Those of us who wish to be of help to people with sexual problems of all kinds, and particularly with problems as sensitive as matters of sexual identity, need to learn something more than theology. We need four skills:

1. We need to learn to listen without judging. We must be able to turn "right" and "wrong" off so that we can truly listen without immediately submitting everything we hear to our own value system. The people who have come for counseling are usually judging themselves too harshly already, so much, indeed, that they are cutting themselves off from the love offered by Christ.

2. We need to know enough about sexuality to realize how fluid it is and how easily people can be influenced by what we do, say and are.

People need a place where they can talk, think, readjust their ideas and assess their desires in a loving, caring environment. We can solve many problems by just being with people where they are, treating them with caring openness, and allowing ourselves to become vehicles of the transforming spirit of God.

3.   When we can encourage some to move from promiscuous, un-related or violent sex to a real relationship with a single partner, we will bring them to a sense of the holiness of love (and we will also help them in relation to the legal system). Where people really feel that their truest expression is to accept a permanent homosexual lifestyle, we can encourage them to live it in the most loving, creative way, just as the best hetero-sexual partners do, and we can help integrate them into the Church's life. We need to take people where they are and accompany them on their path. Everything we wrote about long term committed relationships applies here.

4.   When problems are over our heads, we can confess our ignorance or inability to help. We will in such cases try to know available experts in this field whom we have personally contacted, and we will make referrals to them.

It is doubtful whether a Church that does less than this is truly following Jesus, our dying and living Lord of love. The church needs to provide spiritual direction and affirmation to those individuals who discover that they wish to remain in a homosexual adaptation. No group of people in the United States, except blacks in parts of the South, are more rejected by the mainstream of American culture than those living out homosexual preferences. People are ultimately hungry for God and have a basic desire to know and serve the divine Lord, and the Church needs to offer fellowship, the sacraments and pastoral care to *all* who honestly seek them. In doing so, the Church may discover many undreamed-of creative circumstances both for itself and for those it seeks to serve.

CHAPTER TEN

Overcoming Our Sexual Fears
and Directing Our Sexual Energies

For nearly forty years we have been listening to the concerns that people have about themselves and about how they fit into the world. We have listened to the full gamut of human illegalities, hurts, and angers, as well as to the spiritual problems that most people have. In almost every situation the subject of sexuality sooner or later has come up, and almost never have we found anyone—when all the defenses were down—who was totally comfortable with his or her own sexuality.

As we shall show in the next chapter, sexuality touches the very depth of the human soul, and when it is most adequately expressed it is tinged with a numinous, holy attractiveness and power. Unfortunately, though, the whole subject has frequently been wrapped up in ignorance and in ridiculous misinformation. Few people in our Western culture (not counting those poor souls whose controlling ego has broken down altogether) share all their sexual feelings, actions or desires, unless they are undergoing psychological analysis. What is hidden from others, however, separates us from them, and what is repressed and hidden from ourselves has a tendency to separate us from ourselves and cause psychological splits or neuroses; few things are more important for human stability and solidarity than the ability to share.

Sometimes listeners themselves make true sharing impossible. Any of us who wish truly to listen to other people, and so to help bridge the isolation so many of us feel, need to learn *never* to express shock at *any* revelation, story or confession that we hear. This advice applies equally to pastors, doctors, counselors, spiritual directors or friends. There is no better way to cut off a relationship and isolate the other person than to register shock at something that is told in confidence. Shock (inner or outer) can usually be picked up by others; it will either cut off the confession, limit the sharing, or inhibit the growth potential that comes to both listener and sharer in a real relationship. Listeners need to be open, ready to hear, willing to let the other person talk. They need to listen to what is said by the other person without judgmental interruptions as if one were reading a written account, although not so passively. Indeed, if listeners are comfortable enough with the subject they can often by gentle questioning even help others to express what they might not express without this encouragement.

One of the most complex and hidden areas of human life is human sexuality. If we are to be adequate listeners, we need to know something of human sexuality's wide variety of expressions, both in fantasy and in action. We also need to be sensitive to the fact that those brought up within the Judeo-Christian or Muslim religious traditions often have an overlay of guilt about their sexuality caused by all sorts of nonsensical ideas which they have been taught, and that this guilt adds to their isolation. And most people, regardless of their religious background, have some sexual feelings other than those prescribed as "normal" and socially acceptable or have concerns about areas of sexuality that in themselves may be quite common. All who would listen wisely to others need to be knowledgeable in the area of sexuality, and need to know of experts who can deal with problems that are beyond their own competence. The law in California requiring that all counselors be exposed to sexual information is, indeed, a wise one.

A whole book could easily be written on the subject of this chapter. However, we shall limit ourselves to the following subjects. We will first of all cover the problem of short-circuiting full sexuality, then look at the subject of premarital and extra-marital sex. We shall then look at the subject of promiscuity and the diseases which often accompany it. Then we shall discuss masturbation; and, finally, we will examine the paraphilia—some of the less common ways that the sexual interest expresses itself.

SHORT-CIRCUITING FULL SEXUALITY

One of the problems that frequently goes unnamed is the short-circuiting that occurs in sexual relationship when the purely physical level loses its proper priority in the totality of the relationship. Ruth Tiffany Barnhouse (in a series of lectures in which we participated) outlined five levels of sexuality that need to be integrated if sexual relationships are to be ultimately satisfactory; these are: the spiritual, the emotional, the mental, the psychological or instinctual, and the bodily or purely physical.

One of the problems with a relationship that begins on the purely physical level is that such a beginning may prevent the partners from moving on through the other levels. It is easy to get "stuck" in the purely physical attraction and never move above this bodily, instinctual level of relating. Such relations, not surprisingly, seldom last. No two people are going to have a really satisfying, total relationship if *all* the levels are not involved. The idea that sex is purely of the body is an absurd notion that nineteenth- and twentieth-century Western thought has fostered; it is an idea that is related to the materialistic bias of this limited civilization. From the materialistic point of view, only the physical world is ultimately real; the only real—and certainly the only important—aspects of intimate sexual relations would, from such a viewpoint, be physical also: copulation and orgasm. But sexuality pervades a *much* wider range of our experience than that.

Dr. Barnhouse describes various levels of sexual interaction. And she argues that when individuals move beyond the appropriate level—or move too fast they usually run into problems. Dr. Barnhouse's first level of sexuality is "eye to body". Any woman knows that men stare at women, and the more conscious male is also aware when he is appraised by another person. Interestingly, Dr. Barnhouse's second level is "eye to eye"—the moment when two people look at each other without turning away. We would prefer to call this "face to face". One reason for veiling women's faces in Moslem countries is that veiling protects the property rights that men have in their wives; one would have to have an excellent imagination, however, to get so excited over only a set of eyes. The veiling of nuns came to have the same purpose: a warm and attractive woman once showed us pictures of herself in full habit as a nun, and she looked like an utterly different person, formidable and cold.

The next level is "voice to voice". The voice, Dr. Barnhouse reminds us, can express much more than concepts; it can express a great deal of sexuality. (In Judaism at the time of Jesus no man was allowed to talk to a married woman or be alone with one. This custom was one reason the anointing of Jesus by the woman at Simon's party was such a scandal). Then there is "presence to presence", just being in the presence of another person; the presence of another can spark a whole emotional response. Next comes "emotion to emotion", the level which the entire selves of two people—unconscious, conscious and physical—interact.

Up to this stage of physical interaction, sexuality can usually be controlled by people who wish to do so. From this stage on, however, our ability to control the reactions that we set in motion diminishes. At a certain point we set in motion psychological and physiological dynamisms that have almost a life of their own. The desire for union arises, and the touch and the embrace can be symbolic of it. The sexual encounter progresses from "hand to hand" to "hand to skin"—and the skin is a very sensitive and vibrant sexual organ. The "skin to skin" level of sexual interaction brings still more responses into play; then comes "mouth to mouth", "hand to body", "hands to genitals", "genitals to genitals" and finally union and orgasm.

If sexuality does indeed obtain its meaning and value as a function of relationship and love, then purely "recreational sex", for the pure pleasure of it, is a misuse of sexuality. And if this is true, then the level of interpersonal relating appropriate at the merely recreational level should most likely stop at hand-to-hand contact, or at most a perfunctory kiss on the cheek or an embrace. Without such limits, we may find that our sexuality is running us rather than that we are running it. (But the idea that people can be kept from all *levels* of sexual experience, and can then be suddenly introduced to it, is just as dangerous; it can cause all sort of feelings of sexual inadequacy.)

The issue of sexual learning is delicate. Young people need some instruction, some *realistic* instruction, about how far sexual exploration should go. The statistics that we have already given, however, show how few children receive this kind— or any kind—of sexual instruction from their parents. The purpose of dating in our society is to give young people some comfort with the ways in which their emotions and bodies respond to sexual stimuli, but this certainly does not mean that sexual learning needs to involve genital intercourse. Unlimited sexual exploration, just for "kicks", is dangerous in many ways. First of all, it often occurs before people are capable of any kind of deep or mature emotional relationship, and it almost always aborts the possibility of such a relationship developing (particularly where fidelity to one person is not a value of the culture). Such relationships can also involve a lack of responsibility—the bringing of new life into the world. In his book *Love and Will*, Rollo May points out that, for many of the young people whom he has counseled, sexual relationships have become so casual that they have less meaning than a warm handshake. The holy mystery of sexuality has, for such people, been lost, and with it the beauty and mystery of life itself.

On the beach where I run nearly every day, I have seen people copulating in a slightly secluded corner in plain view of gulls and fellow sunbathers. Most people, however, require some privacy for genital sexuality. For most of us, in fact, one of the best ways to avoid inappropriate levels of sexual involvement is to stay away from places where we have the privacy to follow our desires to their conclusion. A touch is powerfully seductive, and we have to take care not to be utterly controlled by it. We have learned from experiments with rats that they will opt for sexuality rather than for food and survival, even when they have been conditioned to know that sexual activity leads to death itself. And there is a little rat in each of us.

PREMARITAL AND EXTRA-MARITAL SEX

We have already shown that marriage is quite different in matrilineal cultures than in our own. Everything in a matrilineal culture is directed toward the raising of the mother's child. But in our society, with its prejudices and patriarchal attitudes, premarital sex that results in conception causes all sorts of problems. It is quite surprising to us that so many people writing on the subject of premarital sexuality fail to see the burdens it places upon the mother and child. We have never known a marriage in which a pregnancy preceded the couple's essential commitment to each other that did not have a rocky time. And women who have been loved, sexually used, and then dropped suffer traumas that they seldom forget. Women who have given up their child for adoption, furthermore, have come to us ten or twenty years later still wishing to work through their guilts. And we have never known an illegitimate child who was adopted out who didn't have more than average psychological problems sooner or later. Of course, it is not the child who is illegitimate; the parents who get involved in irresponsible sexual intercourse are the illegitimate ones.

Just because premarital and extra-marital sex are both extremely common does not mean that they do not create real problems. We need to take a stronger stand on these issues than we are currently doing—as communities and as churches—while at the same time always stressing that we will provide understanding and concern for the individuals involved. This position, however, demands that we strike a delicate balance. We have people at all levels of psychological maturity and understanding both in the church and in society in general, and probably somewhere around forty to fifty percent of them need to be given a definite set of rules to follow. Indeed, everyone needs guidelines to a certain degree; one of the surest ways to make a child neurotic is to give him or her no guidelines. Guidelines provide security and define the world's limits and boundaries. But, paradoxically, nearly all guidelines have exceptions when applied to individuals in concrete situations and we need to be sensitive to this fact as well.

It is most interesting to note that Masters and Johnson, who can hardly be called prudes in sexual matters, write in their book *The Pleasure Bond* that unless the church does it, nobody will provide guidelines on the subject of sexual exploration, promiscuous sex, and sexual relations outside of committed relationships. Masters and Johnson feel that guidelines *must* be provided. Why? What is so traumatic about premarital and extra-marital sex, especially for teenagers?

First of all, there are no absolutely safe methods of contraception—except, perhaps for vasectomy or tubal ligation. Anyone who maintains that the other methods are foolproof simply doesn't have the medical facts. The pill works well for some people most of the time, when properly used, but it is not always medically safe and it is only 99 percent sure—and teenagers can't afford to be only 99 percent sure. The IUD is less than 99 percent sure and, in addition, there are certain side effects and dangers with this form of contraception, so users of IUDs need expert medical advice (which few teenagers have access to). The condom is unreliable; rubber has microscopic holes and sperm cells are microscopic, and sometimes the device breaks during intercourse. It is far better than nothing, but it is only 90 percent safe. Diaphragms, jellies and foams vary in effectiveness from about 75 percent to 98 percent. And the most ineffective method of all is withdrawal or withholding orgasm, because the lubrication on the end of the penis often contains enough sperm cells to impregnate an egg. These are the reasons why there are nearly as many illegitimate children today as in the days before good methods of contraception were developed.

Any teenager who has full sexual relationships is playing Russian roulette with the life of a child. But it *is* possible to draw reasonable and safe guidelines for teenagers and to stick to these guidelines. It's when we tell teenagers that nothing but a kiss should be engaged in that they write us off as ridiculous. Adults are not dealing in this day and age with reality if they treat teenagers like that.

Now, once one has had sexual intercourse in our culture, it becomes very easy to do it a second and third time, and the chances of pregnancy occurring get greater and greater. If a child does result from a teenage affair, there is often the stigma of illegitimacy (even though there shouldn't be) combined with the problems of a mother struggling alone to raise her child, often a rocky path. Otherwise the child is put up for adoption, which causes its own problems. We have seldom known an adopted child who didn't have a harder task adjusting to life than the unadopted child; to realize that your own parents didn't care enough to keep you may be the ultimate rejection. There is just no way around the fact that teenagers who engage in full intercourse are playing a dangerous game. And we have already mentioned that a quick sexual relationship almost always subverts the possibility of a deep, real relationship. (The only birth-control option we haven't mentioned is abortion—and it is often a psychological trauma of a very severe consequence, and it raises moral questions for many sincere and intelligent people. The effects often last for years, even for a lifetime.)

One of the real problems our culture faces is that almost all adolescent boys are insecure about their sexuality, and one of the most effective ways they find to prove to themselves that they are adequate sexual beings is getting a girl pregnant. And the insecurity of adolescent boys is at least partly due to the fact that they usually receive their sexual information from other ill-informed teenagers or from the gutter. We cannot reiterate too strongly that parents have a moral responsibility to give training in sexual responsibility to their sons, and if they won't do this then *someone* needs to provide it. Few young women would get pregnant except for the insistence of their male partners, men usually older than they are. Our churches and our society are ignoring an important issue in not providing information, guidelines and limits. Our experience is that once we have gained their confidence most young people want accurate information and sensible guidelines. But only those comfortable with sexuality and its real value and responsibilities can give such information and be heard. Here again, obviously the matter of communication is crucial. Where there is little communication between parents and children or where parents are afraid to talk about sexuality, the problems of premarital teenage sex loom large.

Single mature adults are in a different position. Sometimes they need to go as far as sexual intercourse in order to get to know each other and overcome their sexual fears. However, this should be after they have come to know each other well and are facing the responsibility they undertake. Our point is that sexual relations should never be taken lightly. Having someone to talk to about this level of experience helps keep one honest.

Much of what has been said about premarital sex is also true of extra-marital sex. Virtually the only people who can accept extra-marital relationships in their partners, as in "open marriages", are extroverted intuitives. These people live in the world of possibility; structure means a lot less to them than it does to the rest of us. If you want a marriage like this, be sure to marry another extroverted intuitive! All married adults should take a look at the Masters and Johnson book we've mentioned already: *The Pleasure Bond*. Cold, hard data is forcefully and honestly presented to show that almost no "swingers" have truly satisfactory sexual relationships. And those who maintain that being limited to one partner stifles personality just don't have the facts on open marriage. Even Dr. Ruth seems to agree with this point of view.

What are some of the reasons for not engaging in extra-marital relationships? First of all, it is against the principles of faithful marriage—it breaks the contract and it causes pain to the other party. If the children find out about it, furthermore it can cause real resentment and anger. And if it results in divorce, it is usually disastrous to children. (Divorce tends to, in any case, be a no-win situation.) In short, infidelity breaks relationship, and can easily be used by the other party as a club whenever one partner finds that he or she needs a weapon. It is much better to work out the dynamics of a relationship *within* that relationship than to go seeking fulfillment elsewhere.

Of course, people can be unfaithful to each other in ways that are not sexual. Sexual problems, including sexual infidelity, are only third in the list of causes of divorce. When unfaithfulness about money or alcohol—or sex—arises, the time has come to seek good counseling: many relationships can be saved when two people want to work them out. However, there *are* situations in which people are so completely mismatched, or in which so much damage has already been done, that divorce is the only sensible answer. But except in the rarest of situations, we advise the couple to try to reconcile before they jump into another situation that may present even worse problems than the first. People have a tendency to be attracted to the same type of person the second time unless they have worked in depth upon themselves and have really learned why their first marriage went wrong. It is not helpful to blame the other person, as it does not help us change ourselves and our attractions to other potential partners.

PROMISCUITY AND PROSTITUTION

In the area when the Mother Goddess was the dominant religious deity, the temple was frequently a place where one sought union with this goddess through sexual union with a holy priestesses. Even daughters of nobles and kings served for a time in these temples. Usually the daughters had little choice; it was part of what was done. Warriors returning from war with blood on their hands and souls visited these temples to be cleansed and purified and reinitiated into the gentler feminine values. (A fine description of the real meaning of this practice is found in the *Utne Reader* by Deena Metzger.[1]) But with the rise of partriarchy and the loss of a sense of the holy, along with the devaluation of women to the position of property, prostitution became an entirely different and quite sinister institution.

We were really quite naive about prostitution until a friend of ours was murdered by three prostitutes, who were probably under the influence of drugs. We were introduced to the whole world of gang-controlled, big business prostitution. Young women coming to the city from the country are picked up at bus stations by pimps and practically enslaved. From the smaller cities throughout the United States they are sent to the anonymous jungles of New York and other major cities. In order to endure their trade, they are introduced to drugs and kept dependent upon them. This is not victimless crime, but a kind of slavery. (Indeed, when one pays for sexual service one makes another a slave for an allotted time.) Most prostitutes come from broken homes, or homes where true caring has been unknown; often they come from poverty and live in poverty, and prostitution is simply a way of staying alive.

Among the people interviewed by Kinsey 70% of the males had visited a prostitute at least once, so there is still a large population of these debased and despised women. We have no answer to the problem, but certainly some centers should be established for the rehabilitation of those trapped in this lifestyle. Our limited experience in counseling with this group is that often prostitutes have only marginal ego strength. And the victims are not only women. There is also a traffic in prostitution with boys and young men, for those interested in homosexual encounters. This kind of practice, too, is often linked with syndicated crime, and the boys are virtual slaves. Father Bruce Ritter has developed havens in New York where such youths are given an opportunity to break out of that way of life, and these centers have spread over the country into many of the major cities.

With the breakdown of sexual morality, promiscuity has grown throughout the Western world. Promiscuous sex can be defined as sex with a person who is not physically unattractive, where there is no interest in or attempt at real relationship. From our point of view, this kind of sexual activity is a misuse of the human sexual capacity and is basically immoral. Usually people are merely using each other in promiscuous relationships, and such activities do not develop human personality or lead one to the divine. In addition, the immune system seems to become overloaded when people are exposed in this intimate physical way to many different people, each with his or her own spectrum of bacteria.

There are several kinds of sexually transmitted diseases about which any sexually knowledgeable person should be acquainted. In *Fundamentals of Human Sexuality*, Katchadourian describes the more common of these diseases—gonorrhea, syphilis, herpes, AIDS (Acquired Immune Deficiency Syndrome) and other less common conditions. In China these diseases, with the exception of AIDS, were practically wiped out in the first years of the People's Republic of China by the elimination of prostitution and by the compulsory treatment of these diseases. But a change in lifestyle will also help. There is good evidence that when women are exposed to sexual intercourse with many partners there is a much larger incidence of cervical cancer. And one gay friend who knows the homosexual community well told us that he felt that the AIDS scare had probably been a good thing for the homosexual community as it had emphasized relationship in sexuality more than recreational sex. (It is important to add, however, that disease is disease; all diseases should be treated sensitively, without moral condemnation.[2])

Prostitution and promiscuity, then, do not lead to personal growth, and they expose one to physical illness as well. Some people find it difficult to keep from having sexual experiences in a society where it is so available. They become almost addicted to sexual experience; their sexuality becomes compulsive. For some such people therapy is helpful, but others find the group experience of Sexaholics Anonymous more helpful, or find that it is more within their financial means. This group uses many of the principles of the 12 steps of Alcoholics Anonymous. We have found people greatly helped by this organization; it is often helpful to work along with other people struggling with a similar problem.[3] This group is helpful for those who find it difficult to say no to offered sexual intercourse, as well as for those struggling with the paraphilia that we shall discuss in a few pages.

MASTURBATION

The word "masturbation" is obscure in origin. Some maintain that it comes from two Latin words, *manus* (hand) and *struprare* (to defile); others claim that it comes of *mas* (seed) and *turbatio* (excitement). But, whatever the word's linguistic derivation, few common, natural human activities have given so much guilt to so many people as masturbation, an individual's stimulation of his or her sexual organs to orgasm. In our counseling experience we have seldom found any people really comfortable about their masturbating practices. Those brought up in the pre-Vatican II Catholic world were taught that "all cases of masturbation are objectively grave moral evils; every act of masturbation done with sufficient reflection and full consent is mortally sinful."[4] In other words, as one frightened college senior told me at Notre Dame: "If I masturbated and was hit by a truck on the way to confession, I would languish in hell forever. It was mortal sin."

One of the "problems" that usually presents itself for discussion in the area of sexuality is masturbation. It's not that masturbation in the great majority of cases is in itself a problem; it's that people regard it as a problem, and so it becomes one. A physician friend of mine once made a memorable statement: "There are two kinds of people; those who masturbate and those who lie." This statement may not be universally true, but it certainly approximates the situation, especially in males. So, if it is so normal, how did masturbation become such an upsetting subject?

The fear that semen would be wasted, a fear predominant in the Judaeo-Christian culture, led to a condemnation of masturbation in men—although there are few commandments against female masturbation. Very possibly the reason for the difference in the attitude toward male and female masturbation was that an actual emission of fluid occurs in one case but not in the other. While it is true that the word "masturbation" is never mentioned in the Bible (and we must never forget that more of the customs in the early Christian Church came from the synagogue and the rabbis than we realize), the rabbis taught that masturbation was a grievious sin. One authority even said it was a crime punishable by death. And one branch of the Christian community ultimately took over this deeply rooted Hebraic point of view. To quote *The Sex Atlas* on the subject:

> Still, in medieval Europe masturbation was not seen as much of a problem. While it was condemned in various penitentials, the other theological and pastoral writings of the time hardly mentioned it at all, or referred to it in a rather oblique fashion. Even the popular catechisms that began to appear in the 16th century contained nothing on the subject. This omission may appear strange at first glance, but it becomes understandable when we remember that . . . they recognized only one kind of activity as being strictly sexual: coitus among adults. It seems, therefore, that at least women and children had no great feelings of guilt about masturbation, but simply thought of it as a way of relieving physical irritations, comparable to scratching.[5]

Nocturnal emissions, however, *were* perceived as a problem. It was thought that when a male had nocturnal emission, it was because a force drew the semen out of him; this force seemed to be connected with the devil. There is a long dissertation in one of the Church fathers about whether nocturnal emissions are sinful. (Oddly, in the Eerdman translation of this Church father, Cassian, the chapter on nocturnal emissions is not included. I was curious and had it translated. It was not very interesting.)

It wasn't until about 1700, however, that masturbation itself was once again considered a major evil. In 1710, an anonymous pamphlet on the heinous sin of self-pollution appeared in England. It gave spiritual and physical advice, and offered readers embellished warnings on the danger of wasting semen. The author referred to masturbation as "Onanism". (You will remember that Onan was the Biblical character who was punished by God for refusing to impregnate his brother's widow. The term "Onanism" is really a misnomer, however, because Onan was more likely practicing contraception by withdrawal, not masturbation.) This pamphlet went through 80 editions.

The treatment of people who were discovered to be masturbating became extremely inhumane. Doctors recommended special diets, much as they prescribe special diets for obesity today. It was also believed that hard mattresses, thin blankets, washing with cold water, and low room temperature were helpful. There was even an attempt to introduce skirts for men so that trousers wouldn't stimulate the genital organs.

In 1867, one of the greatest British physicians of his time, Henry Maudsley, said that masturbation was characterized by extreme perversion and derangement of thought. He also maintained that masturbation was the cause of low intelligence, hallucinations, and suicidal and homocidal tendencies. In other words, masturbators were potential mad killers, and it seemed only wise to have them in asylums. It was also believed that this form of insanity was incurable. Parents were advised to tie the hands of children to their cribs, or to make them wear mittens. Certain protective devices were invented to make the sex organs less accessible. Some physicians even advised a surgical treatment called infibulation—putting a metal ring through the foreskin so one couldn't get an erection. Sometimes cauterization and even castration was performed. And for female masturbation, surgery was performed to remove the clitoris. (Unfortunately, clitorectomies are not unknown today, as we indicated earlier.) Masturbation had become the symbol for all sexual urges, and had taken on many kinds of evil connotations.

This medical attitude became even more somber when a respected Swiss physician named Tissot published an influential book in 1760, a treatise on the disorders produced by masturbation. The author claimed that masturbation was a sin and a crime, and was the cause of such diseases as "consumption, deterioration of the eyesight, disorders of digestion, impotence. . .and insanity." And ultimately a number of physicians all over the Western world came to see masturbation as the basis for many physical problems. For example, Benjamin Rush, who was one of the founders of American psychiatry, published a book in 1812 entitled *Medical Inquiries and Observations Upon The Diseases Of The Mind.* Rush maintained that masturbation caused not only insanity but also seminal weakness, impotence, dyspepsia, dimness of sight, vertigo, epilepsy, loss of memory, and even death. In the late eighteen nineties, Freud and his friend and confidante, Wilhelm Fliess considered masturbation one of the most common causes of neurosis. Freud even approved of Fliess' procedure for dealing with masturbation—an operation *on the nose.*

With this kind of cultural history, it is no wonder that many young people (and older people as well) have found their genitals so dangerous that they have not been able to touch them—particularly when touching them is viewed as mortal sin. And if they cannot touch them, they may have problems allowing their lovers to touch them. This can sometimes put a barrier between partners—a barrier to real physical sharing, to real intimacy—and such a barrier can contribute to frigidity and impotence.

Sometimes, on the other hand, the idea that masturbation is evil may help make the practice compulsive. As we have noted earlier, males can masturbate to orgasm before puberty, and one very brilliant and sensitive youth we knew had begun a practice of daily masturbation sometime between ages three to five; he was taught that this was a mortal sin, but that in no way deterred the practice. The guilt and pain and isolation that he suffered showed the incredible strength of his personality structure. When he could finally talk freely about the subject— and this took several years of counseling—he realized that he was a highly sexual person and that there was nothing wrong with this practice, when it did not isolate him in his relationship with his wife. When he realized how normal it was, the practice diminished and no longer was a major concern. The agony caused to many people by negative ideas about masturbation is incalculable.

We have also discovered that many men and some women continue to masturbate after marriage. Why should people continue the practice after marriage? Occasionally one partner is more highly sexed than the other, and it is agreed between them that this is an acceptable way to handle this. However, the main reason is the lack of free and open communication between committed partners about their sexual feelings and needs. When we are not comfortable with our sexual feelings, it takes great faith to believe that anyone else will accept and value them. The issue is not masturbation, but honest sharing. Tragically, most people in our culture find it easier to *indulge* in sexual play than to *talk* about it.

Another very gifted young man only revealed after a long period of counseling that his greatest concern was that he could not control his masturbation, which often took place in public. Only because of his brilliance and perceptiveness was he able to keep from being discovered and getting into legal trouble. In this situation, as in the one we discussed above, compulsive masturbation became a substitute for relationship, and so was a denial of the essential meaning of sexuality—bringing people into relationship with each other. It bothers most sensitive people to discover that they are unable to stop something that they want to stop, that their actions have become compulsive; the compulsive quality of masturbation, therefore, is far more serious than the act itself. We would conclude that, generally, compulsive television-watching probably causes more damage than compulsive masturbation—because it robs us of much more time and energy that could be used more creatively. Furthermore, after listening to hundreds of people we have found only these two instances in which masturbation really was a serious problem after the facts about it were clearly laid out.

Few subjects reveal how wrong the "experts" can be as well as does the subject of masturbation. As late as 1920 and 1930 we get statements such as: "When the practice (of masturbation) is begun at an early age, both mental and physical development may be notably interfered with. It is often stated that masturbation is the cause of insanity, epilepsy and hysteria. I believe it to be more likely that masturbation is the first manifestation of a developing insanity." This statement comes from a book by Dr. Charles Hunter Dunn, Instructor in Pediatrics at Harvard University and Physician-in-Chief of the Infant's Hospital in Boston. And Hector Charles Cameron in his book *The Nervous Child*, published in 1930, wrote: "At the worst, confinement in porplastic armor, as for spinal caries, or severe poliomyelitis, may be necessary.[6] No wonder that 60 years ago mothers and father were very worried about masturbation.

And yet the most definitive current study of human sexuality, the book by Katchadourian to which we have already referred many times, states: "Masturbation plays an important role in psychosexual development... Starting with self-exploration the child discovers the pleasurable potential of the genitals, which in turn becomes the vehicle for further learning and sexual masturbation. In adolescence, masturbation continues to fulfill a developmental function in self-exploration as well as providing the primary outlet for sexual release and gratification. As a vehicle for learning about the sexual aspects of one's body and one's self, masturbation continues to play a useful role throughout adulthood."[7]

One probable reason for the ridiculous attitude toward masturbation is the logical fallacy of thinking that associated symptoms are casually related. Among many psychotics (partially schizophrenics) and many of the mentally retarded, inhibitions are significantly reduced. If such people feel a nice tickle in the genitals they take care of it, out in public or any place else. And it is probably in this way that mental illness and masturbation got connected. In itself, in other words, masturbation is rarely a problem. Again, in most cases it is the *guilt* about masturbation that causes the real psychological problems. We have dealt with some very intelligent college students who found it much easier to reveal that they had slept around—that they had had affairs, heterosexual and homosexual— than to tell us that they masturbated. We need to deal with this burden of guilt. When we look at the statistics, masturbation occurs in young children and in adolescents, but also in adults (and very few adults whom we've questioned, when we have met them in marriage counseling, do not occasionally indulge in masturbation), and even, as a matter of fact, in older age. Sometimes it becomes the easiest method of sexual exchange and affection between an elderly man and woman. It also serves a purpose in widowhood.

In conclusion, we must stress that it is always helpful to realize that instinctual urges are practically universal, and so are some actions like masturbation. It helps to see that we are not alone in what we may think are "personal problems". Morton remembers clearly the relief he experienced in the first years of analysis when he realized that he was no more peculiar or evil than most people. He remembers precisely when the insight came, in a flash: he was rounding a curve on the Pasadena Freeway. We are all in the same human condition.

THE FEAR OF HOMOSEXUALITY

We have already dealt with the subject of the homosexualities. However, *fear* of homosexuality can cause problems in adolescents and young adults who in fact have only limited interest in the same sex. The fear can, by itself, keep a man from having an erection, and can cause premature ejaculation. Fear of homosexuality can often be really a fear about one's masculine competence and potency. This is very common among teenage males; they strut and make a good noise, but most of them are frightened to death that no woman would ever want to look at them. How this fear affects behavior patterns is sometimes most surprising. We have often (and we have done a lot of teenage counseling) found that teenagers with no particular financial problems, who were caught stealing or breaking into a store, or shooting someone with a BB gun, usually had deep fears about their own sexuality and masculinity. Teenage violence— which seems to be a male phenomenon—is very often an overcompensation for feelings of sexual inadequacy. Even the police in well-informed communities recognize the role of sexuality in teenage crime.

Let us give you a classic example. A young man of about fifteen was picked up by the police because he was caught shooting a lady across the street with a BB gun. The police said that he could go home with his family if some counseling was provided, and Morton was called in while the boy was still in jail. It took several months, but what Morton discovered was that this teenager had for some time had a very active homosexual life with a younger adolescent. He was scared to death that he was not a real macho male, and his violent behavior was his way of denying his fear. As it turned out, there was a homosexual component in him—as in most of us—but he was not basically homosexual in orientation. The distinction is important. He had to have a brush with the law before he could really deal with his experience, but today he is successfully married and has several children. He probably would have had real difficulty in coming to maturity if he had not been able to deal with the homosexual side of himself and with his own inner femininity.

We'll share another story. A young man went off to college. He did quite well the first year, but in the second year at exam time, he came down with pneumonia. He went home, got well, returned to school, and then right before exam time he came down with pneumonia again. He decided a little counseling might help. So he and Morton talked, and Morton asked him whether he had ever had any homosexual experience. No, he said, nothing other than ordinary adolescent playing around. In the first few sessions they didn't seem to be getting very far.

About six weeks later he came in and said, "You know, you asked me if I had ever had any homosexual experiences. In college during my freshman year my roommate and I had almost nightly relationships." This young man had totally repressed this into the unconscious. But it is difficult to repress selectively; he tended to go blank at exam time, and so whenever finals came around and he had to produce he got totally rattled and anxious. His body took him off the hook and he got sick. As a result of honest self-examination, however, he realized that his basic orientation was not homosexual. He didn't want to continue this type of relationship; he made a decision, therefore, and never had pneumonia again; he went on to get a law degree, married and happily as most of us, and has four children.

Sometimes people with almost exclusive heterosexual experience and desires will fear that they have strong homosexual components within them. Dreams of homosexual experience or failure to be adequate sexual partners with the opposite sex bring on fears that are self-defeating. It is important to remember that dreams are symbolic; a man's dream of a homosexual experience may simply be telling him that he needs more connection with his own masculinity. Women's dreams of this same kind are frequently admonishing them to get in touch with their femininity. But the horror with which many people think about homosexual actions or feelings reinforces their fears.

ANOMALIES AND PARAPHILIA

We have already discussed the problems of violent and psychological rape, prostitution, promiscuity and problems raised by lacking control over our sexual involvements. There are also a group of sexual behaviors that Katchadourian describes as paraphilia, "characterized by variant choices of *sexual object* as manifested in pedophilia, zoophilia, fetishism, necrophilia; and variant choices in the *means* of sexual gratification such as in voyeurism, exhibitionism, and sexual sadomasochism."[8]

Both in action and in fantasy these are much more common than most people believe. In our counseling we have experienced all of these except necrophilia and some of them have been brought to us many times.

Before we look at these different variants of sexuality, it is helpful to listen to the wisdom of Guggenbuhl-Craig once again; in a particularly insightful passage he voices his appreciation of Freud's great contribution to our understanding of human sexuality:

> In psychotherapeutic practice it happens again and again that the more differentiated, and not the weaker, the person is, the more we find the so-called sexual aberrations. Exceptions prove the rule. Un-

differentiated people, with minimal affective development and cultural stimulation, possess a "normal" sexuality far more frequently than do affectively and culturally differentiated people.

Furthermore, hardly anyone who has made the attempt to understand sexuality has taken note of the fact that the greatest portion of human sexual life consists of fantasies; in part, these are of the "normal" variety—significantly more remarkable than the actually-lived sexual life.

Sexual life and erotic fantasies are so rich and multifaceted that every possible variant of psychological life can be experienced through this living symbolism. As Jung understood the peculiar activities and images of the alchemists to be images of psychological development and individuation, so we can recognize and follow the process of individuation in sexual life and its variations. In this connection we also understand the greatness of Freud. He believed he could describe sexuality within the biological model, but he described it with unusual differentiation, and he thought that he had discovered in it the foundations of human behavior. Only a psychologist of the Jungian school can grasp Freudian psychology; Freud encountered sexuality and was overwhelmed by its fascinating manifestations. Against his own intentions, so to speak, he created a modern, living sexual mythology. As an example of this, consider again the image of the polymorphously perverse child: it exists in each of us throughout our whole lives. Some aspects of it are repressed, and lead a merely shadow existence in dreams and mysterious fantasies. What is this polymorphously perverse child if not the Self of Jungian psychology, the symbol of the totality of the psyche, the divine core within us which contains everything, all the possibilities and opposites of our psyche?

I want to mention here one further characteristic of sexual life with all of its variations which can only really be understood from the viewpoint of the individuation process. I am thinking of shyness and secrecy. Sexual life, whether lived-out or fantasized, is kept secret by most people. Even in the analytical situation it can take years before the deepest sexual fantasies are surrendered. Most of the sexual images which appear in the dreams of patients are rendered harmless and cleaned up. This desire for secrecy is hardly comprehensible from the viewpoint of reproduction, pleasure or human relationship. Mystery and intimacy are, however, characteristics of the soul and of the individuation process. For a time this process must proceed in a closed vessel; nothing and no one dare disturb it.[9]

FETISHISM

The pain and guilt that is caused by the paraphilia is well demonstrated by a young man who came to see Morton in his office at Notre Dame. He sat down and said, with a sigh, "You know it is bad enough being black, but on top of that I think I am gay." He went on to talk about how negatively the black community looks upon homosexual behavior. He was suicidal. He came in quite often, and his suicidal thoughts lessened. He graduated from college, but kept in touch with Morton. Some two years later in a visit he finally revealed the condition that bothered him far more than either being black or homosexually inclined: he had a leather fetish. The touch and smell of leather elicited a sexual response from him. Although this caused neither him nor others any damage, it was this experience that he found most difficult to share.

In another situation it took a young man two years of counseling before he developed enough trust to share the fact that he stole women's clothing, panties and nightgowns from stores and used them to stir up his own sexual fantasies. (The panty raids at colleges probably are an expression of the same desire.) In *Ego and Archetype*, Edward Edinger describes a young man who could overcome his shyness only by wearing some hidden piece of feminine clothing. Edinger then points the passage in Book V of Homer's *Odyssey* in which the hero is nearly drowning during a horrible storm when Ino, a sea goddess, throws him her veil and tells him that if he wears it around his chest it will save him. Edinger then writes: "Ino's veil is the archetypal image that lies behind the symptom of transvestism. The veil represents the support and containment which the mother archetype can provide the ego during a dangerous activation of the unconscious."[10]

Guggenbuhl-Craig tells a similar story in *Marriage—Dead or Alive*. He was treating a male student who had gotten into trouble with the police for stealing female underwear. The author and the young man worked at trying to find the psychological roots of the problem. One day the student came in and read him the story of Faust meeting Helen of Troy. Here was Faust before the most beautiful woman in the world, and then she disappeared, leaving Faust with her garment and veil in his hands. The student said: "Women are only a symbol anyway. Maybe the experience of meeting the feminine is deeper if one has only a piece of her clothing, an object which symbolizes the woman, rather than the woman herself. At least one never forgets that the fantasy is almost as important as the reality." The author concludes:

> In a certain sense this student was right. He did not equate sexuality with reproduction, with pure pleasure, or with human relationship. He understood it as something symbolic. Through him it became clear to me that sexuality had to be understood differently from the way I had understood it until then. I began to wonder if it is not often the case that sexual deviation comes closer to the phenomenon of sexuality than does so-called normal sexuality. I must repeat: the concepts "normal" and "abnormal" have lost some of their meaning with respect to sexual life. Individuation provides us with the key to *sexuality*, and not to normality or abnormality.[11]

Bestiality, or having relations with animals, is also common in farm communities. The main harm caused by this anomaly is the guilt caused by this action and the horror of it in the Old Testament. Simply talking this over with an understanding counselor can put an end to this practice and remove the guilt.

VOYEURISM AND EXHIBITIONISM

Working in a parish we found that several times we needed legal assistance to help people who ran afoul of the law in these two practices. Voyeurism comes from the French word to look. People who go to nude shows or buy pornographic material for sexual stimulation are certainly looking, but the term is reserved for those who have a compulsive need secretly to observe the opposite sex bathing or undressing. The practice is much more common with men. Such people are called Peeping Toms and are usually quite passive men who find it difficult to make an overt relation with a woman. The name Peeping Tom comes from the story of Lady Godiva who rode naked on her white horse through the city of Coventry. All the people except Tom closed their blinds, but because of his looking he was struck blind. Women, the usual objects of such activity find it extremely annoying and frightening and such behavior is illegal in most places. Where the activity is persistent psychotherapy is advised.

A similar group of males, lacking in aggression and confidence of their masculinity expose themselves to women. One very fine young man was caught once and had his sentence remitted and then became involved again. He was married. After the second instance as he and Morton talked in his office after he had been released by the police. Morton asked him why he did it. His answer was one of the finest examples of how our behavior can be almost entirely unconscious. He said: "I have no idea of why I did what I did." Again long term psychotherapy eventually solved the problem. In still another situation, a college student was referred to Morton. He was very capable, had done excellent work and suddenly his grades and his attitude toward life in general deteriorated. As the two of them talked the young man revealed that he had been exposing himself before college girls in such a way that he was not picked up. The compulsive nature of his affliction had caused him despair and depression. Simply talking the situation over and realizing that this was a way of reaching out to women whom he considered too formidable to relate to in person, released him from his fear. With this understanding and encouragement to start dating his grades and spirits revived and he went on to get a doctoral degree.

The fad of streaking on some campuses during the seventies was another mass example of exhibitionism—showing its deep psychological roots. In one coeducational college the head of a female dormitory suddenly found that a group of some fifty to a hundred stark naked young men stood before her dorm. She was a remarkable nun who quietly confronted the group and told them to go back to their dormitories and put on their clothes. The crowd gradually melted away.

The obscene call is another kind of vocal exhibitionism. Again the caller is usually a timid person who calls to frighten and annoy either men or women depending on their sexual predilection. Again some of the nicest people from an outer appearance have told me that they had been involved in this kind of behavior.

SADOMASOCHISM

Freud and others have pointed out the intrusion of dominance and aggression into sexual relationships. Nothing points out this connection better than both sadism and masochism, the desire to hurt and the desire to be hurt, as part of sexual fantasy and orgasm. Again this is largely male activity and often one of the homosexualities. Women sometimes cooperate, but usually to please their male partner. This practice becomes very serious when such experiences are forced on other people as in rape. Indeed any coercive sex is tinged with a S-M quality as these behaviors are sometimes called. People who cannot control these impulses are dangerous. People who have little ability to deal with their inner violence often use rape as an outlet for sexuality, but most students of the subject feel that rape is more a crime of violence and particularly an expression of hatred toward women than it is a sexual drive. Often people apprehended in rape are people from the lower socio-economic scale with case histories of deprivation and lack of love. People found in this condition need the best of psychotherapeutic help to redeem them and keep society safe from their depravations. Prisons are merely schools in learning further violence. And yet the public must be protected from such violence. Rape is an increasingly serious problem with 73 out of 100,000 reporting such an experience. The true figure is probably much higher.

PEDOPHILIA AND INCEST

Before we enter this last section of our account, we would mention again that nearly anything can attract to it sexual interest, filth, feces, urine. Pyromania (setting fires compulsively) and kleptomania (compulsive stealing) both seem to have for some people a sexual component. We have already noted our experience with vandalism in this regard in an earlier section of this chapter.

The child represents so much that most adults have lost that it is no wonder that sexual interest in the child is found in many people and that children become the object of sexual abuse and attack. Recently a great clamor has arisen about nursery and preschools where such practices were discovered. A campaign at the present time is running wild to give children knowledge to stay away from enticing strangers. A real problem arises in this connection: children under five (as shown by their responses to the Rorschach test) find it very difficult to distinguish between their fantasy and imagination and a reality situation. This causes real problems and some people can be accused and imprisoned who are innocent. This whole matter needs to be taken from the realm of hysteria and viewed with as much objectivity as we can muster. Often the testifying in court of a molested child can do the child more damage than the molestation. In a recent TV program no mother of a molested child would have the child testify if they had it to do over. Both the victim and the molester need to get good psychological help when these situations arise.

Some years ago in a small group session at a conference a very attractive and mature woman was able to share her experience of being sexually used by her father. Many believe that most molestation does occur within the family situation and experience in counseling bears out this truth for us. This woman agreed to write of her experience in a slightly disguised form and we conclude with her letter to us and her suggestions of how both victims in incest can be helped. Our main suggestion is that children be urged to tell the other parent if indeed incestuous experiences occur.

Dear Morton and Barbara,

Thank you for this opportunity to reach across the conspiracy of silence which protects family violence, to refuse to be a part of the silence any longer. I pray that my insights into the dynamics of incest, its effects, and the journey toward wholeness will offer hope to others trapped in situations similar to my own. I have experienced several years of incestuous sexual harassment, my teenage years, years of silence, lies, tension, guilt, pain and fear. It has been a long, hard road to freedom, but in retrospect, I can see God's presence all along the way, although I couldn't always see it at the time. Perhaps my experience can be a gift for others. That gift is a simple message: you are not alone and *there is hope*.

Today my life is rich and full. Years ago, I would not have believed that life could be this good. I am married and have two children. We've been married over ten years; we like each other and plan to stay married. Our children are bright, healthy, busy little people. We're white, Catholic, middle-class, well-educated, liberal—ordinary people.

I am a woman—and I like that—now. I am strong, vulnerable, compassionate, angry, nurturing, energetic, wounded, striving. It has been amazing to me to discover who I am, and to continue to grow in awareness and in relationship to God, self and others. Some of the wounded places deep inside me can still be reopened from time to time, and healed a little stronger and a little better. Perhaps incest is a wound that never completely, perfectly heals. However, I have come to believe that all things are redeemable through grace. I have been changed by my experience and feel a certain depth of understanding and compassion because of it.

My father was possessive, domineering, manipulative, and verbally abusive. I was afraid of him for as long as I can remember. Some of this was out of proportion, I am sure. But in my youth, he seemed to be all-knowing and all-powerful, a malevolent god. He was also very protective, hard-working, generous, highly intelligent, devoutly religious, and respected in the church and business communities. As a child, I wanted very much to please him, to make him proud of me. My mother was totally devoted to him and dependent on him. Theirs was a very traditional, sex-role stereotyped marriage. We appeared to be the model family, spending most of our time together to the exclusion of all others. The Family was our whole world.

My father would call me over to him and run his hand up and down inside my thighs or stroke my fanny appreciatively. We would "wrestle" frequently, and a lot of that wrestling was for real. If no one else was around, he'd try to pull my clothes off. Every morning he demanded a back rub or a warm body to lie next to his. Every night he came into the bedroom my sisters and I shared to fondle us and kiss us goodnight for several minutes. At home, he frequently walked around nude, and I loathed the sight of him. He constantly intruded on the physical or psychological space of each family member; privacy was impossible, even to bathe.

A call or beckoning finger when no one else was home made my blood run cold. Behind locked doors, he wanted to teach me about sex, to awaken some sexual response in me. He wanted to teach me to defend myself from sexual advances on dates ("men only want one thing"). He'd press me to the wall, or lie on me on the bed fully clothed, while I struggled to get free. He would sometimes try to pull my skirt up and pants down, or try to separate my legs—at this point I would be positively furious and frantic. When he stopped, he would laugh and congratulate me for defending myself so well, a skill I would surely need.

Incest is a prison without walls. There were many components of this prison which trapped me. Among these were:

—youth. Although I was a teenager and older than the majority of incest victims, I was very naive, confused and dependent. As trust was eroded, it was replaced by conflict, helplessness and hopelessness.

—illusion of uniqueness. I thought I was the only person in this awful situation. Unfortunately, there are many of us.

—silence. No one said anything. No one saw or heard or suspected.

This didn't happen. It didn't exist. There was an unspoken, unconscious conspiracy. The truth was too painful to face, too confusing to grasp.

—fear. There were threats not to tell anyone. (What would happen to me, to The Family, if I told anyone, even Mom?)

—my own personality. I was willing to be "self-sacrificing", to endure this situation to protect my mother from the truth and to prevent our family from being separated, as I imagined, by some outside intervention if anyone ever found out.

—religion. We were a conservative, religious family. My understanding of our religion included a very negative attitude toward sexuality. A high value was placed on giving, obedience, and being self-less. I adopted these values, and predictably, they became a source of conflict. Religion was used as a weapon in my father's hands, a powerful instrument to manipulate people whose intentions were basically good.

—sex-role. The only sex-role I knew was the very rigid, traditional model affirmed by my mother and the church, a model requiring self-sacrifice for husband, family, God and church. The dependency built into this model led inevitably to the necessity of trading sex for security.

—my father's personality. He seemed to be a basically well-meaning person who wanted desperately to be loved, and who hated the way he was. This dualistic personality contributed to my ambivalent feelings about him, then and now!

—societal attitudes. Victims are often blamed, and viewed as promiscuous, disturbed or incompetent. Also, sex tends to be sensationalized, so the imagined consequences of getting help seemed worse than the original problem.

Incest isn't just sex, and the implications of incest are not just sexual. It is violence, betrayal, physical and psychological abuse. It wasn't sex in my father's mind if there wasn't intercourse. But it just isn't that simple. It's psychological rape, coercion, terror. It's becoming a non-person.

There were literally thousands of sexual incidents between my father and me. Day after day. Week after week. Month after month. Year after year. All the time I was becoming a woman and learning what that meant. Leering, grabbing, touching, wrestling, exploiting, humiliating.

Even as I write this, it is difficult to put this in a balanced perspective. The sexual aspects of the situation were secondary; they were symptoms. The primary problem was being seen as a possession rather than as a person, being constantly pulled down by physical blows, threats, obscenity, cursing, preaching, loading with guilt and blame. The destructive nature of the relationship set the stage for sexual advances. The total experience had far-reaching and devastating consequences.

The immediate results were complex. The tension was constant. I wondered when he would call me, or walk into the room. What would he say or do? I dreamed of running away, but I would lose the rest of the family; I had no self-confidence—running away without money or skills could be as bad or worse than home, and he'd probably find me anyway. Or maybe I could kill myself, but I didn't want to be dead. I always believed that some-day, somehow, life would be better.

Anger and frustration raged inside me. I wanted to scream, but I couldn't. I hated being dependent and being exploited. I hated him. I hated me.

My self-contempt grew. I hated myself for being a big girl and submit-ting to this day after day. I hated myself when he called one of my sisters and I was glad it was her and not me. I hated my breasts for being so visible and touchable; I hated my periods because he kept track of them, invading my privacy, as usual. I hated myself for having sexual fantasies (sin) and for masturbating (big sin) and enjoying it. I hated the subservient role to which my gender relegated me. I hated being silent, like the rest of the family, and being powerless, paralyzed by fear and confusion.

I blamed myself. I went along. I did not consider my youth, fear, con-fusion, and the overwhelming pressure by my father. I just knew I went along. But going along under pressure, extreme pressure, at that, is not the same as consent. When an individual is young, the issue of consent is com-plicated and debatable even in the most liberal of viewpoints. And when coercion is part of a whole package of verbal abuse and destructiveness, consent is out of the question.

My ego boundaries were repeatedly trampled, as my resistance to sex-ual interaction was ignored and overpowered. The verbal assault eroded integrity. I began to feel that I no longer existed as a separate person with The Family. Defending any sense of self was a losing battle. I was so thor-oughly immersed in this situation, I couldn't even see it anymore.

The conflicts that are part of incest cannot be overestimated. The boundary between love and agression is a fuzzy one at best. When sexual interaction takes place in the relationship between parent and child and escalates very gradually, the distinction is hopelessly lost.

Appearing to be a highly moral family while experiencing incest was yet another source of conflict. My father was highly regarded. My mother adored him. He was terrific in everyone's eyes except mine—I must be the crazy one. I couldn't tell my mother—she would be devastated. Besides, she said women who have problems with men have asked for it. He called me a "worthless piece of shit" and that sounded pretty accurate.

It seems important to put this into the context of my whole experience at that time. Even abusive parents are not abusive all the time, and this is at the root of more confusion and ambivalence. My father was also good to me. And my relationship with him was not my whole life. I had my mother and sisters and a brother. School was great; I was a successful student and had friends at school.

Conflicts can become subconscious in order to survive, as defense mechanisms protect our threatened selves. I was able to function quite well and appeared normal to myself and others during this period and several years which followed.

How did I do so well? There is no doubt that my critical years of early childhood were full of tender, loving care. This rich experience of being loved gives strength to cope with whatever life may bring. And, along with the general confusion, denial of the situation, and acceptance of the necessity for trading sex for security that I have already mentioned, I used my imagination to fantasize an inner life full of adventures and misadventures. I also practiced a very devotional form of religion which was a lifeline, knowing Jesus as comforter, primarily. Importantly, I disowned my body as " not me". The dichotomy that our Christian tradition teaches, valuing spirit over body, made it easy. I knew that my body could be hurt, but no one could hurt me, the "real me" (apart from my body).

I dated, although I was tense and afraid of men. Much to my amazement, I discovered they were decent, nice people. My ticket away from home would be marriage.

I met and married my husband, a gentle man who knew nothing about this part of my past. I appeared to be the fun-loving, wholesome, all-American girl. I shelved all those old memories and began a new life.

I've been asked how I could get married. No sweat. My expectations of marriage and sex were very low, but it had to be better than what I was

leaving. Married sex turned out to be a pleasant surprise; we learned together and it was mostly playful and fun. Getting pregnant, giving birth,
and breastfeeding babies was a super high, and being a woman suddenly
felt really, really good.

I grew tremendously in my husband's love and in loving our children.
The past was laid to rest for several years. Visits to my parent's home were
tense and anxious for me, being around my father, loving him and hating
him. No one else knew our "secret", and once I was married, neither he
nor I ever mentioned it. The past was erased.

Or so I thought, until people, events and relationships awakened the
memories. At the time it seemed weird to be remembering and hurting—
it was over—why think about it ever again? Now it seems that some mysterious, graceful presence of God-within disturbs us into peace. The memories
and the anxiety they produced were a not-so-gentle invitation to grow and
be healed.

I told my husband and a close friend about the past, asking their support, and I got into therapy. Therapy was a long and difficult process, a
year and a half of hard work, struggling and growing. Disintegration is an
essential part of reintegration, causing times of exhaustion and discourage-
ment. Being in therapy affects relationships—some friends disappeared,
others became priceless, my marriage was severely strained for a while.

I gradually became a person, learning stress management, self-worth,
discovering what I value, learning to set boundaries once again. It was
wonderfully rewarding work, and it was only the beginning, a prerequisite
for the journey toward wholeness and holiness.

Confrontation was the hardest thing I have ever done. Breaking the
conspiracy of silence is essential to build honest relationships and for every
family member to be freed from the destructiveness and illusions that characterize family violence. Ideally, the one who confronts is strong enough
to speak the truth and stand by it; realistically, the one who confronts is
extremely unsure of herself, vulnerable, and accustomed to taking care of
everyone else, in this case, taking care of their illusions. My own actions
were determined by an inner wisdom and necessity I now call grace, which
preceded my understanding by quite some time.

Confrontation upsets the family dynamics; the purpose is after all, to
end the pattern of destruction, which goes on inside us long after leaving
home. The confronter has borne the weight of the matter long enough
and, consciously or unconsciously, chooses the time for it all to be out in

the open and dealt with. As poorly as she may be prepared, the other family members are prepared even less. Although confrontation is explosive, it can be done lovingly and with the expectation that everyone will need time to heal.

When I confronted my father with the need to deal with our secret and hopefully to reach some reconciliation based on the truth, I was sharply criticized for not having forgiven and forgotten the past. I found that I need-ed to grow in self-knowledge and self-worth to a point where I could be angry, before I could grow beyond that to forgiveness. Like love, forgiveness grows on its own schedule.

One particularly healing event was meeting another incest victim through a serendipitous set of circumstances. Sitting across from her, I could see myself reflected in her, and for once, I could be outraged at the violence done to her and to her self-worth, and understand that my situation was the same.

Therapy, intimate relationship, spiritual guidance, and turning points on the inner journey have all been very healing. The process of becom-ing whole and well has been a profoundly religious experience of rebirth. Incest affects so many aspects of one's life—reconciliations have been needed with my self, with my body, with God, with my family, with my father, with men, with the masculine in me, with the church.

Healing means being made whole, and for me that has included a pro-cess of reclaiming my body. It is not something I could decide to do for myself, but it is something I can allow. I have known that I needed to re-claim my body for myself, I have longed for it, and looking back, I can see that it has been happening; through dreams and symbols, persons and rela-tionships, and body-work, especially exercise and Reike healing. Now I can value my body, not only as a "temple of the Holy Spirit", and a way for God to be present in our world, but also as the body of me, and the way for me to be present here.

It has been very good for me that men and religion, which have had negative effects on me in the past, have been so much a part of my heal-ing. My husband's love brought me to the point where I could begin to face the past and deal with it. A very dear friend is male, and our deep, strong, and platonic friendship has been a source of strength and learning for me. My therapist was a sensitive, wise and compassionate man, to whom I will always be grateful and for whom I have the highest respect. Experi-encing new life created the need to rediscover religion as a way to articulate and celebrate the great mysteries of life. I am deeply saddened and angered by the prevalent misuse of religion.

The path toward wholeness has been a spiral, going ever deeper, touching the same bases again and again. Am I done with it? Whenever I think so, I find I am not. Are we ever "done" and whole and perfectly in relationship with God and ourselves? I can say, however, that my own experience of healing thus far contributes to a very strong faith and hope in the creative potential of any situation.

POST SCRIPT: SOME NOTES ON HELPING INCEST VICTIMS.

Stages of Healing:

—a "hibernation period" of relative calm; a time for growing, getting ready, with occasional, minor anxiety or depression, and low self-esteem.

—a crisis—the wisdom of the unconscious breaks through, probably most often before any conscious understanding of what is going on.

—psychotherapy—becoming a person

—"dealing with it": first, with one's self—through stages of anger, pain, revulsion, and forgiveness; then, with the offender—"the confrontation" and consequently with the affected family.

Typical Errors in Helping:

—wanting to rush to forgiveness, not realizing the depth of the problem and not seeing the need for all the middle stages of healing.

—judgmental attitudes: not so much about what has happened in the past, about how one should think and feel now. Example, "You seem angry and hostile; why haven't you forgiven your parents yet?" (Yes, that does happen in some counseling situations.)

—impatience. This process takes a long, long time. (It has been six years since I got into therapy and simultaneously confronted my father, and my story tells you how I am doing. I consider myself a strong and highly motivated person, so we are talking about many years.)

—rushing a confrontation before one is ready. The person will know when they have to do it, although undoubtedly she will agonize and be extremely reluctant. Gentle encouragement is needed, no pushing.

What Is Needed:

—some understanding of the magnitude of the problem, and a lot of patience

—reduce anxiety, give support, facilitate storytelling and self-discovery

—above all, believe in the person and in the healing process!

If you don't have hope, you can't help at all.[12]

CHAPTER ELEVEN

Love, Spirituality and Sexuality

Over the years we have become increasingly certain that love is the heart, the center of the universe, and that the highest function of human beings is to experience the victorious love of the risen Jesus and to share it and to express it to those around us. Paul's famous chapter on love, I Corinthians 13, states that no matter how many talents or how much knowledge we have, or what spiritual gift we possess, without love we have no worth and, in fact, we are nothing at all. And in mutually intimate relations between committed partners, the genital relationship can be a sacrament of that love.

Whatever our sexual lifestyle—whether single, married, committed partners or celibate—our sexuality needs to be ordered by love. It is valuable or destructive to the degree that it expresses love or does not express love. We need to be more interested in *loving* than in *being loved*, in *caring for*, rather than *being cared for*; yet at the same time we must be willing to be loved and cared for by our partner in whatever way he or she is able to love and care for us. A true ordering of sexuality, furthermore, is seldom possible without a spiritual life which puts sexuality in its proper perspective and gives the nourishment that comes from being in touch with the Divine Lover. The heart and center of celibate life, the heart and center of married life, the heart and center of coupled people with homosexual orientations, the heart and center of committed partners or of *any* life is love; and love is fed by our spiritual life, which, in turn, is deepened by the very love it feeds.

One celibate had a breakdown trying to live a perfectly regulated life in which there was no place for intimacy and caring. In describing his experience he concluded that no one can be genuinely celibate unless he or she loves. Loving is demanding, and we can't continue loving unless we are in touch with and directed by the Divine Lover, who is at the heart and center of the universe. We cannot love consistently and fully, nor can we bear the tensions in which love and sexuality involve us, unless we experience the persistent, tender, loving mercy of the dying, rising God. And yet without human love our spiritual love is likely to dry up and disappear. These two movements to full human and divine intimacy seem to be strangely intertwined.

Many people try to reduce sexuality to pleasure or to an instinctual reproductive process. In his excellent book *Marriage—Dead or Alive*, to which we have already referred, Guggenbuhl-Craig points out the stupidity of these notions. We have read no better discussion of the holiness of sexuality:

> The compelling power of sexuality, the fact that most people devote a great part of their fantasy to sexual themes, the enormous problem that sexuality has been in every age—all of this is not accidental and would be completely unintelligible were it true that it had to do only with the experience of a simple pleasure. Sexuality has always had something of the numinous about it, something uncanny and fascinating. The fact, for instance, that there was temple prostitution in historical times in the Orient does not mean that these peoples perceived sexuality as something "natural", as something that one could experience in a frivolous and pleasurable way. It indicates just the opposite: these peoples experienced sexuality as something so numinous that it could even take place in a temple...
>
> Another no less important task of the individuation process is for men to confront the feminine, and women the masculine, sides of themselves, to have a confrontation with the anima and animus. The struggle with the contrasexual side and the awareness of one's mysterious bond to it provide the opportunity to experience and to understand the polarities of the soul and of the world, of man and woman, human being and God, good and evil, conscious and unconscious, rational and irrational. The so-called *coniunctio oppositorum*, the union or convergence of the opposites is one of the many models and symbols of the goal of individuation...
>
> The individuational aspect of sexuality reveals itself most com-

pellingly in the loving, intense encounter between man and woman, in the momentary, ecstatic fusing together of the love act. This most deeply moving of human experiences cannot be grasped as merely biological copulation. This powerful event in which man and woman become one, physically and psychologically, is to be understood as a living symbol of the *mysterium coniunctionis*, the goal of the way of individuation. The sexual union of the King and Queen was considered by the alchemists to be the crowning of their work. Sexual fusion expresses the bridging in us of all the prevailing oppositions and incompatibilities. To an extent man and woman complete one another, to an extent they are not at all synchronized with one another. In the love act the whole polarity and fragmentation of being is overcome. This is its fascination, not the associated possibility of a reproductive result. The act of love is moreover much more than merely an expression of the personal relationship between a certain man and a certain woman. It is a symbol of something that goes beyond the personal relationship. This explains the frequent appearance of erotic images in the description of religious experiences. The mystical union of God is in part symbolized by the love act. In this sense most of the love stories of the world, the love poems and the songs about the union of man and woman, are not to be understood as merely expression of erotic life, but as religious symbols.[1]

Sexuality, then, is a strange and mysterious aspect of our human nature. At times our sexuality in itself can give a taste of wholeness and even of a mystical union with the Divine. On the other hand, our sexual desires may also drive us out of ourselves to God to find wholeness and understanding. However—and this is a most important "however"—the divine aspect of sexuality seldom arises unless we first turn inward and integrate our sexual beings into the total pattern of our lives. Sexuality seldom brings us to the fullness of love and wholeness, to an experience of God, unless we have a conscious spiritual life and a growing relationship with God into which to integrate it. We might add that we have seen homosexuals who have experienced something of the deepest mystical union with their beloved as fully as those seized by heterosexual love. We have also known celibates whose *inner* contrasexual union has given them this same experience.

We cannot conclude this discussion of sexuality without a description of the spiritual life of which our sexuality can be a sacrament, or toward which our sexual confusion often goads us. The two of us have had two very different kinds of spiritual journeys. For each of us our sexuality, love and spirituality have been one interwoven fabric. So both of us will describe our spiritual pilgrimages. We shall each write in the first person. Morton writes first and offers suggestions for fellowship with the Divine love that originate in his own journey and struggle, a struggle from darkness and doubt to love and hope. Both of our stories illustrate, we think, a general problem: we humans simply do not expect enough from God. We are continually underestimating God's incredible love for us, love which can use sexuality as well as other experiences. This Divine Lover only makes one demand upon us: that we be channels to others of the very love that he gives us.

MORTON'S JOURNEY:
IMAGERY PRAYER AS A WAY TO FELLOWSHIP WITH GOD

The experience of God's love broke in upon me in many different ways. Traumatic experiences in early adulthood had convinced me that love was transient and one dare not rely upon it. Nonetheless as I looked for meaning in a bleak and meaningless world, I entered the priesthood. I had reached the conclusion in seminary that there were as good reasons for believing in God and a meaningful universe as there were for not believing (not exactly a profession of faith, but it was certainly better than having no faith at all). Vocationally I did well in the Church, and I also married and had two wonderful children. Eventually I entered a new parish, where I intended to be the best clergyperson it had ever seen. I was working fourteen hours a day when the Hound of Heaven caught me. Suddenly I came to the end of the road.

Outwardly everything looked fine, but every time I got up to preach in the pulpit, a very persistent voice perching firmly on my left shoulder whispered into my left ear, "But you know you don't believe any of that claptrap." Very disconcerting. I have said since then that most liberal clergy have little integrity and sensitivity unless they have had a neurotic collapse.

And I had ghastly dreams. I'll never forget this one: I had gone to my new church—a magnificently poured concrete North Italian Gothic structure—to prepare for the service. However, the service was being held in the original little old wooden church, that was at the time used as the parish office. I went into this little wooden chapel to begin the Sunday service, and first of all, I couldn't find my place in the prayer book. You know what that means to any liturgically minded person—a fate worse than death. Then

I couldn't find the vestments. That's like being naked. And then, last of all, I couldn't find the sermon. With that preparation I turned around to see the real calamity. A dead tree had fallen through the nave of the church. And now my consternation really struck me. How was I going to have the offering taken up through the branches of the dead tree? My lack of preparation and the cracked church pictured the state of my ministry and my soul.

Shortly after this dream Barbara had to go East with the two children, as her father was sick. I was living as a celibate. When a married person lives a celibate life, it often feels like the end of the world. I was all alone in the rectory, and I never liked being alone at night. I remember that one night the presence of Dracula in a dream was so strong that I wondered if I should get up and put garlic on the windows just to be on the safe side. It was then I knew I should begin learning the meaning of my dreams.

I went to see a Quaker friend of mine, Dorothy Phillips, who had written a book called *The Choice is Always Ours*—a ground breaking book that shows how similar the thinking of C.G. Jung and other modern depth psychologists is to the major Christian writers on the devotional life. My friend Dorothy Phillips gave me the name of somebody I could go and talk to. I was in such a state that he saw me four times the first week—a rarity in Jungian analysis. My analyst was a man who had escaped from a Nazi concentration camp, a German Jew; he understood what anxiety was. He began to point out to me that in these dreams God was trying to draw me to himself. I could hardly believe it, but as I worked on them my anxieties lessened and my life began to come together.

Now, the first dream with which I made my entrance into the analytic world (I had thought I could produce at least a one-act play) consisted of nothing but the image of a pink peach pit. And with this great dream symbol, I entered the office. The analyst asked me, as we began to talk, what I associated with peach pits. The answer was pretty simple—peaches. Then he asked me my association to peaches and I said, "Georgia". And then he asked me my association to Georgia, and I'm not going to tell you because it went straight to the heart of some of my sexual fears, about which I had never talked to any human being. And this at the age of thirty-four! Talk about the wisdom of something that was knocking right at my door. And presenting a major problem in my life as a peach pit, which, if planted, could bring forth a tree—and the very fruit of life. I have learned more about the rich symbolism of the peach tree as each year has passed. Among the Chinese it is an archetypal symbol of beauty and wholeness.

I began to feel as if I were being visited each night by someone who brought to my attention all the problems that were besetting me. There was a wisdom in the dreams that was greater than any wisdom my highly developed, one-sided rational mind could offer. I had heard about God speaking to human beings. I had read about it. I had read a lot of good theology, in fact. Baron von Hugel had been my theological mentor and had given me a structure that had enabled me to enter in the church as a minister. But here there was someone actually knocking at the door of my soul while I was sleeping. And the speech was in a universal language, trying to bring me to the Divine Lover. However, I did need help in learning and interpreting this universal language.

Another dream I had early in my analysis pictured me as a student in a military school. Now if there was any place in the world that I wouldn't have wanted to be, it was in a military school. I once taught in one. How tragic the school was! Most of the students were there because their parents did not want to be bothered with them because they were undisciplined and uncontrollable. So what was this dream trying to tell me? It was saying exactly what that reform-school atmosphere was trying to say: "Morton, you need to get some discipline into your life." These dreams came to me thirty-four years ago, and since then I have recorded ninety-five percent of my dreams. The journal I'm keeping now is number thirty-four or thirty-five—I have lost track of the number.

After another dream, one of those very vivid ones, I awoke absolutely sure that I had heard heavy earth-moving equipment grinding throughout the church camp I was supervising (in the San Bernardino mountains up around Lake Arrowhead). In my groggy, freshly roused state I said to myself, "Are they going to bulldoze right straight through our church camp?" Now here was a dream that reminded me of the biblical passage, "Every valley shall be filled up and every mountain shall be leveled." There was some pretty heavy reconstruction that needed to go on inside of me, but it could only happen if I worked along with the wisdom coming to me from beyond me.

Another dream pictured me in the midst of a swamp. I thought it was telling me that I was caught in a hopeless situation, but my analyst was suprisingly happy with it. He said, "No place teems with more life than a swamp. The swamp is where life came from. You are in a fecund, growing, creative place, and there can be real growth." I thought of that dream as I saw the hero struggle through the swamp in the archetypal film *The Never Ending Story*.

The final dream I want to share pictured me driving our station wagon. There was a *Wizard of Oz* witch fastened onto the front radiator cap on the hood of our old Plymouth station wagon. I was driving like fury trying to get rid of her, but it didn't do any good. I turned the car this way; I turned the car that way. I speeded up and slammed on the brakes—I did everything I could to dislodge her. But finally I realized I had to face her, so I stopped the car and got out. She came toward me, and at that moment I noticed that down at my left side there was a bucket of water. So I baptized her in the name of the Father, and of the Son, and of the Holy Ghost. And she simply melted away like the Wicked Witch of the West in *The Wizard of Oz*. What this dream showed me was that I didn't have to fear a lot of the things that I was fearing. I simply had to take my Christianity seriously, experientially.

What did all these dreams do for me and why am I sharing them with you? They showed me that there was a wisdom in the universe wiser than I, which cared for me more than I could for myself—enough to break into my life and to continue knocking at the door of my soul whether I listened or not. And I realized that the direct experience of this loving wisdom and care was what Christianity was all about. But it is hardly possible to keep in touch with what the Lord has to say to us—through dreams as well as through other means—if we don't keep a journal and write our dreams and inspirations down when they come to us. I doubt if it is possible to assimilate the wise inner voice—the love, mercy and providence the wise inner voice would give us—unless we write down what we experience. These dreams also made me realize that unless I was living love, particularly toward my wife and children, I was going against the grain of the universe.

The second set of experiences I want to share with you was even more dramatic than this set of dreams. I don't know how long I had been working on the dreams, but things were getting better. When my wife got back from her trip East, I had changed so much that she decided she would get into analysis to find out what had changed me so much and to learn about the new person with whom she was living. She had been keeping me together with baling wire and Scotch tape, and now she had lost her job! I could hold myself together. Don't think that doesn't give a wife a shock; she had to find a new profession.

But despite the fact that things were improving, I walked into the analyst's office one day looking like death warmed over. He looked at me and said, "Morton, what's the matter with you? Do you feel as bad as you look?" And I said, "I look only half as bad as I feel." "Well," he said, "What's the trouble?" I said, "Sometimes I can't sleep at night. I slept for four or five hours last night and then I woke up at 2:00 am and tossed and turned and the Lord knows I have a fourteen-hour day today."

And then he said to me, "Why do you think you wake up at night?" I thought this was a silly question; after all, I was paying him good hard cash to solve my problems. I sort of growled and said, "I don't know, you tell me." And he said, "You know why you wake up at night? God wants to talk to you." My reaction was, "Really now. I've been to seminary." "Well," he replied, "that's the way he got in touch with Samuel; do you think he's changed?" "Okay," I said, "I'll even try something as foolish as listening to God in the middle of the night."

That night I went home and, sure enough, four or five hours later I woke up. I gathered myself together, took my journal, which I kept beside my bed with a pencil secured to it, and went to the only warm room in the house. I took out my journal and said, "All right, Lord, what's on your mind?" And very quietly there was an answer within me: "I'd just like a little of your time and attention. I care about you." I said, "At 2:00 a.m.?" And the reply came back, "It's the only time I can get your attention." And this went on for a half hour or so. I had met the Divine Lover. I went back to bed and went to sleep. I have repeated this practice at least five to six nights a week for the last thirty plus years. Not every time do I get a brilliant revelation. But every time I am assuaged. Every time I know I am not alone. Every time I experience love. I have never, ever been received with less than utter graciousness and concern and care.

There is a third way that I have met the saving center of Love—and in some ways it is the most convincing. I've struggled with darkness and depression for most of these last sixty years. I had one of those disastrous childhoods. And frankly, if you have had a disastrous childhood, about the only answer—the only possible answer—is the risen Jesus, one who conquered life and death and Evil. A tramautic childhood wears thin your soul so the forces of darkness can slip in.

The third thing I learned, then, was that when the mood of anger or fear or depression was near, instead of getting busy to avoid the agony of my inner life, I should turn directly into the dark and painful mood and allow these feelings to express themselves in images. Moods and feelings are so amorphous and intangible that there is little that we can do with them.

I have described this process in several places; it is a process similar to Jung's active imagination, and it is also much like the *Spiritual Exercises* of Ignatius Loyola.[2] Teresa of Avila describes a similar way of coming to the saving center of one's being in *The Interior Castle.*

In order to enter into this process we need, first of all, to put off all other concerns, to become totally still. We need to have two to four hours of time free before us, even if we will not use all that time. We allow our moods to present themselves in images and we listen to the dark voices that hound us; at the same time we hang on to the inner determination to continue calling out for help to the one who has conquered life and death and evil. Unless we continue to cry out for help until it comes, we can get caught in the hopeless meaninglessness of Sartre or Camus, and this can lead to spiritual disaster. There is a certain seductive sweetness in hopelessness that needs to be resisted as we strive on through the worst of darkness, never giving up until the light appears. Here is an example of this process which I wrote while working on this manuscript.

So many concerns and fears beset me waking me in the middle of the night. . . Fears of those close to me, fears about my capability, concerns about sexuality stirred up by writing on this subject. These things seem so overwhelming that I don't know what to do with them. . . they wash over me like a tidal wave. . . nothing to hang onto, the struggle seems hardly worth it. I feel like crawling into a hole and dragging the dirt in after me. What is the use of going on? Part of me knows better. What do I do Lord?

INNER VOICE: Sounds like you should listen to these voices hammering at you. . .

ME: I didn't realize they were here. . . fairly productive day yesterday. . .

INNER VOICE: But the night showed them up.

ME: Lord, I am sick of them.

INNER VOICE: So am I, but they have to be faced by you to be dealt with.

ME: Spew on the dark one, vile one. . .

DARK VOICE: Vile am I? You are the vile one. Stop projecting on me. You are one of the most neurotic, miserable, depraved, deformed, ugly monstrous creatures there is or has been. Stop running away and face what you are. . . foul, smelly, fraudulent, hopeless mess, deceiver of people. You go into psychotic oblivion of your real state. . .but look and see where you really are. . .You're in the pit again. Hear the rattling chains, smell the sulfurous fire into which we shall cast you to burn exquisitely, forever. . .Your dear Lord spoke of the tares that would burn and the worthless fish caught in the net that would be thrown into the fire. You are certainly a tare and useless. . .On top of that you are stupid. Life gives you things and you waste them. . .stupid, out of touch with reality, worn out, finished but still able to fool people. . .And then greatest joke of all. . .You, you write about sex. You would be really funny if you did not lead so many people astray. . .away from reality. . .what do you know about it?

ME: If you are the only reality what are you worried about, everything will come to you. You try to swallow people, to make them dependent because you are afraid you'll lose them.

One of the dark one's minions whom I had not seen standing near me strikes me with a hard blow on the face and mouth. . .Again and again the blows come and then others join in. . .all screaming, "You shall pay for talking to our master this way." Finally I crumple under their blows. I thought they might destroy me with their fists and rocks and kicks and then I hear the Dark One him/herself:

DARK VOICE: Go easily, do not kill him, that would be too good for him . . .We have more delicious tortures for him. . .cutting him apart bit by bit. Tie him down, strip off his clothes and we shall proceed.

ME: Lord, here I am. Beaten and tortured. . .They are driving splinters under my nails and into my groin. Come help and deliver. . .

DARK VOICE: Ho, ho, he thinks that he can be rescued from us now. He came here of his own free will. .

Then a voice is heard, a quiet voice, a voice of authority and love. . .

INNER VOICE: He did not come of his own free will. . .You snared him. He belongs to me with all his faults and failures. He makes mistakes, but he keeps on trying. You trouble him because you are afraid of him and of me. I am here among you now. He called and I came.

My tormentors tremble with fear as the voice reverberates through the dark cavern, the yellow fires are quieted. All of them look for a place to flee, but the voice surrounds them and gradually the whole place becomes luminous with white light.

INNER VOICE: Run back to your cracks in the rock. Hide, if you can, from my presence. You have no moment not filled with fear, fear of love, fear and hatred of the light, terrified by your own rebellion and lostness, restlessly trying to drag others into your misery so you can stand it. . .

Then in the center of the cavern the light congeals into a presence, *the risen Presence*. The minions of hell flee into their hiding places. S/he comes to me, kneels down beside me and unties me and then removes the splinters from my face and genitals and hands and feet. S/he tenderly picks me up and carries me on that rugged pathway through the roughhewn rock passage way up out of the pit. . .The sun is shining when we step out of the dark stone tunnel where the only light had been shed by my Lord. I am nearly blinded by the light. A small shelter had been erected near the waterfall, roses are growing up around it and inside it is cool and dark. . .a bed of boughs is covered with sheep skins and a light blanket of soft wool. He lays me down and says. . .Rest here and sleep. I will sit beside you. Fear nothing.

ME: Lord, (I whisper) why again and again?

INNER VOICE: Not now. . .rest and sleep.

He closes my eyes and I fall sleep. I do not know how long I slept, but when I awake I feel human again. I look up at the bough above me and then to my left and there my beloved still sits beside me. He reaches over and takes my hand. It seems too good to be true. Then he lifts me up and embraces me and I feel his love penetrating through me. We walk out into the sun. . .the sun is high in the sky. . .We run together over the meadow blooming with a thousand flowers and then he throws off his robe and I throw off mine and we dive into the warm pool. It is the very water of life and I begin to come to life. He comes over to me and we play in the water, splashing water back and forth.

INNER VOICE: You are so serious. . .Where would you go from here. . . being too serious can keep you out of the kingdom.

ME: A taste of the kingdom Lord. . .that is what I desire.

INNER VOICE: It is right there when you can see it.

At first I can see nothing but rock walls that rise like battlements over on the right side of the stream that flows down to the sea. . .It is further than it looks and between here and there are forests and hills. . .

ME: All I see is a rocky escarpment with columns of rock here and there.

INNER VOICE: Look again. . .

ME: Yes, Lord I begin to see. . .it is a great castle, one of the many places where the King dwells. Can we go up there?

INNER VOICE: Of course, but you can only start toward those goals that you first see. . .

ME: Is it a long journey?

INNER VOICE: It is both very short and very long and a journey we take again and again. It is the place you started from and the place where you are going and is the way. . .all three. Today it will not take you long.

A heavy wind arises and picks us up and takes us to the door of the great castle. The door is open and we see that what we thought was a castle, confined in space, was really a wall and on the other side is a land of incomparable beauty, rolling hills, lakes, forests, meadows. . .and here and there are villages and cities. . .On one great lake is an island, and there is a palace of great simplicity and beauty. Gradually we make our way there.

INNER VOICE: First we to to see Abba and then you can meet those who have come here to live that you have loved. It is the long way to the lake, but the time passes quickly as we talk.

ME: Why, Lord, do I fall again into that darkness without knowing it?

INNER VOICE: Because you are human and live in a world infested with evil and then because you resist the dark one, he wishes you to give up and destroy yourself. You threaten him.

ME: What little I do could not threaten his infernal majesty. . .

INNER VOICE: That one is weaker than you think. . . Are you still frightened and tired?

ME: Yes, Lord, I am still frightened and tired, but being with you makes things much better. . . still tired, but not as frightened. You certainly come when I call.

INNER VOICE: No, I do not come. I am here with you all the time, but when you face your need and then call you give me the opportunity to enter your life and give you the saving help that you need, the love you crave, the direction you seek. . . and here we are. . .

The boat awaits us at the water's edge and we climb in. . . It is a perfect day. The water is warm and I believe that it is the water from this lake that issues forth from the spring that falls into the pool in the secret garden . . . Soon we are at the island and we walk through the streets lined with flowering trees and up to the great central building. . . There we enter and then, after passing through many doors and tapestry curtains woven with strange designs, we enter the great audience hall. . . The light is intense, but it does not hurt the eyes like the sun. . . But I am awed, take off my shoes and fall to the floor and prostate myself. . . I hear my Lord laughing . . . And then I feel his hand lifting me up and his words.

INNER VOICE: It is right that you feel as you do when you come into the presence of the Holy One, but there is nothing to fear, S/he loves you as much as I do.

Here is one who is both an old man, the wise nurturing woman, a beautiful youth, a lovely maiden, a child and something entirely different from all of these. This one envelopes me rather than embracing me and in that all-encompassing encounter I am known in all of me and I know love. . . Then in a voice like crystal bells I hear: "Welcome; it was so good of you to come. Thank you, my beloved, for bringing him. But he is tired. Take him to the room prepared for him from beginning of time and let him rest. Do come again. All that I ask of you is that you share with all those around you the same love you are so freely given." By this time I am nearly asleep on my feet and I am let out of the great hall into the street to a house that bears my name and birthdate. A yard and garden with a fountain playing in it lie behind the house. Angels are awaiting there to minister to me. My lord embraces me again and I am taken to a pool where I bathe and then fall into bed and sleep.

As the images of hopelessness and destruction changed to images of love and healing and transformation, the moods and overwhelming darkness receded, and I was able to gather myself together and go on.

John Welch has written an excellent book, *Spiritual Pilgrim*, that compares *The Interior Castle* of St. Teresa with Carl Jung's depth psychology. And St. Teresa says that until we get to the very center of the interior castle, the pain and agony often increase. And we don't stay at the center long before we go through the snake pit again. From my point of view, this seems like a terrible way for God to have created the universe, but it is the way it seems to be. And so spiritual practice isn't done once and for all. I must return again and again or else I fall into the abyss. But even if I do fall, I don't have to stay there, because there is One who will pull me out.

The realization that there is Someone who cares about me, who will rescue me, who died for me, over whom even death itself has no power, came to me after my brother died. I had suddenly discovered I was afraid of dying, and I sat down and looked death in the face in a meditation. And suddenly death was enclosed in a silken pouch and I realize that *he* was frightened, and that I didn't have to be afraid even of him.

Then came the realization that I had to work at loving those around me, particularly my family, if I was going to stay in touch with the Divine Lover. I described earlier how my son John taught me so much about love. All the members of my family have taught me that love is something we have to work at. Prayer and love are not separate. They are the inner and outer aspects of the same process. What my family and analysis and prayer have taught me about love is too extensive to describe here, but I have put my version of it in my book *Caring: How Can We Love One Another?*[3]

Out of these four experiences—listening in order to touch of the Other in my dreams, listening to the Divine Lover in the silence, using meditations such as the one just shared, and trying to love those around me with the same love that I had been given—I have begun to stay more open to the persistent love of the risen Christ. But don't make the mistake of thinking that this kind of life doesn't require constant discipline—a constant openness to others and to the presence of Christ.

BARBARA'S SPIRITUAL JOURNEY

Barbara has had a very different spiritual journey from Morton's. She writes: I was always aware that I had been a very-much-wanted first child who arrived ten years after my parents were married. My family were church-attending Methodists who believed in a very personal God, and I was taught early to talk with God about about my desires, problems, and hopes, and to give thanks. Most of my very early prayer time was at bedtime, and for me bedtime prayers were a good, permanent habit; each night, even now, I find it helpful and necessary to review the day, ask forgiveness for what has been amiss, give thanks, and pray for those I love and those in need. And I end by asking the Lord to watch over me.

When I was nine years old our family doctor discovered that my mother had cancer; in those days, that was a sentence of death. And in our family, children were not excluded from the joys or the sufferings. For example, I always knew what the family financial situation was, and I was allowed to help decide how what we had would be spent (these were the depression years, and we didn't have very much). So the fact that my mother was considered terminal was shared with my brother and with me. My mother had faith that life continued after death and that her influence on us would also continue. I never questioned this, but the sad years that followed the revelation that she had cancer were years when I pleaded with God nightly not to take our mother from us.

My parents were soulmates and appeared to be deeply in love with each other, and therefore I now realize how much my father was suffering. During the next eight years my mother managed to live in spite of nine operations and deep X-ray therapy, which left her skin burned to a crisp. During all this time I pleaded and pleaded with God. Meanwhile, at the age of nine, it had become my duty to do the cooking and to take care of my mother during the night if she needed care.

At age 17 I went away to college. I had been brought up in a liturgical Methodist Episcopal church and I discovered in my new city that my denomination was not liturgical—did not have formal services or frequent Eucharist. At that time I also discovered how much I needed this more structured outer worship with others at least once a week. The communion service seemed to bring me an experience of the Divine that I received in no other way. So I began to attend the Episcopal Church, which was more like the church in which I was raised.

The day before Thanksgiving during that first year in college, my mother died. I was devastated; I felt let down by God. It seemed to me that just when I left home and turned my back, God let her die. After two weeks of being home I returned to college, and each night I would cry out to God for leaving me without a mother.

For the next several years I kept attending the Episcopal Church, and I finally met Morton the month after he graduated from seminary when I went to him for confirmation instructions. It was not love at first sight. I was engaged to another man, who was away in the war. But I became active in Morton's church and circumstances intervened, and the man I was engaged to was no longer available.

After some time Morton and I were married. Being a priest's wife was a more or less prescribed role forty-plus years ago, and I admit that, though I worked hard at it, many parts of the prescribed role I did not enjoy. At that period in our lives I continued the daily conversational "talking things over" with God, and Morton and I read the Bible each day together. However, we did not pray together. These were busy war years and I taught at school, did case work for the Red Cross, and faithfully attended all meetings and services connected with Church.

As I look back on my life I realize that my great experiences, both positive and negative, were really religious experiences, but at the time I did not interpret them in that way. For me the sexual experience was one in which God was present. In many of the more negative experiences, I railed at God for not hearing me, but I realize now that until I could be honest with God and be angry, I could not be real. Later I often felt guilty for these angry feelings and words, and I had to learn to feel forgiven for them.

My first pregnancy ended in a miscarriage and was a crushing experience, but perhaps the most difficult time for me was shortly after our second child was born. Morton suffered his darkness experience, about which he has already written; most lay people would refer to this experience as a nervous breakdown. I was terrified. Here we were in a parish. I knew something was radically wrong with my husband. I kept up the outer appearances

that everything was all right, but in this time of need I found myself praying ever more intently. I learned to pray just for each day.

At this point in my life my father was taken seriously ill in the East,
and I needed to go and help care for him. I hated to leave Morton, but
he and I decided I had to go; so I took the children, and nine weeks later
I returned and found that Morton had received help, as he has told you,
and that I was living with an entirely different person. Before I had been
needed, but now I had the feeling that Morton was so happy to be able
to stand on his own two feet that he was like an adolescent who wanted
to go his own way. I felt I was no longer central in his life, to his work,
or to his needs. In desperation I went to see his analyst. Over the long period
of time that I was in analysis I discovered that I was more than a wife and
mother—I was me and Morton was Morton, and I just had to allow these
two individuals, ourselves, to work out a new marriage. All of this I now
know was spiritual growth for me, painful as it was, but at the time I hated
having to recognize this and to allow it to happen. Society was not sup-
portive of independent women at that time, and I really had had very little
drive towards independence. But I did learn to let Morton go—railing at
the Lord all the time!

Out of these several years of great trauma for me, I learned that Morton
had discovered a way of having a personal, one-to-one experience of the
Divine. I spent many hours trying to make his method of going to the Lord
work for me as it did for him. The Lord seemed to speak directly with him,
but with me he just didn't seem to want to communicate! About this time
I read most of the devotional classics, and a few gave me some help; the
ones that did just encouraged me to keep up my conversational way of talking it all over with God and telling him honestly what I felt, not what
I thought God would want to hear.

Years later a Roman Catholic priest who had known me for several
years leveled with me and told me that I was a completely different type
of person than Morton, and that I had had such a different childhood and
background that I was wasting my time trying to meditate in the way Morton
did. The priest said that I should find my own way and that not everyone
found images and imagination real for them or a way to God.

I then discovered a way that I call contemplation (only because Morton
labels what he does meditation, and I needed a word to distinguish his from

mine). I observe something closely, preferably in nature (but music and art can be useful also). After asking God to be in this with me, I concentrate for a few minutes on this experience and only this, and then in some mysterious way I experience a real sense of presence. I seem to feel I come into rhythm with the total universe or become one with it.

In *Companions on the Inner Way* I wrote my description of this process.

> The basic idea is that the spiritual and physical worlds are one in the sense that they totally interpenetrate each other. Whenever we touch the physical we are also touching the spiritual. Contemplation (from this point of view) is an attempt to deal with our spiritual lives in the same natural way that we human beings handle most situations in life. This is a threefold process:
>
> 1. We experience something.
>
> 2. We mull it over or think about it.
>
> 3. We try to discern what implications this experience and our consideration of it has for our lives.
>
> As a method of religious discovery, we need first of all to become aware that we have lived all our lives in a society that has given us a sensory overload of noise and smells and colors. We have become desensitized to sensory experience, and we need to learn to truly *experience* once again. We need to concentrate *totally* on a limited area of sensation for a short period of time without blocking any aspect of it and without thinking about it— just experiencing the *what* as it is now. We can usually enter that sensory experience and stay with it for a short period of time. Any analytical thought at that time immediately turns off the process.
>
> The process begins with relaxation, quieting of the body and the mind as much possible. After a few minutes of experiencing and concentrating on the sensory data that is presented, we can then withdraw further into the silence, into the absence of any sensation, and rest in it, just experiencing whatever comes. What comes may be a dazzling darkness, a sense of presence, a deep sense of peace, a cessation of struggle, or we may be presented with a word, a thought, a number, a color, a musical sound, etc.
>
> As we pull out the depth of the quiet we begin to mull over that which has been given, thinking about it, seeing where this experi-

ence leads us. This can go on for several minutes or an hour. The last stage occurs as we pull out of the depth of quiet and try to understand what the experience means to us, how it applies to my everyday life, where I am now, what it tells me about my relationships with God, with other people, and with the world around me and finally what I am going to do about it.[4]

Four years ago I had a severe accident and was literally crushed. I spent months on my back in the hospital and at the home of a friend. I discovered that I did not rail at God so much. I really felt an inner peace (there was little outer peace during that time). I had learned to take each day, one day at a time, to give thanks for the little things that were pleasant (like having my position changed or being given a cold drink) and to say "ouch" to the Lord when I hurt—and I had a sense that he was with me all through that long experience of being helpless and in pain. I seldom felt down or discouraged—I knew that however it turned out, it would be all right. I learned that my contemplative way of coming into his presence was even a good way to control pain. When I was in God's presence I just knew that whatever was to be would be all right. It might not be the way I wanted it or Morton wanted it, and I wasn't even sure it was the way God wanted it, but whatever it was, my Lord, would be there with me. All I needed to do was to stop and become aware of the Presence, and then I knew things would fall in place. In many ways Morton and I are closer in our feelings, in understanding each other's values, in our intimacy and sexuality and in our prayer life than we have ever been before. In meeting together daily in the Eucharist we find that we can be present to each other and with the Divine.

THEOLOGY AND PRAYER

The idea that we human beings could have a direct experience of God such as we have described did not fit into the theology in which Morton had been trained—that of 20th-century liberal Christianity. Although the matter of theology was not a central concern for Barbara, it was for Morton, whose task it was to try to interpret these experiences in terms of the thinking of the Church if he was to preach and teach and write. He had to go back to the theology of the Church fathers of the first six or seven centuries of Christianity to find a congenial framework for these experiences. While Morton was studying at the Jung Institute in Zurich, he considered leaving the active ministry to become a Jungian analyst, because he saw little hope of bringing the experiences that we had had into the life of the church. In Zurich, however, Morton kept dreaming of building Byzantine churches. As he worked on these dreams he realized that his task was to stay in the full ministry, and to try to bring the dimension of direct religious experience common in the Greek Orthodox Church into the theological thinking of contemporary Western Christianity.

The Byzantine Church never fell into the intellectual sterility of scholastic rationalism. Whatever else we have found in the Greek church, we have felt that the sense of the presence and reality of God was never lost. Morton began to see his work as an attempt to answer the question: How can I be an intelligent, 20th-century Christian, believing that God touches our lives in dreams, lifts us up from the abysses into which we fall, converses with us in the silence of the night, comes as an enveloping presence, is living through us as we love and touches us in our deepest sexual experience? Such an ever-present Divine Lover hardly fits into rational theological thought.

It is nearly impossible to love and pray long and consistently unless we have a theology that has a place for a God who loves us, reaches out to communicate with us and would use us as instruments of Love. The picture most often found in theological thinking in the Western world is one of a God who made the natural world, but who is essentially external to it. This God breaks in now and then, but we know the Divine basically through history and inference rather than through experience. Within this theological framework it is very difficult to believe that we can *know* the reality of Love. Prayer, the centrality of love and the holiness of sexuality all disappear within that framework. It was a great comfort to have Carl Jung and Plato on our side, but in our position as a clergy family it was far greater comfort to realize that every major Church father—East and West—had a theological point of view that took the spiritual world very seriously; and these great thinkers also took dreams, prayer, and images— as expressions of divine and sensuous love— very seriously as well. This was the form of Christianity that Baron von Hugel had reintroduced in the first years of the 20th century.[5]

LOVE IN PARTNERSHIP WITH PRAYER

This theological view tells us that both the physical world and the spiritual world are real and vitally important for our psychological and spiritual growth. The risen Jesus expresses the essential nature of the spiritual world; there is, therefore, nothing left to fear. Our task is to stay in touch with this One who has conquered death and evil. We find our meaning—whether we are single, celibate, committed partners or married folk—by being so much in touch with the Divine Lover that both love and Love flow into us and out through us to those closest to us in full intimacy, then with self-giving concern to those whose lives we touch, and finally out to the whole world. This kind of love is not so much our action as it is the action of God, the action of love pouring out *through* us who allow ourselves to be channels of that love.

Few people allow themselves to experience the sensuous images of St. John of the Cross as he speaks of resting on Jesus' breast in his magnificent poem entitled "Songs of the Soul" or "Stanzas of the Soul", but these images are potent and beautiful:

1. On a dark night, Kindled in love with yearnings—
   oh, happy chance!—I went forth without being
   observed, My house being now at rest.

2. In darkness and secure, By the secret ladder, disguised—
   oh, happy chance!—In darkness and in concealment,
   My house being now at rest.

3. In the happy night, In secret, when none saw me,
   Nor I beheld aught, Without light or guide,
   save that which burned in my heart.

4. This light guided me More surely than the light
   of noonday, To the place where he (well I knew who!)
   was awaiting me—A place where none appeared.

5. Oh, night that guided me, Oh, night more lovely
   than the dawn, Oh, night that joined Beloved with lover,
   Lover transformed in the Beloved!

6. Upon my flowery breast, Kept wholly for himself alone,

There he stayed sleeping, and I caressed him, And the
fanning of the cedars made a breeze.

7. The breeze blew from the turret As I parted his locks;
    With his gentle hand he wounded my neck And caused
    all my senses to be suspended.

8. I remained, lost in oblivion; My face I reclined on the
    Beloved. All ceased and I abandoned myself,
    Leaving my cares forgotten among the lilies.[6]

The essential message of Jesus of Nazareth was to provide us the kind of
experience of which St. John of the Cross writes, so that we may be enabled
to have truly close, self-giving relationships with others. To express the
divine-human encounter, this great saint and poet uses the language and
symbolism of human intimacy in such a graphic way that we might look
askance at his language were the writer not so undeniably Christian.

The story of the prodigal son gives us another example of the Divine
Lover. Jesus says that God wants to have the same kind of relationship with
us that the father in that parable has with his prodigal son. After the son
has been perhaps with harlots and definitely around pigsties (according
to Jewish custom you were unclean for thirty days if you were around a pig-
sty), the father welcomes him home and lavishes gifts upon him. It's hard
for us to understand what a radical action it is for this father to bring out
the best cloak in the house as well as a ruby ring (the signet ring probably
gives the son legal rights to what is left of the father's property). But the
most amazing thing about this story, from a Jewish point of view, is that
the father's nose does not get out of joint when his elder son refuses to
come in to the feast celebrating the younger son's return. The elder son's
refusal to join the celebration is actually a worse breach of religious and
social etiquette than anything the prodigal son has done, and yet the father
goes and beseeches the elder son to come in.

What Jesus is telling us is that there is such a one as this abba to whom
we can turn, who will always receive us. It's almost unbelievable. It is too
good to be true. And so most Christians do not even consider this possibility
or respond to this radical message. Jesus said that the kingdom of heaven
is at hand, which means we can enter it *now*. We don't have to wait. We
can do this by following a twofold process. First, instead of seeking God
we must just stop and be silent. As long as we are totally involved in outer

doings, it is nearly impossible to become aware of another realm seeking our attention. All coming into the presence of Love, therefore, starts with silence. That's one of the reasons that God puts his little dramas at night, in our dreams: because our egos are finally put to sleep; our conscious activity has ceased; we are passive. Until we stop and turn inward, we will not know consciously the love that we are capable of knowing, the love that makes celibacy, marriage, committed intimacy and all of life worthwhile.

So the first stage is quiet, and we find we need four kinds of quiet. Some of us like the middle-of-the-night quiet time because we don't have to take time to quiet down. We are quiet already. It usually takes twenty minutes or so to quiet down out of our busy activity. The important thing is this time for reflection and listening. Until we stop and are quiet we cannot consciously reflect on what our relationships with others have been, how we have been loving, where we have gone astray and where we have been on target. Then, as we bring ourselves before the Divine Presence or the risen Christ, we can listen. And often something of real significance comes through. Sometimes we find real insights and inspiration; and sometimes we are simply quieted and restored, or we are directed to further work that we need to do. Morton maintains that most of the basic insights about the spiritual life and the meaning of Scripture have come to him during these times of quiet. Nearly every one of us needs at least half an hour daily to quiet down, center in, reflect and listen.

The second kind of time that we find incredibly helpful is our daily Eucharist which allows us to step into the rich symbolism and liturgical life of Christianity. We confess our failures and sins, we quiet down, praise God, listen to Scriptures, share with one another, give thanks, and then receive the very living presence of the risen Christ. It is difficult for us to remain stuck in our resentments and differences as we share the healing body and blood of Christ. Few people realize the radical love and forgiveness offered in Eucharist; in the fourth book of the *Imitation of Christ*, Thomas a Kempis gives one of the finest expositions of the meaning of Eucharist ever written. All we have to do, no matter what we have been or done, is to recognize and acknowledge our failures, punyness and rebellion, and we are welcomed by the risen Christ and infused with the divine loving Presence of God as we share in this sacred meal.

The Eucharist outwardly and dramatically symbolizes inner encounter, so well described by St. John of the Cross as an experience of being taken into the very arms of Christ. We are well aware that not all churches provide daily Eucharist, and not all households have an ordained clergyperson. However, each couple or household can have a structured time of prayer, quiet, confession, reconciliation, and scripture reading, based on the essential meaning of Eucharist. The rosary can also be used to provide a structured time of quiet and inward turning. This practice can be particularly helpful for people with a Protestant background, who discover this devotion as something new and therefore fresh, without some of the early-childhood hang-ups about the rosary with which many Roman Catholics have been afflicted.

Third, we need, at least every third week, three or four hours during which we promise ourselves that we will do nothing else but turn, alone, to the presence of Christ through either meditation or contemplation, and do a thorough spiritual housecleaning and rearrangement of our inner furniture, seeing what Christ has to offer us, how he can help us adjust our priorities. We have learned that whenever we are struck by darkness and oppression, we are simply silly not to stop immediately for this kind of time and come into the presence of the saving Christ asking for help. After all, Jesus came into the world to defeat evil and save us from the forces of darkness and bring us to the joy and creativity and love of the Kingdom. The imagination, for those who can use it, can be a helpful tool in bringing us into the Divine Presence; Barbara has suggested an alternate way for those who do not use imagination readily.

Fourth, at least once a year we need to make a retreat during which we can review and reset all our priorities and see how far we have strayed from the track. We need at least thirty-six hours—sometimes we need most of a month. Our task is to put aside our outer busyness, become receptive and turn inward to find what the Divine Lover would have us do, where we are supposed to go, what we are to become. Some of us at this time will be able to reflect on the thread of continuity that runs through our lives, which we are unable to see until we look back. (Barbara is aware, for example that God has kept his hand continuously in her life, but often she is not fully conscious of his influence until some time has passed.) And in the depth of this retreat experience, we have never found anything but forgiveness, mercy, compassion and caring love; and at the same time we always hear the mandate that we share this love with others, beginning with those with whom we are most intimate—especially our spouses, partners, children, parents and grandchildren.

To conclude, we will share an image offered by Austin Farrer.[7] He suggests that when I am quiet and come into Christ's presence, Christ takes my head into his wounded hands; though I twist my head and hurt his hands, still he looks at me, still he smiles at me until I can smile at him and then can turn with a smile to the hurting, broken world. When we are treated this way by the center of the universe, we realize that we are out of step with reality until we treat others, particularly our sexual partners, with the same kind of consideration. This means that we need to be able to talk about any aspect of our lives with our committed partners. And when we bring this kind of caring into our intimacy and sexuality, we are often given a taste of the Kingdom.

CHAPTER TWELVE

The Questions We Ask

During several oral presentations of the material that has been presented in this book in a slightly more expanded form, people were encouraged to hand in written and unidentified questions. In each case the questions were frank and honest. We also found that participants in our sessions were as much interested in the answers to the questions as they were in the basic material presented. So we are reproducing some of these questions and the answers we gave to them, though we have also dealt with a number of the questions within the body of what we have written. The groups to which we have spoken have consisted of clergy (celibate and married), men and women from religious orders, and lay people. Sometimes the questions identify the professional status of the questioner, but in most cases we have no knowledge about the person who turned in the questions. (In several instances, however, the questioner later sought us out for further discussion of the questions that had been raised.)

QUESTION: Does one who is homosexual (by this I mean living the active homosexual life) fail morally if he does not wish to change his orientation?

ANSWER: We have listened to and counseled many people with homosexual preferences or desires. The first thing that we need to do is assess whether the person is exclusively interested in homosexual relationships, or if he or she is genuinely interested in sexual relations with both sexes equally or whether the person's homosexual actions and thoughts are rare and sporadic. With regard to the first category, the best studies seem to show that exclusive homosexuality starts early in life and most probably has some genetic root. Changing homosexuals with this exclusive orientation is like changing an apple into an orange. For these people, the idea of genital heterosexual relation is as repulsive as homosexual genital contact is for the person whose orientation is almost entirely heterosexual. It is absurd to condemn such people for living out their sexual life in a mature, loving relationship.

For people in the latter two categories, however, the question remains open. Sometimes people who have bisexual interests or who have had one fleeting experience with either sex are convinced that there are no alternatives to exclusive homosexual or heterosexual lifestyles. They opt, then, for an exclusive lifestyle that does not represent the basic quality and nature of their sexual preferences. It is immoral not to find out who and what one truly is, and then to try to live that out with love and maturity as best one can.

It is immoral for a person to live at a low integrative level of sexual experience, if it is possible for him or her to come to a higher and more integrated and loving form. For instance, the morality of either heterosexual or homosexual activity is questionable if it involves force that is either overt or psychological, if it takes advantage of those who are too young or immature to make a free decision, if it causes damage to the other (like destroying a marriage), if it is promiscuous or fleeting (as public-bathroom sex acts or one-night stands, tend to be), or if it is directed only toward personal satisfaction and not toward relationship. We would question the morality of purely recreational sexual activity that is divorced from relationship. And teenage sexual involvement is not connected to real relationship in most cases, and is usually harmful to the teenagers' sexual development.

The value of sexuality, as we have said many times before, is how much and deeply it is integrated with love. Few of us have come to sexual moral perfection (indeed, we have yet to meet anyone who has, and so none of us in the position to throw the first stone). Those who do most of the judging are often those who are trying to avoid their own sexual confusions by projecting out their problems. Moral matters usually exist on a many-pointed scale; rarely are they black and white. When we have been able to facilitate people to move from public-restroom homosexual acts to a truly loving relationship, we feel that we have been of service; similarly, when we have helped a promiscuous heterosexual man or woman to move into a real relationship with another person, we have accomplished something of value.

Those people living in committed, long-term homosexual relationships are certainly morally superior to heterosexual people given to violence, promiscuity or prostitution.

QUESTION: How did the Church accommodate itself to the barbarians in regard to marriage?

ANSWER: The Church in Western Europe during the collapse of Roman government did not see presiding at a marriage as one of the necessary functions of the clergy until the twelfth century, and a church representative was not even present at weddings unless they were noble and royal nuptuals. Marriage was a secular affair and was not one of the functions of the clergy. The presence of clergy at weddings didn't become common at all until the thirteenth century. However, the church became involved in the matter of the indissolubility of marriage quite early; with the collapse of civil government, the church courts were the only courts left from about 700 A.D. in most of Western Europe. So although the church had little or nothing to do with the forming of marriages, it did decide when marriages could be broken and how property was inherited. But as the Church became central in society, it began to be involved in the marriages themselves. Nonetheless, until nearly 1200 the Church simply accepted the basic barbarian view of marriage and women. Little attempt was made to bring marriage into Jesus' understanding of it. It took Christian nations 1800 years to translate the obvious implication of Jesus' teaching about slavery into action. It's taking even longer to integrate his beliefs about the value of women, marriage, motherhood and children.

QUESTION: I didn't understand what you meant when you talked about the production of testosterone in the adolescent male.

ANSWER: There is a very definite statistical linkage between active aggression—and feelings of hostility—and the beginning of production of testosterone, the male sexual hormone, in the adolescent male. You can make a behavioral and a biological comparison that is highly statistically significant.

QUESTION: Could you say something about sex and anger?

ANSWER: This is a very interesting subject, and it brings in the whole area of sado-masochism. There is a study entitled *Phallos* by a Danish scholar, Thorkil Vanggaard, that shows that the symbol of an erect penis in many mammalian groups is a symbol of power. When a male baboon wants all other baboons to know that they are to remain in their place and stay away from his harem, he confronts challengers with an erection. So there is a strange sort of interconnection between aggressive, hostile anger and male sexuality. Freud in *Civilization and Its Discontents* suggests that there is no heterosexual intercourse which does not have some aggression in it. This, however, may just say something about his own sexual experience; we think that all aggressive action that is not mutual and playful is inadequate sex. But it is certainly true that many a male has to *learn* responsive sexual behavior. Most males have been raised in an aggressive, male-chauvinistic society, and they have to learn to treat women as equals. Indeed, sometimes when their aggression is taken away from them they can become impotent. Among some spiders, however, it is the *female* that is aggressive; she devours the male after being impregnated. Among humans, though, it is the male who tends to be more aggressive, even violent, while the female is usually the victim (an extreme example of this is the act of rape). But males can also be victims of other males. We know of a male who had repeated experiences of sodomy with other males. He recognized a sadistic element in these experiences.

QUESTION: I deal with a lot of Protestants in preparation for mixed marriages. What can you say in a general way about the kind of sexual morality that is taught in mainline Protestant churches?

ANSWER: In most mainline Protestant churches, people would probably get little or no teaching on the subject of sexual morality. The subject is taboo and that in itself is a kind of teaching. Teaching would usually come from families. It is necessary to find out what each person's individual background is before you have any idea how to respond. You may have to simply ask to find out. There is little uniform Protestant teaching about sexuality; there is no magisterium. The subject is largely avoided.

QUESTION: Am I wrong in believing that masturbation in some ways reflects repressed or suppressed sexual feelings? Could it be a way of escaping from a commitment to chastity?

ANSWER: The answer to this question will be dependent upon how one defines celibacy. If one follows the strict line of the magisterium we have discussed earlier, one who masturbates willfully, consciously, is not only breaking the vow of celibacy but is also committing mortal sin and has a one-way ticket to hell. However, we have taken several surveys of celibate clergy and religious and found that less than 10 percent of our samples viewed masturbation as a mortal sin and 80 to 90 percent occasionally practiced this form of solitary sexual release. We have discussed this matter with several mature, sophisticated people in the celibate life. They viewed masturbation as a more-or-less purely physiological release that actually, helped them maintain their celibate lifestyles without repression.

We have listened to hundreds of people, both Catholic and Protestant, speak of their guilts about masturbation. Although some of those raised in mainline Protestant churches have guilt, few have allowed their guilt to keep them from the practice. Among Catholics, the training before Vatican II was so strict that some had never touched themselves and are frightened to death of their own sexual organs, and incidentally of any relation with the opposite sex. Teaching at the University of Notre Dame, I found that most students raised in the parochial school system who came to me with problems would sooner or later discuss their fears about masturbation, and as they became more widely read and knowledgeable, they grew angrier and angrier at the havoc the things they had learned about masturbation had wrecked for them. They also often expressed a real anger for the church that had given them these ideas, and for the individual teachers as well.

We cannot state strongly enough that the facts of psychosexual development and the actual value of explorations of our own bodies, need to be considered more carefully in most churches.

QUESTION: I'm heterosexual and in love with a wonderful lady. She gives me the strength and closeness I need to continue as a priest. We have been sexually intimate and yet I love the priesthood and I want to stay. I need the closeness, intimacy and caring from her to continue. It seems to even heal the terrible hurts received from fellow priests and from the institution. Am I kidding myself? Is it possible to continue with my love and remain a priest?

ANSWER: A deep, painful, honest statement. Many have come to us with similar concerns. The most important advice that we can offer is that people who find themselves in this position must consciously and honestly face the terrible tensions in which such a situation places them. They need to avoid naivete. They need to face the laws of the institution, the hurt that they can cause their parishioners if the matter is discovered, the tension about their vows that they have broken. Such a position is like hanging on a cross. Not facing the dangers of the situation can cause a person unconsciously to reveal the problem, or to split apart inwardly and become neurotic. A person also needs to be very honest with his or her partner in this situation, making sure the partner realizes that marriage and children may never be a possibility, and especially making sure that neither person is using the other. It would be wise, we believe, for people in such circumstances to have a good spiritual director or counselor with whom to talk over tensions, fears, and the whole direction of their lives.

QUESTION: What is the difference between long-term sexual abstinence and celibacy?

ANSWER: Celibacy should be a commitment to abstinence for a purpose. Plain abstinence can occur because of the lack of suitable partner, or because one isn't interested by reason of conditioning or biology, or because it isn't worth the trouble to be involved. One interesting factor emerged during our group meetings: those who were trained in religious orders received during their seminary training some talks on the values of celibacy and how to deal with it, whereas most of those in diocesan seminaries had received almost no training in this area. And this is a situation which, perhaps, a place like Pecos could be a remedy. A workshop on the values of celibacy could be provided for those who find themselves in a celibate vocation and know little about handling it.

How single people who wish for sexual intimacy can deal with *their* sexual experience is another matter, and one that needs far more attention than we can give at this time.

QUESTION: You suggested that St. Paul's teaching on sexuality might be misunderstood today because the Greek was not properly translated. Was this only with reference to homosexuality?

ANSWER: It was homosexuality we had in mind. Exactly what Paul had in mind when he wrote "fornication", I don't really know; what he meant by "the flesh" warring against the spirit is also difficult to pin down. Paul is ambiguous. But homosexuality was not regarded in the Roman era the way it is regarded today. There was no specific word in Greek for "homosexual", as Boswell points out. Let me give you an example. The Emperor Hadrian (about 160 A.D.) was one of the most creative and constructive Roman emperors; he rebuilt the empire so well that it lasted until 400 A.D. He had a well-known and all consuming love affair with a young Greek youth named Antinous. A novel, *The Memoirs of Hadrian*, by Marguerite Yourcenar about this relationship, is a fine study of Hadrian and of homosexuality. This relationship, according to the novel, caused Hadrian many problems with his wife, but women weren't considered important at that time. It is interesting, though, that the Fathers of the Church did not condemn Hadrian for it because they saw that this relationship had humanized the emperor and had a positive effect on the whole empire. Such an attitude on the part of the church in ancient Rome is hard for us even to imagine as we look at the Catholic Church today. All in all, though, we fear that Paul had some negative conditioning about sexuality and did not see it as a sacrament of love or a way toward relationship with God.

QUESTION: In relationship to the model of sexual sharing without orgasm, how about the needs of the other person? Can the other person be led lovingly to a higher level of sexual relationship in such a way that there is no frustration?

ANSWER: It is wise to be very careful about taking another person to that level of relationship until the subject is honestly discussed and mutually agreed upon. This way of sexuality could only be worked out among committed partners, and it most certainly needs to be mutual. It is important that two people in a committed relationship come to a mutual arrangement about sexual practices or their discontinuance.

QUESTION: Would you comment on the practice of *coitus reservatus*, the capacity of maintaining an erection without coming to orgasm?

ANSWER: This practice is found in many of the Eastern societies, where it is considered to give an almost religious quality to intercourse. (It can also be a form of contraception. But I hasten to add that, along with withdrawal, it is a very poor form, because of the sperm cells contained in the secretion that comes out of the penis as the male becomes aroused. Only one of the 500 million sperm cells possible in ejaculation is necessary to fertilize the ovum.) Some societies believe that ejaculations weaken the male, so they advise this practice. One of the best treatments we know of concerning sex for union rather than for orgasm is Jolan Chang's *The Tao of Love and Sex—The Ancient Chinese Way to Ecstasy.* Katchadourian also describes this practice in the book to which we have referred several times.

QUESTION: Sometimes I feel that my celibacy, as much as I find it difficult to handle, opens the door to deeper intimacy with others, both men and women. I'm on an intimate level with perhaps thirty or forty people. Is it a blessing or a curse?

ANSWER: Who knows? It would depend on the results in spiritual and psychological growth both for them and for you. It would be quite important to have a peer with whom one could review these situations. Some of the wisest counselors, both clergy and psychologists, have found their relationships getting out of hand and primarily serving *their* needs rather than the needs of others. There is nothing wrong with our receiving something from a relationship, as long as the needs of the other are primary. The need to be needed can be very strong. I doubt, for example, whether we should act as confessors for people with whom we are in such relationships. We need to stay within our human limitations and not play God.

A major problem facing married priests and clergy is the resentment on the part of the husband or wife and children when too much intimacy is given to other people and they feel deprived of it. Morton, too, is probably on a fairly intimate level of relationship with somewhere between twenty and forty people. Before he began to deal with it, this problem caused more tensions in our family life than any other single issue. The celibate is freer —but he or she also can lack the objective assessment that a committed relationship provides.

QUESTION: Am I correct in assuming that a priest can't take money for doing spiritual direction? And if he can't, how should the question of reciprocity be handled?

ANSWER: That is correct; I doubt if a parish or order priest should give spiritual direction for a stipulated fee. Still, the issue of reciprocity remains important. Morton was a priest in a parish, and many people came to him for spiritual direction; if they were members of the parish he gently—and sometimes not quite so gently—suggested that if they didn't tithe, they needed to do so. All he was doing, though, was bringing them to where they ought to be anyway. And it made them take the direction much more seriously. For others it was a matter of voluntary gifts, and they were usually generous. There is a real problem about giving people something for nothing. It can be unhealthy for both the giver and receiver. It can put unconscious chains on a relationship. (Morton has an ideal situation. He has met with an analyst-priest friend, John Sanford, and over the years he has listened to John for an hour. Then John listens to Morton for an hour. It works magnificently; it really does the job. But if Morton didn't give John the definite continuous time and John didn't do the same, it probably wouldn't work out.) Many counselors have no regular source of income, and they need reimbursement for their help. And most people wish to give something in return if their needs are met.

QUESTION: Will you please recommend to me or to us some reliable, clear and simple dictionary of Jungian psychological terms?

ANSWER: There isn't any. The best way to come to an understanding would be to read the following five books of Jung, in the following order: *Memories, Dreams, Reflections*, Jung's autobiography: *Analytical Psychology: Its Theory and Practice* (The Tavistock Lectures); *Man and His Symbols*; *Modern Man in Search of a Soul*; and *Two Essays in Analytical Psychology*. All of these books are available in paperback. In the back of Jung's *Psychological Types* there is a glossary that helps with his terminology. Reading a good, general introduction to psychology is also helpful in providing background. The general index to the nineteen volumes of *The Collected Works* by Jung will show Jung's treatment of most terms. But understanding Jung without understanding Freud is difficult, and Freud has summarized his thinking in *A General Introduction to Psychoanalysis*. There is, in short, no easy way to learn about modern psychological thought. It is like learning a new language. (In regard specifically to Jung, by the way, we believe that it is better to read Jung himself than books about him.)

QUESTION: I am a priest who, as long as I can remember, has had a homo-sexual orientation and I cannot understand the reasons for this. I have never allowed myself to have a genital relationship with another man, though on occasion I have shown great affection for some men. Some have respond-ed in kind and others have not. My question or problem is that even though this does not cause me guilt, it is a desire that surfaces at times. I know that I consciously look at men in much the same way that the heterosex-ual looks at women. I am sure that this does continue bringing sexual thoughts to my mind. I find that my orientation has helped me in counsel-ing many men because I am in tune with some feelings and stimuli that other males may not notice. And so for that reason I accept my situation and know that the Lord uses it and is in the process of making me whole. One of my major problems, though, is relating to groups of males. In the parish we have male groups with whom we relate on the surface— discuss-ing sports, crops from a farm community, and other things typically male that do not always interest me. I have fears that I will not come across to them as a male leader of the community communicating Jesus Christ to them. And conversely, there are times I am sure that I could come across to some women as rather cold, whereas a heterosexual male would pick up and notice these women and maybe be more responsive and helpful. I also know that at times I seem to resent other homosexuals or those whom I might consider effeminate. I mention these areas as you may wish to com-ment on them in a way that may help my ministry or that of other priests.

ANSWER: Thank you for that honesty and straight forward sharing. I had a very interesting letter from an Anglican Bishop in Australia whom I met when I was there some years ago. His Anglican diocese had been studying the subject of homosexuality and had come to the conclusion that there is no reason why a celibate homosexual shouldn't be a priest as well as a celibate heterosexual. (The diocese couldn't see, however, how there could be a homosexual priest who was active genitally—but our question has to do with a celibate homosexual.) There is no question that the person sen-sitive in this area can help people who are troubled about similar problems.

Let us give in more detail the example we have already used of a friend who is a psychologist and a priest. He has had a long history of homosex-ual feelings, though he has not lived out homosexual action. He was working in a hospital in a large medical clinic. He is a specialist in dealing with specific psychological problems. He developed a very real attraction to one of the patients, a young man with whom he worked; he really came to care for the man. He made no physical or sexual advances, but his feelings bothered him so much, that he finally went to his supervisor suggesting he be taken off of the case. His supervisor listened to the whole story and then asked the therapist, "Have you noticed that your patient is beginning to get well? It is probably the very love you have for him that has helped in the creation of a new attitude towards himself. Love is healing: stay with the situation." In this case this priest's sexual attraction allowed him to feel a depth of love and concern that was never expressed in any genital or outwardly affectionate way, but was experienced as caring by the youth and had a healing effect upon him. He was open and conscious enough to discuss it with his supervisor, who kept the therapist in the situation until the young man was discharged. The tension of the situation also fostered a real growth in the therapist, as he dealt with and integrated his feelings. We are not responsible for our feelings, but we *are* responsible for our actions.

To respond to your fear of not being helpful to women, there is a far greater danger in heterosexually starved celibate or married priests being too friendly to women parishioners and giving them *too much* affection than the other way around. As a matter of fact, many women prefer a homosexual male as a friend. They know that that relationship will stay on a friendship level. We have heard this again and again. Few women have the same kind of negativity to the homosexual male that men do; women do not find them threatening. As far as leading men's groups, one just has to learn a little bit more about the crops and sports. This just entails dealing with people where they are and trying to be to others what they need. Your situation is difficult but probably no more difficult than that of heterosexual celibate or married priest.

We have two last comments to make on this subject. First, individuals who are not aware of some bisexual orientation or homoerotic feelings are rarely able to listen to, understand and help those who are struggling with such feelings; Second, celibate priests are not the only clergy who have strong attractions for the same sex. Jung pointed out that the male with a mother complex is not sick; such a person has gifts which others don't have. One of the results of being in close touch with the anima (one's feminine side) is that through the anima one is opened to the depth of the unconscious. This means that the person can also be open to religious experience and inspiration, and so can develop a profound religious interest. Our experience is that many males who are drawn to the ministry have a close contact with the anima, and so they tend also to have erotic feelings toward both sexes. Our experience is that this is as true of married clergy as it is of celibate priests. Although we have no detailed statistics, we have discovered that some thirty percent of both categories are aware of bisexual or homoerotic feelings, and most feel some guilt about them. We arrive at this figure from several self-report samples that we have taken, and from generalization from our experience in counseling.

QUESTION: In your presentation, did you imply that it is more in keeping with nature if a person is a healthy bisexual—or is it merely a decision that one must make?

ANSWER: First of all, we need to realize that there are some people who have only a very small heterosexual component within them, and then there is a much larger group of both men and women who have little or no contact with any conscious homoerotic feelings. Then there is a large group who are aware of both homoerotic and heteroerotic feelings within themselves. If we are comfortable with a lifestyle that is exclusively homoerotic or heteroerotic, then we should probably not dig around to find what we can find. But if we belong in the middle group who have had feelings or experiences in both directions, then we need to work out a healthy acceptance of who we are and come to a conscious choice about how we should deal with our sexual inclinations; it is unhealthy to deny the reality of any aspect of our psyche that is calling attention to itself. We also need to remember that there is a difference between having occasional feelings, or having performed a single or occasional act in the past, and having persistent feelings and actions in the present. Feelings themselves need not be lived out, except in fantasy. Living out both aspects of bisexuality can cause many problems for those in a celibate vocation, or in committed long-term relationships, or in marriage. And one last comment: most heterosexually or homosexually oriented people need deal with the contrasexual side of themselves only if they develop severe psychological problems and find that they must become aware of what is being repressed within them in order to solve their problems.

QUESTION: How does a celibate begin to deal with his/her contrasexual side?

ANSWER: First of all, one needs to identify what one's contrasexual side is like. We can do so by examining those who carry our hate and our infatuation. Then we can watch for dreams of people of the opposite sex who carry emotional power for us. Secondly, we can have an imaginative dialogue with our inner complement and get to know this inner figure. The man can have a dialogue with his inner woman, and the woman can dialogue with her inner man. (Jung used to say he often had an inner conversation with Miss Jung.) These inner figures are real and complex. As we get to know them better we are not so likely to be possessed by them or to project their characteristics onto others. Hugh of St. Victor, a priest of the Middle Ages, wrote a most perceptive dialogue with his soul, pictured as a worldly and sexual woman.

QUESTION: Would you describe again the difference between falling in love and loving?

ANSWER: In falling in love, "A" experiences a rosy glow just looking at "B", perhaps before "A" even knows "B". The psychoanalytic notion of "transference" is quite similar. Transference is falling in love, and falling in love is projecting something within us out upon another person. When a man falls in love he suddenly (as in a great insight) perceives his own inner femininity tinged with angelic light within a particular woman. When the woman perceives her inner knight in white armour suffused with the Holy in the same man who has projected upon her, we have what might be called a double whammy. But the actual person upon whom we project this image need not bear any more resemblance to our image than a hat does to the hook we hang it on. It is difficult for us to believe that we can fall into such irrationality, but most of us do, and tens of thousands of novels, plays and movies describe the process. (Esther Harding gives an excellent picture of this process psychologically for women in her book *The Way of All Women*.) When the man sees his beloved in curlers or she sees his chauvinistic ways, the image may fall off as quickly as it fell on. But for all their problems, projection and falling in love are not entirely bad, immature or wrong. Perhaps God gave us the capacity to project so two people with their own bad self images and their fears of relationship could be drawn into living with each other. For many people, real committed relationship would simply be too threatening without the sauce of falling in love.

Almost all the studies, however, show that until two people can move beyond these romantic feelings, through genuine communication, to a state of knowing and appreciating each other, their relationship is not likely to last. Of course, some of the romantic feelings may remain, but they may go up and down like a roller coaster. In true loving we have some residual in-love feelings, but we begin to recognize the faults and failures of those we love; we forgive them for hurting us and are able to see through all their unpleasant characteristics the genuinely divine spark that dwells in the depth of every human soul. We also recognize that we are no prizes ourselves, and we try to give to those we love the kind of love that God has given to us. . . .even if they are as unworthy of our love as we are of God's.

QUESTION: If a woman throws herself at a priest and threatens his celibacy, how should he handle it?

ANSWER: First of all, most priests are men, and I know of very few cases of a male rape by a woman. Such a situation requires more than acquiescence by a man. (Women priests might have more to worry about in this area.) So this question really involves three related issues. The first concern whether the woman has placed a transference upon a priest without any encouragement from him, or whether the priest himself has encouraged it. Some people go to church and immediately place a transference upon the priest. (Psychologists, doctors and counselors are also sitting ducks for projection.) This is why priests who are counselors need *always*, and we don't very often say "always", to limit the counseling time that they give to a parishioner to one hour in a neutral and unsuggestive setting, and to set limits before counseling relationships can go any further. The most mature people can fall into a mess in a powerful mutual transference. Second, this problem extends to married clergy. Don't think the problem is any easier for a married man, dear celibate friends. Monogamy is not instinctual. No matter how much we learn and deal with our projections they can rise up and seize us. In some ways celibacy may have somewhat fewer tensions than living in a committed relationship and counseling in depth with others. The celibate with little genital experience and a conscious commitment to the celibate state may feel less temptation in counseling. Married Protestant ministers and Roman Catholic priests, in other words, have similar problems. The only difference is that for married ministers it is the vow of marriage that may be threatened, while for celibate priests it is the vow of celibacy.

Third, we need to be *very careful* whom we take on in a long-term counseling relationship. We should listen for Divine guidance before we take anybody on a long-term basis. We can take on people for questionable motives. But once we are actually in an in-depth counseling relationship, we have to bear the tension if a strong transference takes place; we can destroy the person if we break the transference and refuse to see a person with whom a deep transference has occurred. If one feels a great attraction to the counselee when he or she first appears, it may be wiser not to let this become a long-term counseling assignment. One must be able to refer the over-attractive person on to someone else.

QUESTION: What is the difference between suppressed sexuality and repressed sexuality?

ANSWER: Repressed sexuality is the kind that is dangerous; suppressed sexuality is not. The difference between a state of repression and one of suppression is that in the first case I am entirely unaware of an unacted-upon part of myself, but in the second case I am in control. When we don't even know about a part of ourselves, we have no way of using safety valves to let out the pressure that this aspect of ourselves may cause. It makes a big difference, for example, whether we are entirely unaware of a problem of latent homosexuality, which then drives us to certain forms of behavior, or whether we consciously bear the tension caused by our knowledge that a part of us can be attracted to another person of the same sex. Not knowing is repression; bearing the tension consciously is suppression. Consciousness allows me to keep an eye on this side of myself and to handle the situation with my own will. Repressed sexuality—a denial of sexuality altogether—can cause almost any psychic or physical trauma, or even a bizarre episode of acting out. So one of our most important tasks is getting to know ourselves, accepting ourselves, and bringing the totality of ourselves to the Christ. We find in this experience that we are still valuable and are given strength to bear the tension of the conflicting emotions and impulses within us.

QUESTION: How much should a counselor give to a counselee, emotionally speaking?

ANSWER: We think it is very wise, when dealing with the average counselee—who is coming in because he or she is emotionally disturbed—within the privacy of a closed-door office, to go no further than a friendly, reassuring handshake. We can listen, and give understanding and compassion, but we must not abuse the act of touch. Touch can signify different things to different people. An embrace in public, as in a public worship service, is a very different thing from an embrace in the privacy of a closed office. Much more friendly touching, in other words, is permissible in public than in private. We doubt if we can go beyond a caring embrace *at the end* of a session in which an individual has expressed great pain without conveying more than pastoral concern. One particular counselor told us that one of the reasons he got deeply involved with a counselee was that the other person sought a deep, mouth-to-mouth contact, a deep kiss, and from then on it was simply a matter of time before the relationship became intensely sexual.

This isn't inevitable. We can make our limits at *any* point, especially if we have a deeply developed and disciplined spiritual life. But we need to decide how far we can go *before* we get into a counseling situation. We have known people who have gone to the level of the deep kiss and maintained it for years and years. They have never broken this boundary because it would have been to them a full violation of their celibacy, and this they would not do. (Homosexual transferences, of course, pose the same dangers if the counselor is open to them, and they require the same limits.)

It is particularly dangerous for men, either married or celibate, to give unmarried or unhappily married women a great deal of affection and warmth, as this may suggest to the woman that there is much more commitment than there really is. Our experience is that women are much more prone than are men, particularly in our patriarchal society, to find counseling situations a legitimate way of initiating a real relationship. The priest figure is a holy image and carries a numinous quality—in addition to being male. Deep within the unconscious of many women is a holy, priestly figure, just as many men have a goddess or holy nurturer within them. These priestly images are very easy to project out.

There are two final determinants to guide my behavior in counseling situations. First, how will that behavior affect the other person? Second, how is the behavior going to affect me, my spiritual life, and my growth and development and my other relationships? If the relationship is going to be creative both for the other person and for me and mine, and is under Christ, then the relationship may be permissible. But if it is going to be creative only for me and damaging for the other person, then I should break it off before a transference develops. And if it is going to be creative for the other person and not for me, I should refer him or her elsewhere. We need always be aware that our unconscious desires can play tricks on our judgment.

QUESTION: What are the characteristics of an ideal relationship?

ANSWER: We have said a lot about the ideal relationship, but it would certainly help to summarize the essential qualities of any intimate, long range bond between two people—although it takes courage for two fallible humans to speak on such a subject.

1.   Unless two people share a common vision of the nature of reality and how we come to maturity within it, they can seldom have the deepest kind of relationship. We have already pointed out the dangers that beset two people with little or no religious framework at all; it is very difficult not to deify either oneself or the other. Daily Eucharist has been for us a point of meeting, sharing, relating, forgiving and being forgiven that has done wonders for our own marriage. Also, a religious framework that does not see the intimate human bond as expressing the nature and life of God will offer quite a different ideal of intimacy and love than the one we have offered.

2.   The relationship will approach the ideal to the degree that the partners can communicate on any subject—from finances, to use of time, to work habits, to sex. Without the development of a comfort with total communication, the ideal relationship is rarely approached.

3.   Giving love and caring are a part of the ideal. Paul describes the nature of Christian love in I Corinthians 13. As the Prayer of St. Francis reminds us we need to be more concerned with understanding, counseling, forgiving and loving than in receiving these things from our partner. Caring requires time, effort, imagination and constancy. When the two of us are travelling separately, we always try to call each other by phone daily. We try to think about each other, to be considerate, and to digest our angers and disappointments before we spit them out; the thoughtless person speaks without taking thought.

4.   In real relationship one suffers when the other suffers, and rejoices with the other's joys. There is an emptiness when the other is gone and

a lilt in one's inner song when the other appears. There is real attractedness to each other.

5.   Last of all, there is the physical joy of bodily affection and warmth, and of sexuality in which the two become one in a certain real sense—a union that is indeed a sacrament of love and of the oneness of the Godhead. This is natural, good and holy, and it gives release and joy to both people. (This level can be put aside, however, if it is not in the best interest of either party.)

QUESTION: Someone has written: "The man who enters a life of consecrated celibacy enters a condition in which nowadays, especially, his whole emotional life is going to be profoundly affected." Do you agree with such a statement?

ANSWER: We do, but we would also say that any person who enters a long-term committed relationship enters a condition in which nowadays, especially, his or her whole emotional life is going to be profoundly affected. We cannot emphasize strongly enough that both celibacy (bringing the contrasexual elements into union within us) and committed relationships (coming to inner wholeness through interaction with another person) require total emotional involvement and commitment.

QUESTION: How much choice is involved in one's sexual orientation?

ANSWER: For some people there is little choice. This statement is true for four to ten percent of those whose orientation is largely homosexual and for nearly fifty percent of those whose sexual predilections are almost entirely heterosexual. For the forty percent or so of those who are somewhat capable of responding to members of either sex, it is important not to be influenced by either heterosexual or homosexual propaganda; these people must truly find out who they are and what their own sexual way of life should be.

As to the matter of acting out one's sexuality, some people with weak egos have little choice. Furthermore, where cultural mores give us little reason for bringing our sexuality into a relationship based on caring and love, there is little reason for control. However, when people find that their sexuality is running them and that they are unable to control it, it is time to seek psychological help. Uncontrolled sexuality can bring serious legal and social problems—as well as psychological and religious ones.

Two questions were asked that addressed the same problem in slightly different ways, and we shall answer them together.

QUESTION ONE: When any man falls in love with a woman, a real desire for union with the beloved usually follows. When that man also happens to be a priest with a commitment to celibacy, these feelings, needless to say, cause conflict. What steps would you consider to be wholesome in dealing with a situation like this for the good of both the priest and the woman (a single woman) involved?

QUESTION TWO: What steps would you consider wholesome in dealing with a projection situation between a celibate priest and a woman?

ANSWER: First of all, let us recommend several books on this subject, and then we will give some practical suggestions as to what those in this situation can do to avoid disastrous consequences. It is good to remember that married priests (male or female) can also fall into this situation, and that nearly everything we suggest applies to them also. Christopher Kiesling has two excellent chapters on this very subject in his book, *Celibacy, Prayer and Friendship—A Making-Sense-Out-of Life Approach*. Also, the last chapter of *Urgent Longings* by Thomas Tyrrell deals specifically with the situation described in the questions. Tyrrell's thesis is that repression of our capacity for romantic attachment and love can do people irreparable damage and make them less than human. Dr. Tyrrell works with a group that is dedicated to helping celibates become open to deep relationships and yet remain within the celibate lifestyle. (We wonder as we survey our own experience, however, if Tyrrell is not a bit overly optimistic about the ease with which people can maintain the celibate state and have real intimacy.) A third book, *A Young Man of Forty, An Experience of Celibacy* by Keith Clark, is a personal account of dealing with the tension between having deep relationships with others and maintaining the celibate way of life. Clark also emphasizes that people without deep relations with others will probably not remain healthy.

Our first suggestion is that when we find ourselves getting involved we stop and reflect; we should do nothing until we have taken the time (away from our involvement) carefully to think through what is happening to us. A most important consideration in this matter is that we not use or damage the other person. Men, on the whole, can with some ease fall in and out of love. But, women, as Candace Pert points out in a passage we quoted in an earlier chapter, find it more difficult to fall in and out of love. Celibate men need to keep this in mind. If men are celibates and intend to remain in that state (or in priesthood in the Roman Catholic Church), they do not offer any woman much of a future. The needs for family, children and home are probably stronger in women; a long-lasting affair is not nearly as satisfying for most women as it can be for men. A celibate male can keep a woman from other relationships which may be more fulfilling for her just by hanging on to the relationship to fulfill his own needs.

If the woman is married, all sorts of other problems arise. Sometimes women may protest that they are not being taken care of sexually. This claim brings people into a shadowy area in which these people need to be very frank, open and honest with each other. A relationship between a celibate male and a married woman requires that both partners bear a lot of tension. Relationships with an older woman or a divorcee, however, may be quite different from those with a married or a younger woman; and then there is the relationship that two committed celibates may have with one another. These situations are all different and they all can cause various amounts of damage. When we find ourselves becoming emotionally and sexually involved, it is very difficult not to forget our good intentions; we are dealing with a primal life force. We need to be extremely careful and thoughtful if we are not to hurt ourselves or others in such relationships, whether the partners be celibates, married men, or women, or female priests. Much pain and tension already exists in the world; we do not wish to add to it by our thoughtless emotional and sexual involvements. In any intense emotional relationship, both people need to discuss and set the limits to which their relationship can move, and then each person needs to abide by his or her own limits and respect and support the limits of the other. But we know that this is easier said than done.

Abiding with the limits of celibate life is, from our experience, easier for members of religious communities than for diocesan priests. The celibate community member has more or less consciously and willingly chosen his or her life style, and such a person usually has the support of other community members. Many diocesan priests, however, have chosen to serve God, and they have had celibacy forced upon them while at the same time they are placed in situations of intense isolation and loneliness.

To remain vitally alive—to be open to others in depth while remaining celibate (or, for the married priests, monogamous)—is an heroic vocation; when we do not see it as an heroic vocation, the monogamy or celibacy can quickly go down the tubes.

QUESTION: What does a man do who is married and has two children and suddenly the girl of his dreams appears?

ANSWER: Our answer is very simple: Don't do anything quickly and before one does anything one should seek out competent objective counsel. This answer also applies to a married woman who falls in love with another man. There is no easy solution to such a problem. When people come to us in this situation we usually counsel them to move slowly, and usually to stay with their spouses, to whom they are married and with whom they have had children. Too often the new love will have within him or her the same problems that have made the present partner seem unattractive. Children's lives are also at stake. One couple with whom we have been close maintained a difficult marriage until the children were essentially grown up; then the two separated and each found a partner who met their needs. However, they did not part for another person; they separated, rather, because after twenty years of marriage they discovered that they were not meeting each other's needs.

Each situation of this kind should be dealt with individually and in depth, and precipitous action is almost never advised.

Again we need to emphasize that the wisest and most mature people can be taken in by projection. A delightful story is told of John Stuart Mill, the great 19th century philosopher, who really believed that he obtained his ideas and inspiration from a rather frowsy woman from the East End of London. He truly believed that after he had visited her, she stimulated him with brilliant ideas. What Mill came into touch with was his own incredibly creative anima, his wise feminine side, which this woman somehow mirrored and made available for him.

QUESTION: I was confused by your discussion of nudity and the Amazon natives. Will you explain?

ANSWER: What we were trying to illustrate was that many of our sexual attitudes are conditioned by our social mores and are not necessarily connected with religious ideas. Here was someone who had never before been nude in public, and yet it was very easy for him to be comfortable with these natives, for whom nudity was the cultural norm and did not signify an orgy. In our culture, nudity on the whole means something quite different. The movie *The Emerald Forest* was rated R largely because it showed the nudity of an actual Amazon tribe. We saw nothing offensive in it. We quote that description of Amazon natives to stress the relativity of mores on this matter. When in Japan, Morton stayed in a Japanese hotel in which there was a common male bath. As he got out of the bath, an unknown Oriental spoke to a Japanese friend of ours saying: "This is the first time I have ever been in a bath with an Occidental." Our point is that many matters are relative.

QUESTION: We would like to have some solid spiritual direction on how to deal with our sexuality. Will you deal with that?

ANSWER: Although we have covered this matter before, it is a good way to end our discussion. We see six different elements in dealing with our sexuality spiritually, in integrating our spirituality and sexuality.

1.   Ignorance seldom helps any growth. Ignorance about sexuality is no exception. We need to know and understand and be comfortable with our own bodies and how they function, and also to realize the depth and pervasiveness of our sexual needs and desires. We need also to understand and become comfortable with the sexual difference between us and the opposite sex.

2.   If there is to be intimacy, the area of sexuality needs to be open to full and comfortable verbal communication. If we are not free to discuss our sexuality, then it cannot truly be shared; thus there cannot, in that case, be a real sharing of love, and so neither sexuality nor love can achieve their spiritual potential.

Communication needs to extend beyond our concerns with sexuality to all aspects of life. When there is any area of our lives that we cannot share, we make our sexual communication and union themselves less significant.

3.   Sexuality needs to be linked with caring, genuine caring. We need to be as concerned with giving as we are with receiving. Sexuality not related to genuine mutual love is inferior sexuality—and is also inferior spirituality.

4.   People have psychological and theological ideas even when they are not aware of them. Indeed, it is difficult to separate our psychology, philosophy, and theology. If we would have a place for sexuality in our

spiritual direction, we need a theology that sees sexuality as one possible way of being nudged further into our communion with God.

5.   We must be reflective and abandon any sexual practice that is damaging either to us or to another person. When sexuality is damaging to another person, it does not foster spiritual growth.

6.   We need to be comfortable bringing our sexual lives to God and bringing God and prayer into our sexual experience. If God created our sexuality, made it good, and freed it from being tied just to periods of conception, then this aspect of our lives can be as much a part of our spirituality as any other part.

CONCLUSION

We conclude our questions and answers, and our reflections on love and sexuality, with these words of the great Anglican poet George Herbert in a poem entitled "Love".

Love bade me welcome; yet my soul drew back,
    Guilty of dust and sin.
But quick-eyed Love, observing me grow slack
    From my first entrance in,
Drew nearer to me, sweetly questioning
    if I lacked anything.

"A guest," I answered, "worthy to be here."
    Love said, "You shall be he."
"I, the unkind, ungrateful? Ah, my dear
    I cannot look on thee."
Love took my hand, and smilingly did reply,
    "Who made the eyes but I?"

"Truth, Lord, but I have marred them; let my shame
    Go where it doth deserve."
"And I know you not," said Love, "who bore the blame?"
    "My dear, then I will serve."
"You must sit down," said Love, "and taste my meat."
    So I did sit and eat.

Notes

Introduction

1. A 4th Edition of this work was published under the name of Horant A. Katchadourian, M.D., without the cooperation of Donald T. Lunde, M.D. in 1985. It came into our hands half way through our work in this book. The last six chapters of this book refer to this new edition.

Chapter One

1. Erwin J. Haeberle, *The Sex Atlas* (New York: The Seabury Press, 1977), p. 125.

2. Ibid., p. 124.

3. Ibid., p. 126.

4. Gerhard Adler, ed., *C.G. Jung Letters, 1:1906-1950* (Princeton: Princeton University Press, 1973), p. 377.

5. See Chapter 7, Richard Coan, *Hero, Artist, Sage or Saint?* (New York: Columbia University Press, 1977).

6. We use the word neurosis well aware that the official handbook of the American Psychiatric profession, DMS III, describing mental sickness no longer uses this classification, but we find it helpful when discussing Freud and also in distinguishing certain types of symptoms from psychosis.

7. A major conflict has raged around Freud's shift from the seduction theory to his theory of the innate Oedipus complex. The Freud archives are closed to public inspection from

289

a few years beyond the point of donations to the archives to the year 2102. The former keeper of the archives, Jeffrey M. Masson, found evidence that orthodox Freudianism had tried to conceal the fact that Freud did not always hold to the Oedipal theory. His views were published in a book *The Assault on Truth: Freud's Suppression of the Seduction Theory* and is summarized in the February 1984 *Atlantic Monthly*. A complete account of the controversy is provided by Janet Malcolm in *The New Yorker*, December 5 and 12, 1983 and has since been published in book form.

8.   Op. cit., p. 67.

9.   Susan Schiefelbein, "The Miracle of Regeneration: Can Human Limbs Grow Back?" *The Saturday Review of Literature*, July 8, 1978.

10.   Katchadourian and Lunde, op. cit., pp. 96-7, 99-100, 103-5, 477.

11.   Ibid., pp. 476-7 and the chapter on Aggression in Melvin Konner, *The Tangled Wing: Biological Constraints on the Human Spirit* (New York: Holt, Rinehart and Winston, 1982).

12.   The word hermaphrodite comes from the Greek god Hermaphroditus, the son of Hermes and Aphrodite. Actual physical hermaphrodites are very rare, with only sixty reported in twentieth century medical annals. They have both testicular and ovarian tissue.

13.   Melvin Konner in *The Tangled Wing*.

14.   Carole Offir, *Human Sexuality* (New York: Harcourt Brace Jovanovich, 1982), p. 129.

15.   C.S. Ford and F.A. Beach, *Patterns of Sexual Behavior* (New York: Harper and Row, 1951).

Chapter Two

1.   Carol Offir, *Human Sexuality* (New York: Harcourt Brace Jovanovich, 1982) provides on pages 305-337 an excellent summary of available data and draws heavily upon Gagnon and Simon, "On Psychosexual Development" in D. A. Goslin, ed., *Handbook of Socialization Theory and Research* (Chicago: Rand McNally, 1969) and *Sexual Conduct: The Social Sources of Human Sexuality* (Chicago: Aldine, 1973). She also draws upon A. Hass, *Teenage Sexuality* (New York: Macmillan, 1979), and upon M. Hunt, *Sexual Behavior in the 1970's* (Chicago: Playboy Press, 1974). The data in the text is taken from Hunt.

2.   Sylvia Brinton Perera, *Descent to the Goddess, A Way of Initiation for Women* (Toronto: Inner City Books, 1981), p. 11.

3.   Two excellent books for children are written by Peter Mayle, *"Where Did I Come From?"* and *"What's Happening to Me?"* (Secaucus, N.J.: Lyle Stuart, Inc., 1975). Our daughter has used these books with our grandchildren very effectively.

4.   Carol Offir, op. cit., p. 149.

5.   A.C. Kinsey et al., *Sexual Behavior in the Human Male* (Philadelphia: Saunders, 1953), p. 470.

6.   Ibid.

7. Katchadourian and Lunde, op. cit., pp. 210-218.

8. Linda Schierse Leonard, *The Wounded Woman: Healing the Father-Daughter Relationship* (Boulder, Colorado: Shamahala Publications, 1982).

9. John Moore, *Sexuality and Spirituality* (San Francisco: Harper and Row, 1980), pp. 4-7.

10. Gilbert Herdt, *Guardians of the Flutes* (New York: McGraw-Hill, 1981).

Chapter Three

1. Jolan Chang, *The Tao of Love and Sex: The Ancient Chinese Way to Ecstasy* (New York: E.P. Dutton, 1977).

2. The romanticization of love is dealt with in Philip Keane, S.S., *Sexual Morality: A Catholic Perspective* (Dublin: Gill and Macmillan, 1980), pp. 10-12. H.W. Richardson, *Nun, Witch, Playmate* (New York: Harper and Row, 1971) devotes Chapter VI to exploring the historical meaning of this romanticism.

3. I have described the basic difference between East and West in several places: in *The Other Side of Silence* (New York: Paulist Press, 1976), ch. 13 and in *Companions on the Inner Way* (New York: Crossroad, 1983), ch. 2.

4. William Johnston discusses Zen madness in *The Still Point* and friends living in Japan tell us that it still presents a serious problem. Two positive accounts of the meaning of the Eastern way are found in Richard Coan's *Hero, Artist, Sage or Saint?* (New York: Columbia University Press, 1977) and in Paul and Janet Clasper's *The Ox-Herder Pictures, Zen Buddhism's Version of "The Pilgrim's Progress"* (Hong Kong: The Lotus-Logos Press, undated).

5. In my book *Companions on the Inner Way*, pp. 22-29, I sketch the implications of this point of view for spiritual life and action.

6. Plato was pessimistic about the ultimate nature of matter, yet he believed that the Ideas (archetypes) could be expressed in matter. He also believed that these ultimate non-physical forms were apprehended not through intellect but through prophetic inspiration, artistic inspiration, cathartic (healing) power and love. Friedlander in his excellent study, *Plato* (New York: Harper and Row, 1960), shows how central love was to Plato's thought.

7. Philip Keane, op. cit., p. 9.

8. *The Documents of Vatican II* (New York: America Press, 1966), p. 253f.

9. Herbert Richardson, op. cit., p. 74.

10. Katchadourian and Lunde, op. cit., provides an excellent summary of Freudian theory of sexual development, pp. 189-196, and also of the learning theory in sexual development in the pages that follow the discussion of Freud.

11. Katchadourian and Lunde, op. cit., p. 176.

12. Ibid., pp. 166-171.

13. Carol Offir, op. cit., p. 329.

Chapter Four

1. A fine summary of the biological differences between men and women is found in Melvin Konner, op. cit., Chapter 6, "The Beast with Two Backs." He draws heavily on the work of Eleanor Maccoby and Carol Jacklin, The Psychology of Sex Differences (Stanford: Stanford University Press, 1974). He also draws attention to an excellent survey of these differences, comprising the entire issue of Science, March 20, 1981. We draw heavily and gratefully upon the data Konner has accumulated in these excellent twenty-one pages.

2. Summarized by Konner, op. cit., p. 111.

3. Omni, Feb. 1982, Vol. 4, No. 5: 111-2.

4. C.S. Lewis, Surprised by Joy (London: Fontana, 1959), p. 13.

5. An excellent pictorial exposition of this truth is found in National Geographic, June 1984: 774-813.

6. William Irwin Thompson, The Time Falling Bodies Take to Light: Mythology, Sexuality & the Origins of Culture (New York: St. Martin's Press, 1981), p. 156. Thompson has provided an erudite and somewhat esoteric study of the development of patriarchal society. His accumulation of data is most impressive and we rely heavily upon it.

7. Gilbert Herdt, Guardians of the Flutes (New York: McGraw-Hill, 1981).

8. See Mary Daly, Gyn/ecology, The Metaethics of Radical Feminism (Boston: Beacon Press, 1978), chapters three through six.

9. Katchadourian and Lunde, op. cit., p. 36.

10. In my book, Myth, History and Faith (Ramsey, NJ: Paulist Press, 1974), Ch. IV, particularly pp. 63-65, I deal with the myth of the dying and rising god of Asia Minor and with Yahweh's kinship with this god.

11. In my book Resurrection, Release from Oppression I have dealt with our loving response to Jesus' resurrection as an integral part of assimilating the meaning of the event.

12. Clare Fischer, Betsy Brenneman, and Anne Bennett (eds.), Women in a Strange Land (Philadelphia: Fortress Press, 1975), pp. 84-85.

13. Betty Roszak and Theodore Roszak, (eds.), Masculine/Feminine, Readings in Sexual Mythology and the Liberation of Women (New York: Harper and Row, 1969), p. 20.

14. C.J. Jung, Civilization in Transition, vol. 10 of the Collected Works (Princeton, NJ: Princeton University Press, 1975), p. 121.

15. Veravon der Heydt, Jung and Religion, Lecture 215 (London: Guild of Pastoral Psychology.

Chapter Five

1. Donald Goergen, a Catholic priest, has written an excellent survey on these different attitudes in The Sexual Celibate (New York: Seabury Press, 1974).

2. Ruth 3:1-15, 4:1-6, 9-12, Jerusalem Bible.

3. Psychology Today (Feb. 1985): 22ff.

4. This great elegy is found in II Samuel 1:17-27. The account of David's life which follows is a great piece of historical writing. II Samuel 9-20 is not only magnificent classic Hebrew but probably a contemporary account of David's reign and describes his loving greatness and his failings.

5. Leviticus 19:18, 34.

6. Matthew 5:39.

7. I have discussed this subject at length in my book, *Healing and Christianity*.

8. For the full implications of the importance of touch see James Lynch, *The Broken Heart: The Medical Consequences of Loneliness* (New York: Basic Books, 1977) and also in Chapter 9 of Morton's book, *Prophetic Ministry*.

9. Matthew 19:12. This passage occurs along with the story of the rich young ruler and Jesus' statement about divorce and children.

10. According to Exodus 21, Leviticus 25 and Deuteronomy 15, Hebrews might not keep Hebrew slaves in bondage for more than seven years, *unless* they wanted to stay in bondage, then it was for life. No limit was set for the servitude of foreigners. The law even prescribes freedom for slaves who have been so badly beaten that they lose an eye or a tooth!

11. St. Ambrose, *Concerning Virgins*, Book I.

12. Augustine, *The Good of Marriage*, Vol. 27 of The Fathers of the Church (Washington, DC: The Catholic University of America Press, 1957), chapters 3 and 7. Donald Goergen provides an excellent critique of Augustine in *The Sexual Celibate*.

13. Irenaeus, *Against Heresies*, 1:24.

14. Eusebius, *Ecclesiastical History*, ix, xxix, 3.

15. A concise treatment of the history of Christian celibacy is given in James Hastings, (ed.), *Encyclopedia of Religion and Ethics*, Vol. 3 (New York: Scribners, n.d.), pp. 271-277.

16. Philip S. Keane, S.S., *Sexual Morality, A Catholic Perspective* (Dublin: Gill and Mac-millan, 1980), p. 58. This book was given the Imprimatur by the Archbishop of Seattle in 1977. For anyone wanting a scholarly survey and critique of the Catholic view on sexuality, we know of no better book.

17. Op. cit., p. 4.

18. An excellent survey of religious attitudes toward sexuality is found in Sylvia Chavez-Garcia and Daniel A. Helminiac, "Sexuality and Spirituality: Friends, Not Foes," in *The Journal of Pastoral Care* (Vol. XXXIX, no. 2, June 1985). Although the article makes much the same point that we are making, the authors fail to point out the root reason for the fear of sexuality in Christianity and at the same time they do not acknowledge how much of this attitude still remains within the Roman Catholic Church.

19. In the Eastern Orthodox Church, where church and state were more closely related than in the West, the priest became a part of the valid wedding service. See W. K. Lowther Clarke, (ed.), *Liturgy and Worship* (London: SPCK, 1954), pp. 461-2 for Pope Nicolas' description of a wedding in 866.

20.   Chapter 16 of Katchadourian and Lunde, op. cit., pp. 42ff. and Morris Plascowe, *Sex and the Law* (New York: Prentice Hall, 1951).

Chapter Six

1.   Ann Landers, *Newsday* (New York, N.Y., Jan. 14, 15, 1985).

2.   Aldous Huxley, *Tomorrow and Tomorrow and Tomorrow, and Other Essays* (New York: Harper and Row, 1956), p. 68.

3.   Peck, M. Scott. New York: Simon and Schuster, 1978.

4.   Sylvia Chavez-Garcia and Daniel A. Heliniak, "Sexuality and Spirituality: Friends, Not Foes" in *The Journal of Pastoral Care* (Vol. XXXIX, No. 2, June 1985): 161-2.

5.   Much of this explanation has been drawn from my account of falling in love in *Caring* (Ramsey, N.J.: Paulist Press, 1981), pp. 126-9.

6.   John A. Sanford, *The Invisible Partners* (Ramsey, N.J.: Paulist Press, 1980), p. 13.

7.   Ibid., pp. 17-18.

8.   Adolf Guggenbuhl-Craig, *Marriage—Dead or Alive* (Zurich: Spring Publications, 1977), pp. 9-10.

9.   Ibid., pp. 41-45.

10.   March-April 1982, p. 15.

11.   Charles Williams, *The Forgiveness of Sins* (London: Geoffrey Bles: Centenary Press, 1942).

Chapter Seven

1.   Jared Diamond, "Everything *Else* You Always Wanted to Know About Sex, But That You'd Never Ask," in *Discover* (April 1985): 73-74.

2.   Susan Brownmiller, *Against Our Will. Men, Women and Rape* (New York: Bantam, 1981).

3.   Oliver M. Butterfield, *Sexual Harmony in Marriage* (Buchanan, New York: Emerson Books, 1977—first published in this present form in 1953).

4.   William H. Masters and Virginia E. Johnson, *The Pleasure Bond* (New York: Bantam Books, 1970), p. 195.

5.   The Berkeley Sex Therapy Group, 2614 Telegraph Ave., Berkeley, California, 94704, has privately published some selected papers that outline their theory and practice, entitled *Expanding the Boundaries of Sex Therapy.*

6.   Ibid., p. 10.

7.   Op. cit.

Chapter Eight

1. Donald Goergen, *The Sexual Celibate* (New York: The Seabury Press, 1974), p. 184.

2. *TV Guide* (March 23, 1983): 3-5.

3. Henry C. Lea, *Sacredotal Celibacy in the Christian Church* (no city mentioned: University Books, Inc., 1966).

4. James Hastings, ed., *Encyclopedia of Religion and Ethics* (New York: Charles Scribners Sons, n.d.), p. 274.

5. The Documents of Vatican II, Walter Abbott, S.J., ed. (New York: American Press, 1966), p. 565.

6. Barbara has contributed a chapter on types in Morton's book, *Christo-Psychology* (New York: Crossroad, 1982), pp. 68-90. The relevant literature is reviewed in this article.

7. Morton has written widely on these gifts of the spirit as he discovered that most modern theology had little room for these direct gifts of God to human beings. His first book was on the gift of Tongues, *Tongue Speaking* and other books followed: *God, Dreams and Revelation* and *Dreams, A Way to Listen to God*, *The Other Side of Silence*, and *Afterlife* deal with the gift of revelation; *Encounter with God* and *Companions on the Inner Way* provide a theological framework in which the gifts make sense; *The Christian and the Supernatural* describes the gifts of wisdom and knowledge; *Transcend* gives a summary treatment of many of these gifts.

8. John Dourley, *The Illness That We Are: A Jungian Critique of Christianity* (Toronto: Inner City Book, 1984), p. 67.

Chapter Nine

1. Much of the material in this chapter was published in Chapter 6 of Morton's book *Prophetic Ministry*, New York: Crossroad, 1982, under the title "Ministry to the Homosexual". It was first published in much that form in the *Journal of Religion and Health*, Vol. 7, No. 1, January 1986.

2. Mutual masturbation refers to a host of practices by which orgasm is achieved by stimulation of the clitoris or penis by the hand or other part of the body. Fellatio & cunnilingus is the practice of obtaining orgasm through the use of mouth to genital contact. This term can be used to refer to this experience among males or females in homosexual play or the same practice in heterosexual experiences. Sodomy is the insertion of the penis in the anus (obviously impossible in female homosexual activity) in either homosexual activity or heterosexual activity. There is some evidence that the release of the male semen into the rectal cavity is related to the development of AIDS and may be quite dangerous physiologically. The tearing of the walls of the rectal cavity in anal intercourse also is clearly connected with passing on the AIDS virus.

3. An excellent and up to date survey of the data is provided by H.A. Katchadourian, *The Fundamentals of Human Sexuality*, Fourth Edition, New York: Holt, Rinehart and Winston, Inc., 1985, pp. 334-5 and pp. 338-9.

4. William R. Stayton, Th.D., *Your Church*, Jan/Feb. 1975, "0-1-2-3-4-5-6- Changing Attitudes Toward Sexuality".

5. Op. Cit., pp. 90-91, p. 207.

6. C.G. Jung, *Collected Works*, Vol X, *Civilization in Transition*, Princeton, N.J.: Princeton University Press, 1979, p. 107.

7. New York: Arbor House Publishing Company, 1978.

8. *The Homosexual in Our Society*, The transcript of a program broadcast on November 24, 1958, by radio station KPFA-FM, Berkeley, San Francisco: PanGraphic Press, 1959, p. 6.

9. Many studies have been published about the Biblical attitudes to homosexualities. One of the best is D.S. Bailey, *Homosexuality and the Western Christian Tradition*, London: Longmans, Green, 1955. James B. Nelson, *Embodiment*, Minneapolis: Augsburg Publishing House, 1978, also gives an excellent survey.

10. We have already mentioned the ambiguity of Jesus' treatment of the Jewish Law. At one point he says nothing in it can be changed and in another he makes changes (and rather radical ones) that need to be made—the treatment of women, divorce, the equality of human beings. It is said that a Red Guard Chinese Youth was burning books during the cultural revolution; a copy of the Bible somehow survived. He read it and was converted. When asked what brought him over to Christianity he replied that three of Jesus basic teachings touched the core of him: "Individual autonomy, compassion for the welfare of others, and respect for personality."

11. Chicago: Chicago University Press, 1980.

12. From a letter written by Daniel Berrigan, S. J., William Sloane Coffin Jr., Morton Kelsey, Virginia Mollenkott, James B. Nelson, Robert Raines and Walter Wink on July 3, 1985 to the editor of *Sojourners* in regard to an article published in the July issue of *Sojourners*.

13. This subject of Christianity and Healing has been discussed in depth by Morton in *Healing and Christianity*, New York: Harper and Row, 1976.

14. Paul Friedlander, *Plato: An Introduction*. Trans. by Hans Meyerhoff, New York: Harper & Row, for the Bollingen Foundation, Inc., 1964. Josef Pieper, *Love and Inspiration: A Study of Plato's Phaedrus*, London: Faber & Faber, 1964.

15. *The Collected Works of C.G. Jung*, trans. by R.F.C. Hull, Vol. 9, part 1, *The Archetypes and the Collective Unconscious*. Copyright by Bollingen Foundation, New York, 1959. Bollingen Series XX.9.1. Distributed by Princeton University Press. pp. 86-87.

16. Ibid. p. 71.

17. *Someday I'll Find You*, London: Fount Paperbacks, 1984, p. 124.

18. The finest short statement of the Biblical stance toward homosexualities was written by Walter Wink, the New Testament scholar, entitled "Biblical Perspectives on Homosexuality", *Christian Century*, Nov. 7, 1979. The most careful study of the New Testa-

ment texts, their language and the Graeco-Roman milieu to which this language referred is Robin Scroggs, *The New Testament and Homosexuality*, Philadelphia: Fortress Press, 1983. This book, however, is flawed by the author's reliance upon George Devereaux's Freudian interpretation of the homosexualities and his lack of knowledge about current homosexual practice.

Chapter Ten

1. *Utne Reader*, no. 11, Aug./Sept. 1985, pp. 120-44.

2. Ibid., pp. 177-90. In addition Katchadourian has an excellent discussion of other diseases of the sexual organs pp. 165-177.

3. Those interested can write to S.A., Box 300, Simi Valley, CA 93063. The group is a nonprofit group and so send self-addressed stamped envelopes for reply.

4. Keene, op. cit., p. 59.

5. Op. cit., p. 185. Much of the following material was gleaned from Haeberle's excellent historical treatment, pp. 185-9.

6. Christopher Cerf and Victor Navasky, *The Experts Speak*, New York: Pantheon Books, 1984, pp. 17–18.

7. Op. cit., p. 271.

8. Ibid., p. 257.

9. Op. cit., pp. 78, 79, 92, 93.

10. Edward Edinger, *Ego and Archetype*, New York: G.P. Putnams's Sons, 1972, p. 115.

11. Op. cit., p. 85.

12. From a letter, whose author wishes to remain anonymous, to the two of us. Some of the situations are changed to maintain the anonymity of all the persons involved.

Chapter Eleven

1. Op. Cit., pp. 79-81, 91-92.

2. Morton has described this process at great length in *The Other Side of Silence: A Guide to Christian Meditation* and given several examples of this process in the last chapter of that book. He has also given briefer descriptions of this method in Chapter 8 and 9 of *Adventure Inward: Christian Growth through Personal Journal Writing* and also in chapter 7 of *Companions on the Inner Way: The Art of Spiritual Guidance*.

3. Morton has also provided there a list of fifteen rules for dealing with sexual feelings in loving situations.

4. Op. cit.

5. In his book *Companions on the Inner Way: The Art of Spiritual Guidance and in Encounter with God* Morton has described this theological framework in detail.

6. St. John of the Cross, *Dark Night of the Soul*, trans. E. Allison Peers, Garden City, N.Y.: Doubleday & Company, Inc., 1959, pp. 33-4.

7. Austin Ferrer, *A Faith of Our Own*, Cleveland; The World Publishing Company, 1960, p. 68.

Bibliography

St. Ambrose. *Duties of the Clergy*.

_____. *Concerning Virgins*, Book I.

An Account of the Experience and Recovery of Incestuous Sexual Abuse. Anonymous unpublished paper.

Apfelbaum, Bernard, ed. *Expanding the Boundaries of Sex Therapy*, Berkeley: Berkeley Sex Therapy Group.

Appleton, Jane and William (M.D.) *How Not to Split Up*. Berkeley: Berkeley Publishing Corporation, 1978.

St. Augustine. *The Good of Marriage* Vol. 27 of *The Fathers of the Church*. Washington D.C.: Catholic University of America Press, 1957.

Baars, Conrad W. *The Role of the Church in the Causation, Treatment and Prevention of the Crisis in the Priesthood*. unpublished paper.

Bailey, D.S. *Homosexuality and the Western Christian Tradition*. London: Longmans, Green, 1955.

Bausch, Rev. William J. *Masturbation, Practical Guidance and Advice for the Catholic Teenage Boy*. Chicago: Claretian Publications, no date.

Bell, Alan and Martin S. Weinburg. *Homosexualities: A Study of Diversity Among Men and Women*. New York: Simon and Schuster, 1978.

Bell, Alan. *Sexual Preference: Its Development in Men and Women*. Indianapolis: Indiana University Press, 1981.

Bergler, Edmund (M.D.) *The Revolt of the Middle-aged Man*. New York: Grosset and Dunlap, 1954, 1957.

Borhek, Mary V. *My Son Eric*. New York: Pilgrim Press, 1979.

Boswell, John. *Christianity, Social Tolerance, and Homosexuality*. Chicago: University of Chicago Press, 1980.

Briggs-Myers, Isabel. *Gifts Differing*. Palo Alto, CA: Consulting Psychologist Press, Inc. 1980.

Brown, Helen Gurley. *Sex and the Single Girl*. New York: Bernard Geis Associates, 1962.

Brown, Norman O. *Love's Body*. New York: Vintage Books, 1966.

Brownmiller, Susan. *Against Our Will, Men, Women and Rape*. New York: Bantam Books, 1975.

Burtchaell, James Tunstead (C. S. C.) and others. *Marriage Among Christians—A Curious Tradition*. Notre Dame, Ind: Ave Maria Press, 1977.

Butterfield, Oliver M. (PhD.). *Sexual Harmony in Marriage*. New York: Emerson Books, Inc., 1967.

Calvin, John. *Institutes of the Christian Religion*. Trans by J. Albau, Philadelphia: Presbyterian Board of Christian Education, 1928.

Campbell, Joseph. *Myths to Live By*. New York: Bantam, 1973.

Cartwright, Rosalind D., Lynda Weiner Tipton, Jane Wicklund. "Focusing on Dreams— A Preparation Program for Psychotherapy", *Archives General of Psychiatry*, vol. 37, March 1980.

Cerf, Christopher and Victor Navasky. *The Experts Speak*. New York: Pantheon Books, 1984.

Chang, Jolan. *The Tao of Love and Sex, The Ancient Chinese Way to Ecstasy*. New York: E.P. Dutton, 1977.

Chartham, Robert. *The Sensuous Couple*. New York: Penthouse International, Ltd., 1971.

Clark, Keith. *An Experience of Celibacy: A Creative Reflection on Intimacy, Loneliness, Sexuality and Commitment*. Notre Dame, Ind: Ave Maria Press, 1982.

Clark, Kenneth. *The Nude, A Study in Ideal Form*. Garden City, N.Y.: Doubleday Anchor Books, 1956.

Clasper, Paul and Janet. *The Ox-herder Pictures, Zen Buddhism's Version of "The Pilgrim's Progress"*. Hong Kong: The Lotus-Logos Press, no date.

Coan, Richard. *Hero, Artist, Sage, or Saint?* New York: Columbia University Press, 1977.

Cory, Donald Webster. *Homosexuality, A Cross Cultural Approach*. New York: The Julian Press, Inc. Publishers, 1956.

Daly, Mary. *Gyn/ecology, The Metaethnics of Radical Feminism*. Boston: Beacon Press, 1978.

Dante (Alighieri). *Divine Comedy*. Trans. by Dorothy L. Sayers and Barbara Reynolds. Baltimore: Penguin Books, 1962.

Dantec, Francois. *Love is Life—A Catholic Marriage Handbook*. Notre Dame, Ind.: University of Notre Dame Press, 1963.

Death to Life. Chicago: Argus Communications, 1968.

De Rougemont, Dennis. *Love in the Western World*. Trans. by Montgomery Belgion. New York: Pantheon, 1956.

de Saint Exupery, Antoine. *The Little Prince*. New York: Harcourt Brace and World, Inc., 1943.

Dignity. A national publication of the gay Catholic Community. (Vol VI, No. 2, Feb. 1975). 755 Boylston St. Room 514, Boston, MA 02116.

The Documents of Vatican II. New York: America Press, 1966.

Dourley, John. *The Illness That We Are: A Jungian Critique of Christianity*. Toronto, Canada: Inner City Books, 1984.

Dufresne, Edward R. *Partnership—Marriage and the Committed Life*. New York: Paulist Press, 1975.

Eichenlaub, John E., M.D. *The Marriage Art*. New York: Dell Publishing Company, Inc., 1961.

Encyclopedia of Religion and Ethics. ed. by James Hastings, Vol. 3, New York: Scribners, no date.

Epstein, Joseph. "Homo/Hetero: The Struggle for Sexual Identity", Harper's Magazine, September 1970.

Evely, Louis. The Man is You. New York: Paulist Press, 1966.

Fairchild, Roy W. Christians in Families. Atlanta: John Knox Press, 1964.

Farrer, Austin. A Faith of Our Own. Cleveland: The World Publishing Company, 1960.

Fiorenza, Elizabeth Schussler. In Memory of Her: A Feminist Reconstruction of Christian Origins. New York: Crossroad, 1984.

Fletcher, Joseph. The Ethics of Genetic Control. Garden City, NY.: Anchor Books, 1974.

Ford, C.S. and F.A. Beach. Patterns of Sexual Behavior. New York: Harper and Row, 1951.

Forster, E.M. Maurice. Toronto: MacMillan of Canada. 1971.

Fortunato, John E. Embracing the Exile, Healing Journeys of Gay Christians. New York: The Seabury Press, 1982.

Fourez, Gerard. Christian Celibacy: Mystery of Death and Resurrection. An unpublished paper.

Fracchia, Charles A. Living Together Alone. San Francisco: Harper and Row, 1979.

French, Marilyn. The Woman's Room. New York: Jove Publishers, 1980.

Freud, Sigmund. The Interpretation of Dreams. Trans. by James Strachey. New York: Avon, 1967.

_____. Three Essays on the Theory of Sexuality. Trans. by James Strachey. New York: Basic Books, 1962.

Friedlander, Paul. Plato: An Introduction. Trans. by Hans Meyerhoff. New York: Harper and Row, 1964.

Gannon, Timothy J. Emotional Development and Spiritual Growth. Chicago: Franciscan Herald Press, 1965.

Gardella, Peter. Innocent Ecstasy. Oxford University Press, 1985.

Gelman, David. "Finding the Hidden Freud", Newsweek. November 30, 1981.

Gelpi, Donald. Charism and Sacrament: A Theology of Christian Conversion, SPCK, 1977.

Gibran, Kahlil. Thoughts and Meditations. Trans. by Anthony R. Ferris. New York: Citadel Press, 1967.

Goergen, Donald. The Sexual Celibate. New York: The Seabury Press, 1974.

Goldberg, Herb. The Hazards of Being Male—Surviving the Myth of Masculine Privilege. New York: New American Library, Inc., 1976.

Goslin, D.A. Sexual Conduct: The Social Sources of Human Sexuality. Chicago: Aldine, 1973.

Guggenbuhl-Craig, Adolf. Marriage—Dead or Alive. Zurich: Spring Publications, 1977.

_____. Power in the Helping Professions. Irving, Texas, 1971.

Gustafson, Jane. Celibate Passion. New York: Harper and Row, 1978.

Haas, A. Teenage Sexuality. New York: MacMillan, 1979.

Haeberle, Erwin J. The Sex Atlas, A New Illustrated Guide. New York: The Seabury Press, 1978.

Haley, Jay. Strategies of Psychotherapy. New York: Grune and Straton, 1963.

Hamilton, Eleanor. Sex with Love, A Guide for Young People. Boston: Beacon Press, 1978.

Hanaghan, Jonathan. The Courage to be Married. St. Meinrad, Ind: Abbey Press, 1976

Handbook of Socialization Theory and Research. Ed. D.A. Goslin. Chicago: Rand McNally, 1967.

Herdt, Gilbert. Guardians of the Flutes. New York: McGraw-Hill, 1981.

Heron, Alastair. Towards a Quaker View of Sex. Friends Home Service Committee: London, 1963.

Hite, Shere. The Hite Report. New York: Dell, 1981.

Homosexuality and Ethics. Ed. by Edward Batchelor, Jr. New York: Pilgrim Press, 1980.

Hooker, Evelyn. "A Preliminary Analysis of Group Behavior of Homosexuals", *The Journal of Psychology.* Vol. 42, 1956.

_____. "Male Homosexuality in the Rorschach", *Journal of Projective Techniques,* Vol. 22, No. 1, 1958.

_____. "The Adjustment of the Male Overt Homosexual", *Journal of Projective Techniques.* Vol. 21, No. 1, 1957.

Hope for the Homosexual. Forward Movement Publications: Cincinnati, 1966.

Human Sexuality: New Directions in American Catholic Thought. A Study Commissioned by the Catholic Theological Society of America. New York: Paulist Press, 1977.

Hunt, M. *Sexual Behavior in the 1970's.* Chicago: Playboy Press, 1974.

St. Ignatius of Loyola. *Spiritual Exercises.* Trans. by Thomas Corbishley. New York: Kenedy, 1963.

The Jesus-Caritas Union of Priests. The American Experience Presentation No. 2, (Fourth Edition: March 1972.)

St. John of the Cross. *Dark Night of the Soul.* Trans. by E. Allison Peers. Garden City, N.Y.: Doubleday and Company, Inc., 1959.

Johnson, Robert. *He.* King of Prussia, Penn.: Religious Publishing Co., 1974.

Jones, Clinton R. *Homosexuality and Counseling.* Philadelphia: Fortress Press, 1974.

Jones, H. Kimball, *Toward a Christian Understanding of the Homosexual.* New York: Association Press, 1966.

Jung, C.G., *Letters, 1: 1906-1950.* Ed. Gerhard Adler. Princeton, N.J.: Princeton University Press, 1973.

_____. *Collected Works,* Princeton, N.J.: Princeton University Press, 1979. Vol. 10, *Civilization in Transition*

_____. *Collected Works.* New York: Pantheon Books for the Bollingen Foundation. Vol. 11, *Answer to Job.*

_____. *Memories, Dreams, Reflections.* Recorded and edited by Aniela Jaffe. New York: Pantheon Books, 1963.

_____. *Modern Man in Search of a Soul.* New York: Harcourt Brace Jovanovich, Inc., 1955.

Katchadourian, Horant A., M.D. *Fundamentals of Human Sexuality.* (4th edition). New York: Holt, Rinehart and Winston, Inc., 1985.

Katchadourian, Horant A. and Donald T. Lunde. *Fundamentals of Human Sexuality.* New York: Holt, Rinehart and Winston, 1972.

Kazantzakis, Nikos. *Report to Greco.* New York: Simon and Schuster, no date.

Keane, Philip S., S.S. *Sexual Morality. A Catholic Perspective.* New York: Paulist Press, 1977.

Kelsey, Morton. *Adventure Inward: Christian Growth Through Personal Journal Writing.* Minneapolis, Minn: Augsburg Publishing House, 1980.

_____. *Afterlife: The Other Side of Dying.* New York: Paulist Press, 1980.

_____. *Caring: How Can We Love One Another?* Ramsey, N.J.: Paulist Press, 1981.

_____. *Christo-Psychology.* New York: Crossroad, 1982.

_____. *Christ Speaks to the Family.* Pecos, N.M.: Dove Publications, 1975.

_____. *The Christian and the Supernatural.* Minneapolis: Augsburg, 1976.

_____. *Companions on the Inner Way.* New York: Crossroad, 1983.

_____. *Discernment: A Study in Ecstasy and Evil.* New York: Paulist Press, 1978.

_____. *Myth, History, and Faith.* New York: Paulist Press, 1974.

_____. *The Other Side of Silence: A Guide to Christian Meditation.* New York: Paulist Press, 1976.

————. *Prophetic Ministry*. New York: Crossroad, 1982.

————. *Resurrection: Release from Oppression*. New York: Paulist Press, 1985.

————. *What is a Real Man?* Pecos N.M.: Dove Publications, 1980.

————. *Woman's Unique Gifts*. Pecos, N.M.: Dove Publications, 1980.

Kerenyi, Karl. *Hermes—Guide of Souls, The Mythologem of the Masculine Source of Life*. Zurich: Spring Publications, 1976.

Kiersey, David and Marilyn Bates. *Please Understand Me*. Del Mar, Cal.: Promethean Books, Inc., 1978.

Kiesling, Christopher, O.P. *Celibacy, Prayer and Friendship—A Making-Sense-Out-of-Life Approach*. New York: Alba House, 1978.

Kinsey, A.C. *Sexual Behavior in the Human Male*. Philadelphia: Saunders, 1948.

Konner, Melvin. *The Tangled Wing: Biological Constraints on the Human Spirit*. New York: Holt, Rinehart and Winston, 1982.

L'Abate, Luciano. "Intimacy is Sharing Hurt Feelings: A Reply to David Mace." *The Journal of Marriage and Family Counseling*, Vol. 3, No. 2.

LaHaye, Tim and Beverly. *The Act of Marriage, The Beauty of Sexual Love*. Grand Rapids, Mich.: Zondervan Publishing House, 1976.

Lair, Jess. *Sex: If I Didn't Laugh I'd Cry*. New York: Fawcett Crest, 1979.

Lawrence, Gordon. *People Types and Tiger Stripes*. Gainesville, Fla.: Center for Applications of Psychological Type, Inc., 1979.

Lea, Henry C. *Sacredotal Celibacy in the Christian Church*. (No city listed): University Books, 1966.

Leclercq, Jean. *Monks and Love in Twelfth Century France*. Oxford: Clarendon Press, 1979.

————. *Monks on Marriage: A Twelfth Century View*. New York: The Seabury Press, 1982.

Lehrman, Nat. *Masters and Johnson Explained*. Chicago: Playboy Press, 1970.

Leonard, Linda Schierse. *The Wounded Woman: Healing the Father-Daughter Relationship*. Boulder, Col.: Shamahala Publications, 1982.

Lewis, C. S. *The Lion, the Witch and the Wardrobe*. Middlesex, England: Penguin Books, 1950.

————. *Surprised by Joy*. London: Fontana, 1959.

Lowen, Alexander, *The Betrayal of the Body*. New York: Collier Books, 1967.

Lynch, James. *The Broken Heart: The Medical Consequences of Loneliness*. New York: Basic Books, 1977.

Maccoby, Eleanor and Carol Jacklin. *The Psychology of Sex Differences*. Stanford: Stanford University Press, 1974

Martos, Joseph. *Doors to the Sacred: A Historical Introduction to Sacraments in the Catholic Church*. Image Books, 1982.

Masculine/Feminine, Readings in Sexual Mythology and the Liberation of Women. Ed. by Betty and Theodore Rosnak. New York: Harper and Row, 1969.

Masson, Jeffrey M. *The Assault on Truth: Freud's Suppression of the Seduction Theory*. New York: Farrar, Straus and Giroux, 1984.

Masters, William H. and Virginia E. Johnson. *Human Sexual Inadequacy*. Boston: Little, Brown and Company, 1970.

————. *Human Sexual Response*. Boston: Little, Brown and Company, 1966.

————. *The Pleasure Bond: A New Look at Sexuality and Commitment*. Boston: Little, Brown and Company, 1974.

May, Rollo. *Love and Will*. New York: W.W. Norton and Company, Inc., 1969.

Mayle, Peter. *Where Did I Come From?* Secaucus, N.J.: Lyle Stuart, Inc., 1975.

_____. *What's Happening to Me?* Secaucus, N.J.: Lyle Stuart, Inc., 1975.

McTaggart, Joe. *Some Reflections on Celibacy.* Unpublished paper.

Mead, Margaret. *Male and Female: A Study of the Sexes in a Changing World.* Greenwood, 1977.

Meister Eckhart. Trans. by R. B. Blakney. New York: Harper and Row, 1941.

Miller, Alice. *The Drama of the Gifted Child.* New York: Basic Books, 1981. 1981.

Miller Arthur. *After the Fall.* New York: The Viking Press, 1964.

Money, John. *The Destroying Angel.* Del Mar, Cal: Prometheus Books, 1985.

Moore, John. *Sexuality and Spirituality. The Interplay of Masculine and Feminine in Human Development.* San Francisco: Harper and Row, 1980.

Needham, Joseph. "The Tao-Illuminations and Corrections of the Way," *Theology.* July 1978.

Nelson, James B. *Embodiment—An Approach to Sexuality and Christian Theology.* Minneapolis, MN: Augsburg Publishing House, 1978.

Newcomb, Franc Johnson. *Hosteen Klah: Navaho Medicine Man and Sand Painter.* Norman: University of Oklahoma Press, 1964.

Nouwen, Henry J. M. *Intimacy—Pastoral Psychological Essays.* Notre Dame, Ind.: Fides Publisher Inc., 1969.

_____. *The Wounded Healer.* Garden City, N.Y.: Doubleday and Company, 1972.

O'Connor, Elizabeth. *Search for Silence.* Waco, Texas: Word Books, 1972.

Offir, Carole Wade. *Human Sexuality.* New York: Harcourt Brace Jonavich, 1982.

On Being a Good Listener. Cincinnati: Forward Movement Publications, no date.

One—The Homosexual Viewpoint. May 1959, vol VII no. 5, February 1960, vol VIII, no. 2.

One Institute Quarterly: Homophile Studies. Winter 1959, Vol II, No.1; Spring 1959, Vol II, No.2; Summer 1959, Vol. II, No.3; Fall 1959, Vol II, No.4; Spring 1962, Vol. V, No.2; Summer 1962, Vol V, No.3; Fall 1962, Vol. II, No.4.

O'Neill, Nena and George. *Open Marriage—A New Lifestyle for Couples.* New York: M. Evans and Company, Inc., 1972.

Pable, Martin. *Celibacy and Personal Growth.* Unpublished paper.

Payne, Leanne. *The Broken Image, Restoring Personal Wholeness Through Healing Prayer.* Westchester, Ill.: Cornerstone Books, 1981.

Peck, M. Scott. *The Road Less Traveled: The Psychology of Spiritual Growth.* New York: Simon and Schuster, 1978.

Perera, Sylvia Brinton. *Descent to the Goddess, A Way of Initiation for Women.* Toronto: Inner City Books, 1981.

Peterson, James A. *Married Love in the Middle Years.* New York: Association Press, 1968.

Phillips, Dorothy. *The Choice is Always Ours.* Theosophical Publishing House, 1975.

Pittenger, Norman. *Time for Consent? A Christian's Approach to Homosexuality.* London: SCM Press Ltd., 1967.

Plato. *Phaedrus.* Ed. by R. Hackforth. Cambridge: Cambridge University Press, 1972.

_____. *Symposium.* Trans. by Benjamin Fowett jr. New York: Bobbs, 1956.

Ploscowe, Morris. *Sex and the Law.* New York: Prentice-Hall, 1951.

Reavis, John W., Jr. *The Rejected.* A transcript of A National Educational Television Network Presentation. September 11, 1961. KQED. San Francisco.

Regan, Rev. Dennis M. "Toward a Theology of Human Sexuality" Prepared for Pre-Synod Consultation, University of Notre Dame, June 15-18, 1980.

Renault, Mary. *The Last of the Wine.* New York: Random, 1975.

Richardson, Herbert. *Nun, Witch and Playmate, The Americanization of Sex*. New York: Harper and Row, 1971.

Robson, Kenneth S. "The Role of Eye-to-Eye Contact in Maternal-Infant Attachment," *Journal of Child Psychology and Psychiatry*, Vol 8, 1967. Pergamon Press, Ltd., Great Britain.

Rose, Phyllis. *Parallel Lives, Five Victorian Marriages*. New York: A Knopf, 1983.

Ruether, Rosemary Radford. *Sexism and God Talk*. Boston: Beacon Press, 1983.

The Same Sex, An Appraisal of Homosexuality. Ed. by Ralph W. Weltge, Philadelphia: Pilgrim Press, 1969.

Sanford, John. *Evil: A Psychological and Religious Perspective*. New York: Crossroad, 1981.

_____. *The Invisible Partners—How the Male and Female in Each of Us Affects our Relationships*. New York: Paulist Press, 1980.

_____. *The Kingdom Within*. Philadelphia and New York: Lippincott Co., 1970.

Sapp, Stephen. *Sexuality, the Bible and Science*. Philadelphia: Fortress Press, 1977.

Schofield, Michael. *Sociological Aspects of Homosexuality, A Comparative Study of Three Types of Homosexuals*. London: Longmans, 1965.

Shoham, S. Giora. *Salvation Through the Gutters, Deviance and Transcendence*. Washington: Hemisphere Publishing Corporation, 1979.

Short, Ray E. *Sex, Love or Infatuation*. Minneapolis: Augsburg Publishing House, 1978.

Smith, Morton. *The Secret Gospel*. New York: Harper and Row Publishers, 1973.

Smoke, Jim. *Growing Through Divorce*. Irvine, Cal.: Harvest House Publishers, 1976.

Socarides, Charles W., M.D. *Beyond Sexual Freedom*. New York: The New York Times Book Company, 1975.

_____. "Homosexuality and Medicine", *Journal of the American Medical Association*. May 18, 1970. Vol. 212.

Social Action. December 1967. Vol. XXXIV, No. 4.

Social Progress, A Journal of Church and Society. Nov./Dec. 1967.

Stayton, William R. "0-1-2-3-4-5-6 Changing Attitudes Toward Sexuality", *Your Church*. Jan./Feb. 1975.

Steiner, Rudolf. *Knowledge of the Higher World and its Attainment*. New York: Anthropoophic Press, 1947.

Strage, Mark. *The Durable Fig Leaf*. New York: William Morrow and Company, Inc., 1980.

St. Teresa of Avila. *The Collected Works of St. Teresa of Avila*. Trans. by Kieran Kavanaugh, O.C.D. and Otilio Rodriguez, O.C.D., Washington D.C.: ICS Publications Institute of Carmelite Studies.

_____. *The Interior Castle*. Trans. by E. Allison Peers from the critical edition of P. Silverio de Santa Teresa. Garden City, New York: Images, 1961.

Thompson, William Irwin. *The Time Falling Bodies Take to Light: Mythology, Sexuality and The Origins of Culture*. New York: St. Martins Press, 1981.

Treese, Rev. Dr. Robert L. "Homosexuality: A Contemporary View of the Biblical Perspective". Prepared for the Consultation on Theology and the Homosexual, Glide Urban Center and The Council on Religion and the Homosexual in San Francisco, August 22-24, 1966.

Tripp, C.A. *The Homosexual Matrix*. New York: New American Library-A Signet Book, 1975.

Tyrrell, Bernard J. "The Sexual Celibate and Masturbation", *Review for Religious*. Vol. 35, 1976.

Tyrell, Thomas J. *Urgent Longings: Reflections on the Experience of Infatuation, Human Intimacy and Contemplative Love*. Whitinsville, Mass.: Affirmation Books, 1980.

Van der Post, Laurens. *The Face Beside the Fire*. New York: William Morrow and Company, Inc., 1953.

Vanggaard, Thorkil. *Phallos—A Symbol and Its History in the Male World*. New York: International Universities Press, Inc., 1972.

von der Heydt, Vera. "Jung and Religion". A Lecture for the Guild of Pastoral Psychology, London.

Webb, Lance. *Making Love Grow*. Nashville, Tenn.: The Upper Room, 1983.

Welch, John. *Spiritual Pilgrims, Carl Jung and Teresa of Avila*. New York: Paulist, 1983.

Western Spirituality: Historical Roots, Ecumenical Routes. Ed. by Matthew Fox. Notre Dame, Ind.: Fides Clarentian, 1979.

Williams, Charles. *All Hallow's Eve*. New York: Farrar, Straus and Giroux, 1963.

_____. *Descent Into Hell*. New York: Eerdmans, 1949.

_____. *The Figure of Beatrice: A Study in Dante*. New York: Octagon Books, 1980.

_____. *The Forgiveness of Sins*. London: Geoffrey Bles: Centenary Press, 1942.

_____. *The Greater Trumps*. New York: Farrar, Straus and Giroux, 1963.

Women in a Strange Land. Ed. by Clare Fischer, Betsy Brennenman, Anne Bennett. Philadelphia: Fortress Press, 1975.

Yourcenar, Marguerite. *Memories of Hadrian*. New York: Farrar, Straus and Giroux, 1963.

Index

307